OF SLASH PINES AND MANATEES

UNIVERSITY PRESS OF FLORIDA

Florida A&M University, Tallahassee
Florida Atlantic University, Boca Raton
Florida Gulf Coast University, Ft. Myers
Florida International University, Miami
Florida State University, Tallahassee
New College of Florida, Sarasota
University of Central Florida, Orlando
University of Florida, Gainesville
University of North Florida, Jacksonville
University of South Florida, Tampa
University of West Florida, Pensacola

Of Slash Pines and Manatees

A Highly Selective Field Guide to My Suburban Wilderness

Andrew Furman

UNIVERSITY PRESS OF FLORIDA

Gainesville · Tallahassee · Tampa · Boca Raton
Pensacola · Orlando · Miami · Jacksonville · Ft. Myers · Sarasota

Funding for this publication was provided through a grant from Florida Humanities with funds from the National Endowment for the Humanities. Any views, findings, conclusions or recommendations expressed in this publication do not necessarily represent those of Florida Humanities or the National Endowment for the Humanities. As the non-profit, state affiliate of the National Endowment for the Humanities, Florida Humanities supports programs and resources that explore the history and culture of Florida and encourage a lifelong appreciation of literature, literacy, and learning.

Cover: Kim Heise, *Slash Pine and Red-Bellied Woodpecker.*

Copyright 2025 by Andrew Furman
All rights reserved
Published in the United States of America

30 29 28 27 26 25   6 5 4 3 2 1

Library of Congress Cataloging-in-Publication Data
Names: Furman, Andrew, 1968– author.
Title: Of slash pines and manatees : a highly selective field guide to my suburban wilderness / Andrew Furman.
Description: Gainesville : University Press of Florida, 2025. | Includes bibliographical references.
Identifiers: LCCN 2024038733 (print) | LCCN 2024038734 (ebook) | ISBN 9780813080963 (paperback) | ISBN 9780813073712 (ebook)
Subjects: LCSH: Human ecology—Florida, South. | Landscape changes—Florida, South. | Suburban life—Florida, South. | Suburban animals—Florida, South. | Suburban plants—Florida, South. | Florida, South—Environmental conditions. | Furman, Andrew, 1968– | BISAC: NATURE / Essays | BIOGRAPHY & AUTOBIOGRAPHY / Personal Memoirs
Classification: LCC GF504.F6 F87 2025 (print) | LCC GF504.F6 (ebook) | DDC 304.209759—dc23/eng/20241031
LC record available at https://lccn.loc.gov/2024038733
LC ebook record available at https://lccn.loc.gov/2024038734

The University Press of Florida is the scholarly publishing agency for the State University System of Florida, comprising Florida A&M University, Florida Atlantic University, Florida Gulf Coast University, Florida International University, Florida State University, New College of Florida, University of Central Florida, University of Florida, University of North Florida, University of South Florida, and University of West Florida.

 University Press of Florida
2046 NE Waldo Road
Suite 2100
Gainesville, FL 32609
http://upress.ufl.edu

To Wendy,

For making Florida home

CONTENTS

Introduction: Hawk and Dove and Me 1

BEING WITH PLANTS

1. Starting from Seed 13
2. The Last Patch of Florida Land 30
3. The End of Orange Juice? 38
4. Slashed 42
5. The Nature of the University 55
6. Macroalgae Matters 62
7. My Garden Tour 74

BEING WITH ANIMALS

8. The Problem with Pretty Birds 87
9. Summer Animals 98
10. Yellow-Crowned Night-Heron 112
11. Gone, Fishing 127
12. Stingray 130
13. This Is Not a Chapter on Manatees 142
14. Fox 158

BEING WITH YOURSELF

15. A Highly Selective Field Guide to Florida's Feral Creatures 177

Acknowledgments 193
Works Cited 195

Introduction

Hawk and Dove and Me

Here I was, at home in my small study one recent morning trying to write lines on my computer—not these lines—when I was jolted by the thud of a dove against the window just beyond the computer screen. This first thud was followed almost immediately by the second thud of a hawk. My eyes adjusted to the depth of field just in time to recognize dove (mourning? white-winged?) and hawk (Cooper's? sharp-shinned?), prey and predator, caroming off the window, both somehow recovering from the blow to continue their ancient dance. On my feet now, straining my neck to keep the pair in view for as long as possible, I watched them beeline over my neighbor's mango tree. Such a chilling, if fleeting, scene to witness. My eyes shifted back to the window, the spot of impact, where the residue of the struggle remained, several small feathers, like snowflakes, the dove's feathers I was pretty sure, adhering to the glass. My heart had leapt to my throat, where I could still feel it thumping.

Thump. Thump. Thump.

I sat back down to catch my breath, felt my heart return to its comfortable grotto in my chest. Did the dove escape, or did the hawk seize its prey beneath its razor-sharp talons somewhere beyond the mango tree? In either case, there was no way I could return to whatever words I was writing indoors after witnessing the life-and-death goings on, outdoors. I marveled for a while over the essential animal business taking place right outside my window. So much going on out there. How little we see of it, even those of us who fancy ourselves solid seers, sealed as most of us are inside climate-controlled interiors too many hours of the day. It was hard, sitting there, reckoning my mostly indoor life, this "sivilized" life, as Huck Finn put it, with the greater liveliness outdoors. *Fraud!* I heard in the imagined echoes of hawk and dove against my window.

A lot of us in the developed world of the Anthropocene, I think, fear that the lives we lead are fraudulent lives. We suspect that a more authentic life must be somewhere else, over there, or there. We know, even those of us who haven't read Thoreau (by which I mean most of us), that life is fleeting and dear, too fleeting and too dear to spare a second living a not-life. Those of us who write a lot about nature and the environment probably suffer from this anxiety more acutely than most people. After all, we pose the question to ourselves, if we're so enraptured by the outdoors, if we know in our heart of hearts that that's where it's at, the real stuff, so to speak, what the hell are we doing so many hours of the day with our noses pressed up against books and computer screens?

Wild animals (by contrast to us human animals) don't fret so much about such matters. They're too busy living. Consider my hawk and dove literally flying for their lives. Again, I'm not sure how things worked out for the creatures. I only know that they certainly weren't wondering about me. Wild creatures don't concern themselves much with the human lives on the other side of a house window. Notable exceptions notwithstanding (recent books and documentaries on foxes, octopuses, and goshawks come to mind), most wild creatures don't care a fig about us. Yet it seemed like a big deal, all the same, that I'd been here to witness this essential outdoor scene. It seemed miraculous, the very simultaneity of our lives, that while I carry on a rather coddled human life in one of the world's wealthiest countries, animals and plants under my very nose in this asphalt-frosted region of South Florida carry on their life business with such fierce urgency.

These realms, the wild and the human, are separate realms, we like to think, yet maybe not so separate after all, the border between thinner than a pane of glass. In this brief moment, it occurred to me, I glimpsed the environmental ethic that has informed my own way of *being* in Florida these many years, the ethic that inspires each of the chapters in this book you hold in your hands, an ethic that acknowledges and embraces the radical intermingling between realms we have long seen in opposition to each other.

* * *

I'm not the first writer, of course, to marvel over the proximity and simultaneity of human and nonhuman animal lives on the planet. The creation stories, current literatures, and lives of Native Americans—from the Seminoles of my southeast corner to the Tlingit of the Pacific Northwest—betray an ecological vision of interconnectedness. Such insight comes harder for most non-Indigenous North Americans, like me, raised on various versions of that alternative creation story that emphasizes the dominion of humankind over the rest of creation more so than interconnectedness. Yet Mary Oliver, a far more attentive seer than I can ever hope to be (a Floridian too, during her later years), recounts in *Owls and Other Fantasies: Poems and Essays* (2003) a scene in which she searches out and listens for the cries of an owl and rabbit, predator and prey, hearing in their harsh cries the terror that she cannot fully deny in her comparatively placid and sunny life. "The world where the owl is endlessly hungry and endlessly on the hunt," Oliver writes, "is the world in which I live too. There is only one world." To hear rabbit and owl for Oliver is to put a finger on the pulse of her own wild life. I'm not sure that most of us, I'm not sure that I, will ever fully realize what Oliver realizes in the ecstatic predator and prey sounds of owl and rabbit. The triumph of her book, and of much of her oeuvre, boils down to a triumph of the imagination, her powerful act of witness and revelation in this one world.

Truth is, I wasn't really thinking about Native American creation stories or Oliver's writing the moment after I glimpsed hawk and dove. But I was thinking about Emerson's "The American Scholar," particularly his lines about a true scholar grudging "every opportunity of action past by [sic], as a loss of power." I love this Emerson nugget and recall it often. I love the encouragement it gives to my inclinations. Emboldened by his admonition, I fled the study and looked around for my dog, Storm. "Time for a walk," I announced, having found him sprawled out on the couch in the family room, his tongue dripping out his mouth. My increasingly lazy, medium-sized black-and-white mutt gave me the side-eye as he had already completed his regular morning walk and his afternoon walk ought to have still been hours away. Stirred by that fleeting vision of hawk and dove, however, I was anxious to get outdoors to see more of the "wild spectacle" within arm's reach, to borrow a phrase from the environmental writer, Janisse Ray. Time for this scholar to pursue some action.

What did I see when I went outside? Not much. It was September and still too darned hot in South Florida. Most of our winter creatures hadn't yet migrated southward to us from their more temperate climes. Our year-round furred, feathered, and scaled residents, for their part, were lying low, doing their best to beat the heat until the mercy of sundown. But even an uneventful walk outdoors is a good walk, I say. There's always something to witness outside: tree and shrub and sky, at the very least. The skies may be the most underrated feature of the Florida outdoors, such dazzling subtropical sights closer by to distract us: manatee and Geiger tree and yellow-crowned night-heron and painted bunting and fox (to list a few of the Florida plants and animals that take up some of the following pages). Who has the time or inclination to look up at the sunlight oranging tiny clouds scalloped across the sky? Who thinks it worthwhile to take a moment to track the progress of those scallops sliding toward the western horizon? Well, me, for one. To study in earnest the manifold instantiations of a Florida cloud is to be convinced once and for all, per Joni Mitchell, that you've never known clouds at all.

I've grown to appreciate more and more the ordinary and everyday sights, sounds, and smells of the physical world close at hand, and I dedicate plenty of attention in this book to these more commonplace and underappreciated outposts of the Florida outdoors. (Consider, for example, my meditations on seaweed.) Part of this might have to do, simply, with the different brain and body I occupy well into middle age, an organic slowing of my gait and gaze. But part of this surely has something to do with the COVID-19 pandemic that descended upon the globe as I was writing this book. For a time there, during the most stringent period of quarantine and lockdown, life slowed down for everyone. Well, I want to be careful here. It slowed down for those of us fortunate enough to remain unafflicted and to survive, and for those of us who weren't deemed "essential workers" in the various service and healthcare fields, those of us who were granted the luxury (let's just call it what it was) of remote work for weeks, or months. Planes, trains, automobiles, and boats quieted as many of us, to curb the spread of the virus, were asked only to stay at home.

During this period, our carbon emissions dropped precipitously along with the roar of our human presence. Wild creatures took note and decamped from the safety and seclusion of their warrens, terrestrial and aquatic, to enjoy the strange new terms of their earth business. Many of us, judging by the social media posts alone, delighted in this new world, the tighter circuit of our daily migrations, home the center of a shorter radius. Many of us, suddenly, had time on our hands as well. The dailiness of our lives, that is, had shifted both spatially and temporally. And so we looked. And so we listened. A lot of us were living lives a lot closer to Thoreau's recipe for a life lived in full, as David Gessner recognizes and reflects upon in *Quiet Desperation, Savage Delight: Sheltering with Thoreau in the Age of Crisis* (2021). The only shame was that it took a catastrophic pandemic that claimed millions of human lives and counting to precipitate this greater wakefulness, and, well, that this wakefulness was so ephemeral. Sadly, as the pandemic ebbed, and despite the spikes that continued to ravage so many, most global citizens in the developed world—impelled by internal or external forces (i.e., employers)—returned to those former patterns of car commutes and climate-controlled workdays. As I write these lines, we've mostly resumed our old habits so toxic to both our external and internal weather. It took very little time, the climate data suggests, for our carbon footprint to return to its previous size, setting the globe back on its perilous course to exceed the two degrees Celsius warming that the Intergovernmental Panel on Climate Change predicts will trigger catastrophic and unprecedented heat waves, droughts, water stress, and extreme weather events, generally. Still, glimmerings of hope remain in the greater mindfulness that obtains in various pockets, both individually and collectively. It's so little, really, to ask. Rethink and revise the terms of what we call life in the Anthropocene.

What does all this have to do with the morning glimpse of hawk and dove that provoked these reflections? Well, nothing, and everything. For even before the pandemic, I'd been looking at and listening to the outside world near at hand in an ongoing effort to sort out the terms of my citizenship in this state, nation, and planet during this perilous earth-time I happen to be alive. I've long courted what wildness remains in my zip code (ever tilting toward the urban) by ripping out the useless, chemical-dependent sod at our home and tending, instead, to upward of fifty varieties of native trees and plants, several of which I've started by seed; I've been a passionate watcher of our local birds for over thirty years; I continually build, install, and rebuild nest boxes for our resident screech owls and red-bellied woodpeckers, which frequently segue to squirrel-boxes and bee-boxes; I haven't eaten meat in years—mostly on account of its horrific carbon footprint—and (I won't lie) I miss it terribly. The pandemic, however, imbued an added frisson of urgency to these activities, deeply aware as I suddenly was (especially pre-vaccine) that I was living, that we were all living, precarious hawk and dove lives.

* * *

I've tended thus far in these ruminations to underscore the centrality of the outdoors, what we once called nature without equivocation (before Bill McKibben alerted us to its demise), and to the exclusion of the social realm. So I ought to return, here, to describe in further detail what I mean by this environmental ethic of radical intermingling, which more truly seeks to resist the wild/social, outdoors/indoors, nature/culture dichotomies that continue to hold sway over our imaginations. To be sure, I truly am fascinated with stingrays and herons and hardwood hammocks, in and of themselves, and these chapters offer abundant detail on these and other nonhuman phenomena. Yet I fear that the opening hawk and dove anecdote that I've shared, and maybe even the way I've framed Oliver's owl and rabbit meditations, tend to position the outdoors in all its manifestations as a place of retreat from the noise, the burdens, the thinness, of my and our indoor (i.e., social) lives. While I wouldn't completely deny the outdoors this role—because, sure, sometimes I do light out to my nearby ocean or park simply to clear my head of the tumult of other people—nature as retreat ranks rather low on the menu as I ponder the nourishment the Florida outdoors has offered me. The far more salient and salutary role the outdoors plays in my own life, what I've found worth writing about, resides in those glimmering correspondences I've recognized between the realms on either side of my window. Put another way, my immersions in Florida's "wild," "nature," "real" (these are all freighted and imperfect terms) invariably color, and are colored by, my experiences as a husband, father, son, brother, neighbor, and friend; too, by my privilege of navigating as a white male a southern state with a tortured and often overlooked racial history. (See, especially, my chapter on slash pines.) Okay, so let me try to put it yet another way. My forays into the great outdoors—as the chapters that follow, with any hope, illustrate—do not represent escapes from the climate-controlled interiors of my domestic and workplace life so much as they serve as a mode of engagement with these crucial aspects of my identity. I invite readers to contemplate how the very braided structure of most of these chapters blur those boundaries we've grown so accustomed to. I sit in my small study half the time thinking hawk and dove thoughts; I scour the scruffy outposts of my neighborhood in the predawn darkness seeking a meeting with a gray fox, thinking all the while of the feral creature still fast asleep at home, our youngest child, Eva.

    I welcome and even court the porousness between my outdoors and indoors life. I've always been more a Thoreau than an Emerson guy, but I keep an Emerson quotation from "Self-Reliance" taped to the lower edge of my computer monitor. I'm looking at it now. "My book," Emerson writes, "should smell of pines and resound with the hum of insects. The swallow over my window should interweave that thread or straw he carries in his bill into my web also." I love the way this passage revels in images evoking the permeability between outdoors and indoors, this radical intermingling. A pine-smelling book. A book abuzz like a bug. This one world. Just think of it!

* * *

The chapters here, broadly speaking, document my ongoing negotiation over the terms of my human *being* in Florida, one of the most overdeveloped states in the nation *and* one of the most naturally and uniquely beautiful states in the nation. Of course, there are all sorts of ways that other people conduct this negotiation, both within and without Florida. Some people keep a journal, or practice yoga, or read, or seek therapy, or surf, or do volunteer work, or partake of controlled substances. I do a few of these things, too. But mostly, vis-à-vis Emerson, I study nature. Strategies through which to "study nature," of course, vary widely too. I have a friend, some years older than myself, who's determined before he dies to lay eyes on the manifold breathtaking environmental sights the world has on offer. "The volcano is erupting again in Iceland!" he texted me just weeks ago, then announced that he and his wife were booking their airplane tickets. I would be treated to some pretty amazing photographs of the Fagradalsfjall Volcano in the weeks ahead, which, sure, I marveled over and appreciated. I wouldn't begrudge my friend his mode of engagement with the outdoors, just as I wouldn't begrudge a boar hunter or a skydiver or a jet-skier (well, as an open-water swimmer, I begrudge jet-skiers just a little). Yet I've always been more a depth than breadth fellow when it comes to my environmental excursions. I don't go in much for worldwide, or even continent-wide, travel. There's plenty to explore close to home, I say.

When I'm feeling defensive about my inclinations to hunker down, I sometimes trot out my green motivations. We face a climate crisis unparalleled in human history, as everyone either knows or should know, and jet fuel is a carbon dioxide pollutant of the most horrendous sort. I don't truly feel that any of us should be hopping on airplanes as frequently as we do for work or play. That said, I'm a homebody by nature, regardless of our climate crisis, a nature-lover and writer of the most domesticated sort. My guiding lights, nature writingwise, have *not* been those often very popular books shelved under Travel and Adventure. I still remember my visceral reaction upon reading Peter Matthiessen's *The Snow Leopard* (1978), the nature writing classic in which Matthiessen documents his spiritual journey to the Himalayas in Nepal, where he hopes to glimpse the rare snow leopard. At one point of the book, he recounts how fiercely his young son back in the United States misses him, which made me nearly shout at the inanimate paperback pages: *Pete, what the hell are you doing in Nepal when your child needs you at home?*

No, the books that move me more are those other volumes that deeply mine often humble, hardscrabble home territories for all they might teach us about living a human life in full. To name just a few: Thoreau's *Walden* (1854) and his multivolume Journal, Scott Russell Sanders's *Staying Put: Making a Home in a Restless World* (1993), Annie Dillard's *Pilgrim at Tinker Creek* (1974), Terry Tempest Williams's *Refuge: An Unnatural History of Family and Place* (1991), Janisse Ray's *Ecology of a Cracker Childhood* (1999), Ellen Meloy's *The Anthropology of Turquoise: Reflections on Desert, Sea, Stone, and Sky* (2002), Robin Wall Kimmerer's *Braiding Sweetgrass* (2013), Lauret Savoy's *Trace: Memory, History, Race, and the American Landscape* (2015), J. Drew Lanham's *The Home Place: Memoirs of a Colored Man's Love Affair with Nature* (2016), Michael Branch's *Raising Wild: Dispatches from a Home in the Wilderness* (2016), Margaret Renkl's *Late Migrations: A Natural History of Love and Loss* (2019) and *The Comfort of Crows: A Backyard Year* (2023), Susan Cerulean's *I Have Been Assigned the Single Bird: A Daughter's Memoir* (2020), Catherine Raven's *Fox & I* (2021), and, well, anything Rachel Carson wrote about the sea and Wendell Berry writes about the farm. Just as these books and authors continue to inspire me, I only hope that my contribution here inspires readers to undertake their own journeys of homeplace, wherever that may be, their own negotiations with this one world close at hand.

* * *

My own homeplace, Florida, of course, is one of the most imagined and misimagined states in the nation. This may partly be on account of the unfortunate events that tend to merit national news coverage, events ranging from spring break debauchery to horrific acts of gun violence, catastrophic hurricanes, and other climate-related disasters, to "Florida-men" (and women) stories, the crisis of undocumented immigrants braving the Florida straits on unseaworthy dinghies (often to fatal consequence) to the various lesser crises on our behemoth cruise ships. Currently, the Sunshine State also sits at ground-zero in our culture wars over all manner of incendiary issues, including (but not limited to) abortion, book bans, COVID-19 countermeasures, and LGBTQ+ rights. Most longtime Floridians I know lament the suspicion, distrust, and plain old meanness that increasingly seems to pepper our daily transactions with one another out and about, while friends who live in other states (and nations) increasingly ask how I can still *be* in Florida. Well, *this* is how, the chapters that follow suggest.

This is how I can be here.

I'm under no illusions that the environmental ethic I advance in these pages stands the chance to unite our dis-united state or nation, much less solve our climate crisis. But I will say that I've been delighted to discover, in my excursions to engage with the Florida outdoors close at hand, a surprising number of fellow travelers, ecowise, who don't share my politics regarding most other matters. While I might not see eye-to-eye with my neighbor on, say, the efficacy of vaccines, we do share a love for the wild animals making a go of it in the scruffy outposts of our subdivision. It's something we *can* talk about together. I cherish these moments with my fellow Floridians—who plant political signs on their lawns in direct opposition to my own signs—when it's felt like we've stood more on common ground than ground-zero. A first step, anyway, toward healing the civic dysfunction that ails us may reside in our radical intermingling with others who don't always think as we do.

* * *

Meanwhile, in the wake of my brief encounter with hawk and dove, I enlisted our younger daughter, Eva—our only child still living full time at home—to help me place various stickers on most of our windows to preclude future unfortunate avian collisions against the unforgiving hurricane-resistant glass. Some of these stickers happen to be Halloween-themed and will surely inspire the mockery of our neighbors during the non-fall months. But that's okay. Eva delighted, also, in sponging tempera paint in a curlicue pattern (per the advice on the American Bird Conservancy website) against the tall glass on our front door. Further, we now keep our yard lights off at night during the peak weeks of fall and spring migration. During these weeks, millions of birds under the cover of night streak past my home, which happens to be smack in the middle of a flyway for many of them between nesting grounds as far north as Canada's and Alaska's boreal forest and overwintering grounds as far south as the

Antarctic. I've done the research. The ABA (American Birding Association) estimates, conservatively, that bird strikes against glass kill up to one billion birds per year in the United States alone!

The mere thought of it is enough to make me queasy with guilt—a blackpoll warbler in September, say, weighing barely twelve grams hoping to survive its extraordinary three-day journey from Denali National Park in Alaska to its overwintering grounds on some coffee plantation in Columbia, but perishing after striking one of my stupid windows. The least I can do, it seems to me, is rally my resources to minimize the threat that my concrete and glass house poses to these heroic migrants and maximize the benefit my property provides, plantwise, in this *one* world that we share. All of which is to say that looking at hawk and dove, seeing them and thinking about them, gleaning what I might from this brief episode and acting accordingly, represents one small episode in which I've tried to conduct mindfully my blessed life as a Floridian. This same spirit impelled all the chapters collected here into being.

Being with Plants

1

Starting from Seed

> Though I do not believe that a plant will spring up where no seed has been, I have great faith in a seed,—a, to me, equally mysterious origin for it. Convince me that you have a seed there, and I am prepared to expect wonders.
> —Henry David Thoreau, From "The Succession of Forest Trees"

It was mostly a pecuniary matter at first, propagating native plants by seed.

Shortly after we moved into our new home, I spent a fair bit of money (or, according to my wife, an exorbitant amount of money) on handsome shrubs and small trees indigenous to South Florida. The previous owners of our house had maintained the half-acre yard after a fashion; specifically, they had crowded the live and laurel oak understory with a tangle of exotic and invasive plants—philodendra, bougainvillea, schefflera, croton, oyster—which they must have liked. I set about making improvements, at least to my mind, inspired by a rival aesthetic to privilege native flora and its associated birds, butterflies, tree-snails, and whatnot.

There was a lot of work to do.

* * *

Executive Order 11987, Section 1(d), at the federal level, defines "native species" as "all species of plants and animals naturally occurring, either presently or historically, in any ecosystem of the United States." Florida statute 5B-40.00 further defines a native plant as a "plant species that is presumed to have been present in Florida before European contact." The Florida Native Plant Society provides a somewhat more nuanced definition: "It includes those species understood as indigenous, occurring in natural associations in habitats that existed prior to significant human impacts and alterations of the landscape."

* * *

Much of my leisure time over the first two years at the new house was taken up by grubbing out the "exotic organisms" (defined by Executive Order 11987), those meddlesome and unwelcome interlopers, some of which offered terrific resistance against my efforts with a sub-par shovel. I deposited various native shrubs and trees in place of the exotics I uprooted and babied those new plantings with copious doses of water and fertilizer. Within a matter of weeks I was on a first name basis with our nearby native nursery owners, Carl and Donna, which probably reinforces my wife's impression of my extravagant cash outlay.

In any case, the place was looking up after those first couple years. My little patch of Florida was finally picking up its former tune, expressing itself in tender new shoots of fiddlewood and wild coffee and marlberry and firebush and necklace pod and beautyberry and Jamaican caper and seven-year apple and cinnamon bark and strongbark and bloodberry and coontie. But there was still a lot of work to do. I was about to head to the native plant nursery to lay some coin on Carl and Donna when it hit me, probably because I was watering the caper and coffee out front and it was early fall and several of the plants of both species were just starting to advertise their fruit—on the caper, brown string bean–shaped pods that had burst open to reveal bright orange insides from which sticky berry-bracelets dangled, and on the coffee, drooping clusters of oval, blood-red berries. There were some smaller, bright orange berries on my strongbark shrub too, I noticed. I had worked pretty hard to see those first-generation plants through to the point where they had established their roots, put out new growth, and were now hoping to broadcast their genes about via the digestive tracts of our resident blue jays, mockingbirds, catbirds, squirrels, and raccoons. Why was I still planning to pay for new plants when I could just plant them myself now from seed?

So, as I've said, it was mostly a pecuniary matter at first, propagating native plants by seed.

* * *

You may detect a malodorous whiff of xenophobia, racism, and colonialism in all this native plant business. If so, you're not the only one. Michael Pollan and others have noted these troubling resonances in the language of doctrinaire advocates for native gardening (see Pollan's "Against Nativism" in the May 15, 1994, issue of the *New York Times Magazine*). And it's certainly true, as scholars have documented, that the prevailing German aesthetic of the "natural garden" during National Socialism—which called for the elimination of foreign plants from German soil—was part and parcel with the Nazi plan to rid Germany of Jews and other non-Aryan human beings it deemed "foreign" to the soil. And, yes, it's likely true that the Sierra Club, when it took a hard line against immigration to the United States in the 1980s, ostensibly to curb unsustainable population growth that threatens indigenous ecosystems, succumbed to xenophobia instead. Yet, while it's impossible to prove that privileging native flora over exotic flora in one's landscaping plan does *not* rise from nefarious motives—the whole proving a negative thing—I still believe that it's the soundest landscaping ethic for where I find myself living today, a onetime pine flatwoods mostly cleared of its slash pine and live oak and dozens of understory plants to make room for my subdivision, to make room for me. Strongbark, in particular, is listed as endangered by the State of Florida.

* * *

I collected my berries, depulped the seeds (which is a fancy way of saying that I squished the fruits between my fingers to extract the kernels inside), and tucked them away in three separate business envelopes marked JAMAICAN CAPER, WILD COFFEE, and STRONGBARK.

* * *

I am an exotic specimen, both to the United States and to Florida—borderline invasive, given my modest but significant reproductive efforts. Who knows where my progeny might spread their seed? My native soil, or the closest to it I can determine, ranges from various backwaters of the Jewish Pale of Settlement in Eastern Europe. Riga. Medzilaborce. Genetic memory in the Furman/Dickstein/Goodman/Trucker clan is terrifically short, owing to multiple voluntary and involuntary displacements over the past century or so. In 1996, I arrived in Florida via Pittsburgh, via Los Angeles, via Philadelphia, via Scranton, via South Orange, via Manhattan. I don't want to make too much of the connection between my non-native status as a human being in Florida and my gardening ethic that privileges native Florida plants. But I don't want to make too little of it, either. I carry a palpable sense of dislocation, of not-quite-at-homeness, to all the places I have lived. I bring to Florida an acute sensitivity to the weight and impact of my strange footfalls here. It's a sensibility, in my view, that pretty much all current Floridians ought to share, with the exception of the Seminole and Miccosukee. Most people here who call themselves "native Floridians" (without intending harm, I hasten to add) suffer from a peculiar case of myopia. In any case, my lingering sense of outsiderness has played a definite—and, I hope, constructive—role in my gardening proclivities, my visceral desire to make my little half-acre patch of suburbia more closely resemble the pine flatwoods of its recent past.

* * *

Pecuniary matters aside, I suppose I had a lot riding on those native plant seeds.

* * *

"Seeds are extraordinary objects," Brian Capon writes in *Botany for Gardeners* (2010). "They are compact, easily stored, and capable of survival through freezing temperatures or prolonged drought, conditions that usually kill the parent plants."

In 2007, a Russian team of scientists unearthed 32,000-year-old seeds of the Siberian flowering plant, *Silene stenophylla*, from deep below the permafrost near the Kolyma River. An Ice Age squirrel, apparently, had buried the cache. The scientists successfully germinated some of the new seeds, which grew into plants, which bore flowers slightly different from modern *S. stenophylla*, and which, after a year, produced new seed. In photographs, the white, five-petaled flowers look pretty and surprisingly dainty.

* * *

Wendy thought that I had lost my mind when I showed her my seed collection. Wasn't I spending enough time digging holes already? Plus, and placing far too much confidence in me, "What the heck are we going to do with all those plants once you get them started?"

Carl, unlike Wendy (and whom I didn't abandon, entirely), encouraged my efforts, vis-à-vis my native seeds. He was awfully nice, too, about donating a few plastic seed-flats he had lying around. "It'll be a great project for our three-year-old, Eva," I blurted out toward his back as he milled through various plastic pots and such near giant mounds of his soil blends, feeling, for whatever reason, that some sort of explanation was required. "Sure," he said, turning to hand me the stack of flats. They seemed like giant black ice cube trays. He chided me (only half-sarcastically) that I better not be planning on starting my own nursery and going into competition with him. I sort of laughed it off as I set the trays down in my trunk, asked if there was anything special I ought to know about planting wild coffee, Jamaican caper, and strongbark seeds. He told me no, that I didn't need to scarify them or anything, at which point my blank stare, followed by my bemused utterance, "Uh, scarify?" made him snort with laughter. I think he realized then that he and his wife needn't fear my competition. Clearly, I had a lot to learn about this whole seed business.

* * *

"The process," according to *The Encyclopedia of Organic Gardening* (1978), "by which the coat is altered and made permeable to gases and water is called scarification. In nature, scarification is the natural result of the seed's exposure to prolonged periods of freezing and thawing or to wind and rain. When the gardener or seedsman gathers seeds at the end of a season and places them in storage, he eliminates this period of natural weathering and must find other ways to break down the seed coat." In *A Gardener's Guide to Florida's Native Plants* (2001), Rufino Osorio recommends that the seedsman file seeds to nick a small hole. Sandpaper will suffice for smaller, more delicate seeds.

Various additional horticultural methods have been developed to facilitate or hasten germination, depending upon the plant and its peccadilloes, as Miranda Smith describes in *The Plant Propagator's Bible* (2007). These methods include leaching, stratifying, soaking, or exposing to fire. Leaching involves a laborious cycle of soaking seeds in water, straining, and running (or leaching) water over the seeds; stratification involves chilling seeds in a refrigerator or freezer. Soaking is simple enough, but if you oversoak them, Smith warns, your seeds will rot.

Osorio painstakingly describes a home-method to simulate fire so that Floridians might start seeds of the finicky redroot plant. It may be best simply to buy these shrubs from your local native plant nursery.

* * *

Beware of bad seed. The melaleuca tree, introduced to South Florida from Australia in the first decades of the twentieth century, is now considered a "noxious weed" by federal and state agencies. A hundred years ago, however, the "progressive" idea was to drain the Everglades to make it fit for agriculture and habitation, to thereby "redeem" the swamp. It seems almost apocryphal from the current vantage, but state officials in the 1930s hovered over the sawgrass in airplanes and intentionally scattered fistfuls of melaleuca seed to dry up the Everglades and "stabilize" the soil. The pale, papery-barked trees can produce over a million seeds a year and the seeds, unsurprisingly, grew into immense and impenetrable forests. By 1994, melaleuca stands, propagated by seed, had usurped nearly 500,000 acres of the Everglades. These dense monocultures, which I routinely glimpse during my Everglades excursions, form an ecological wasteland as the trees do not support any native species, but *do* host the lobate lac scale, an invasive pest from India. In recent years, various state and environmental agencies in Florida have spent millions of dollars to reduce melaleuca coverage on public lands.

You reap what you sow.

* * *

While the young characters, Emil and Marie, enjoy apricots in the wild, unkempt orchard in Willa Cather's *O Pioneers!* (1913), Alexandra Bergson, the novel's hero, reminisces upon the origins of those trees: "There was a man in the streets selling apricots, and we had never seen any before. . . . They cheered us a good deal, and we saved all the seeds and planted them." Emil and Marie will later enjoy adulterous sex in the weed-choked orchard only to be caught and savagely murdered by Marie's husband. Cather, in this novel anyway, didn't quite know how to feel about wild, unmanaged land, or unmanaged bodies, or those luscious apricots planted by seed.

You reap what you sow, she suggests in the Emil-Marie plotline.

* * *

The Sierra Club, I should mention, continues to revisit its stance on non-native persons. The organization adopted a neutral position on international immigration in the 1990s and today supports comprehensive immigration reform for undocumented immigrants. Further, the Sierra Club now devotes substantial resources toward environmental justice and gender equity. In 2022, its Board of Directors appointed Ben Jealous, the former president and CEO of the NAACP, as its new executive director.

* * *

I decided to start off my project with only one seed flat, figuring that those sixty cubes would offer ample sprouts to keep me busy. For the growing medium, I didn't settle for store-bought potting mix, which would have felt like cheating. Having decided to start plants from seed, I had decided to reduce gardening to its lowest common denominator. This included the soil. And so I blended my own concoction of peat moss, sand (gathered from my nearby beach), topsoil, and perlite (expanded volcanic rock to enhance drainage and aeration). Enlisting Eva's help—who never passes up the opportunity to dirty her hands—we filled each of the cubes with the mix on a flimsy card table beneath a small, covered area of our back patio, then saturated the cubes with a healthy dose of hose-water, setting the nozzle to its "mist" setting for the first time. I didn't leach or scarify or stratify or soak my seeds, as Carl claimed it was unnecessary. Even so, depositing the sixty seeds beneath a blanket of soil at the appropriate depth (no deeper than their diameter, various online sources contended) turned out to be trickier than I had anticipated. I tried using the wet end of a chopstick, "a professional grower's technique," according to *The Plant Propagator's Bible*. The idea is that the seeds are supposed to adhere to the wet wood of the chopstick and then stick better to the potting mix, as it's even wetter. I figured it would seem like a magic trick to Eva, making the seeds stick to the end of the chopstick, then disappear into the soil. But the seeds wouldn't stick to the darned chopstick, no matter how hard I tried. I grew frustrated leaning over the card table, stifled my curses. Eva, bored, began grabbing at the seeds indiscriminately, confusing the coffee pile with the caper and strongbark piles. It's not for nothing that we call our youngest, "Eva Destruction." She soon grew sick of my chastisements and went inside. Substituting my clumsy fingers for the chopstick, finally, I managed pretty much to poke the seeds beneath the skin of the rich soil.

I probably should have scarified the strongbark and caper seeds, at least. The Institute for Regional Conservation website—which I didn't consult until weeks after I planted the seeds—claims that one must, in fact, scarify strongbark and caper seeds. Fucking Carl.

The Russian scientists coaxed life from those 32,000-year-old damaged seeds through a complicated in vitro technique involving tissue extraction and test tubes and various chemicals—techniques, of course, utterly beyond my capacities.

* * *

At the time, anyway, I was feeling pretty good about myself, starting plants from seed. Why hadn't I tried this, earlier? Anticipating my success, I began to approach colleagues at work, asking them if they'd like some native plants once I got them started. Most said "Sure." How else to respond tactfully to my strange ebullience? I can't quite explain my sudden ardor for those sixty seeds, but I think it had something to do with the simplicity of the enterprise. It seemed so fundamental, so earthy, so (and I realize how odd this sounds) gosh-darned cool, misting the seed flat each morning over the next several days, waiting patiently for those first green shoots to show themselves. I felt as if I had tapped into something essential and true.

* * *

We, and our world, all start from seed, planted in the perfect medium. It's an old knowledge. Several Native American creation stories (I'm thinking of an Iroquois version here) feature seeds from the Sky World nourished over the granddaughter of the Sky Woman on what would become earth. From the body of this granddaughter comes the sacred tobacco, strawberry, and sweetgrass. There's plenty of attention to seed in the Hebrew Bible, too—Abraham's seed and what have you. Matthew, in the New Testament, compares the entire Kingdom of God to a mustard seed, the smallest seed, which nonetheless grows into a well-established tree. Dewey Dell, in William Faulkner's *As I Lay Dying* (1930), feels "like a wet seed wild in the hot blind earth." Things, alas, don't come out so great for poor Dewey Dell. Zora Neale Hurston's Janie in *Their Eyes Were Watching God* (1937) "often spoke to falling seeds and said, 'Ah hope you fall on soft ground,' because she had heard seeds saying that to each other as they passed." Fewer and fewer of us, I suspect, manage to retain our innate sympathy with seeds.

* * *

A week passed. Then two weeks. I diligently tended my seeds, misting the soil to keep everything moist. But there wasn't an awful lot to do, truthfully. I had plenty of time to ruminate on my seeds.

* * *

The first of the six orders of the Mishna—itself the first written recording of the "oral law," or Talmud—is called *Zera'im* (Seeds), and deals, specifically, with the agricultural laws and blessings pertaining to the Jews of Palestine. That "seeds" represents the very first section of the Mishnah betrays the rabbis' poetic sensibilities, to be sure. But what most strikes me upon studying the various tractates of *Zera'im* is the literal nature of the rabbis' concerns vis-à-vis our treatment and handling of seeds, plants, and their fruit, the intense level of discourse and debate surrounding, for example, the maintenance of one's fields, which particular fruit ought to be tithed or offered as gifts to the Temple, and in what quantities, the seasons during which fields and trees ought to be left fallow, which particular crops could and could not be mixed. The Talmud, as a whole, represents an astounding document, crafted collectively over centuries, delineating in extraordinary detail, and across every conceivable arena of human affairs, an ethical code of behavior governing our existence in the here and now. First comes first, the rabbis seem to be saying in *Zera'im*. Let us tend our seeds.

* * *

A couple more weeks passed. My seeds showed no signs that they had germinated. I continued to carry out my seedsman's duties. Each morning, I misted the seed flat on the patio with the hose. I began to fiddle a bit with the tray's location, scooting the card table to the edge of its protective cover on clear days to offer the seeds a bit more light, rotating the tray clockwise or counterclockwise.

"It sure is taking a long time for them to sprout," Wendy observed one morning as I fussed over the seeds.

"They can take up to a couple months to germinate," I explained, exaggerating somewhat, my faith just beginning to flag. I might have taken heart in the following passage from Ecclesiastes: "In the morning sow thy seed, And in the evening withhold not thine hand; For thou knowest not whether shall prosper, either this or that, Or whether they both shall be alike good." But I didn't know the passage at the time, which I love for its simplicity, and which continues, "And the light is sweet, And a pleasant thing it is for the eyes to behold the sun."

I probably should have scarified those darned seeds, is what I mostly thought.

* * *

William Bartram was a great collector and grower of seeds. Collecting the seeds of the wondrous flora he comes across in the Carolinas, Georgia, and Florida was essential to his project of knowing his new country. "Having completed my Hortus Siccus," he writes in his famous *Travels* (1791), "and made up my collections of seeds and growing roots, the fruits of my late western tour, and sent them to Charleston, to be forwarded to Europe, I spent the remaining part of this season in botanical excursions to the low countries, between Carolina and East Florida, and collected seeds, roots, and specimens, making drawings of such curious subjects as could not be preserved in their native state of excellence."

Flash forward two hundred years or so. The Norwegian government, in association with the Consultative Group on International Agricultural Research and the Global Crop Diversity Trust, currently maintains the Svalbard Global Seed Vault, commonly referred to as the "doomsday vault." Located inside a mountain just over 800 miles from the North Pole on an island on the Arctic Svalbard Archipelago, scientists involved with the project gather and store duplicates of all seed samples from throughout the planet's crop collection. The vault acts as a backup system for the genetic diversity of the planet's food supply in the event of "natural or manmade disasters," as the Global Crop Diversity Trust website puts it, alluding to such diverse threats as war, climate change, hurricanes, tidal waves, and modern industrial farming that trends increasingly toward monoculture.

Closer to home, the writer and ethnobiologist Gary Paul Nabhan co-founded Native-Seeds-Search in 1983, a nonprofit organization that maintains seed banks of indigenous southwestern U.S. plants to conserve the agro-biodiversity of the region. The organization hopes to preserve the genetic diversity of southwestern crops both to preclude a potential food crisis and to support the essential land- and food-based rituals of the region's Native American tribes. Nabhan and his colleagues have preserved nearly 2,000 varieties of seed, to date, promoting their use and conservation through educational programming—their high-demand Seed School sessions in Tucson—and an online and retail store. Other U.S. nonprofits striving to preserve Indigenous and African derived foodways include the Cherokee Nation Seed Bank, the Hawai'i Public Seed Initiative, the Native American Food Sovereignty Alliance, and Sistah Seeds.

What all these seed-savers are up against, mostly, is industrial agriculture, or Big Ag, as seed-saver Janisse Ray documents chillingly in *The Seed Underground: A Growing Revolution to Save Food* (2012). The development of hybrids in the mid-twentieth century offered corporations the first opportunity to reap immense profits off seeds as the seeds of hybrid plants do not grow "true." Farmers and gardeners, lured by the attractive features of hybrids, could no longer collect the seeds of their plants to produce a new crop next season. Suddenly, they were forced to buy new seeds each year from a corporate supplier. The advent of genetically modified seed technology in the 1990s—and intellectual property litigation favorable, thus far, to Big Ag—has only further concentrated corporate control over the ever-winnowing array of seeds that farmers worldwide can afford to plant.

* * *

My seeds, meantime, might as well have been scattered across the arid southwest, or buried deep below the Arctic permafrost. A month into my project and there were still no signs of nascent coffee or caper or strongbark plants in those sixty cubes of hand-mixed soil. In the merciless way that these things transpire, Eva came home from preschool about this time with a small tray of her own seeds planted in soil: parsley seeds and pea seeds and corn seeds. The idea was to celebrate through these eventual shoots Tu B'shvat, a minor agricultural holiday marking the New Year for trees, which has sort of morphed into a Jewish version of Earth Day. Wendy set Eva's small plastic tray right down next to my flat of wild coffee and Jamaican caper and strongbark seeds. I think it was at precisely this moment that I saw the flat of native seeds as being *my* seeds, my enterprise, while those other seeds represented Eva's (and Wendy's) rival experiment. I wasn't a poor sport about things. I misted Eva's seeds right along with my own seeds, but I can't say I was exactly rooting (no pun intended) for them. Of course, with staggering rapidity—two, three days tops—parsley and pea and corn shoots burst through the soil of Eva's tray, which delighted her.

"Ta-daaa!" she said, joining me on the patio as I misted her seedlings, my seeds. Eva took to joining me out on the patio every morning before I drove her to preschool as I tended the trays. "Ta-daaa!" she exclaimed, repeatedly, as she loomed over her seedlings, my stubborn seeds, opening her palms theatrically toward her thriving colony, flashing her little corn-niblet teeth. I can't be sure about this, and so I hesitate to say anything, and I should first mention that I love my younger daughter to pieces (heck, I love all three of my kids), and think the world of Eva, truly, she's a real pistol, adorable too with bouncy brown curls . . . and yet, having said all this, I'm pretty sure that Eva knew that she was being something of a little jerk the way she gloated over her plants every morning as I labored fruitlessly over my larger flat of sleepy seeds.

"Ta-daaa!"

But I was in no rush, I kept reminding myself. I wouldn't let my daughter psych me out. I would be patient.

* * *

Patience. During my early travails as a seedsman, it was impressed upon me in countless small ways that the patience the endeavor required of me was hopelessly out of step with the spirit of the times. Driving Eva to preschool one morning in the midst of my project, I stopped for one of those big yellow school buses on the other side of the street that was flashing its red lights, its miniature STOP sign propped at its side from a mechanical arm. A minivan approached from behind at a fast clip (which is why I probably noticed it in the rearview mirror), swerved over, and screeched to a halt beside me. A septuagenarian driver motioned for me to roll down my window and then chastised me for stopping. "The rule is," he irascibly explained, "if there's a three-foot gap and you're driving on the other side of the road, you don't have to stop for the buses." Before I could even respond, the septuagenarian in the minivan had sped off toward wherever he was rushing.

The bus eventually folded back its little stop sign and drove off, and I sped off too. A voice brayed on the radio, "Metro PCS believes that *everyone* should have 4G LTE service." A bumper sticker on the Subaru in front of me, I noticed, featured a familiar graphic of a hiker in mid-stride brandishing a walking stick, but an incongruous slogan, "Hike Faster." Later that week, Amazon CEO Jeff Bezos announced that his company planned to offer, in the not-too-distant future, thirty-minute home-delivery of packages via drone-like "octocopters," presumably so consumers needn't wait a whole day or two to receive purchases below a certain weight and volume.

* * *

It was the seventh week after planting my seeds that I noticed the first hint of green in one of the strongbark cubes, just barely parting the dark soil at the surface. Eventually, and over several days, fourteen additional seeds that I had planted would sprout into slowly unfurling leaves perched on hopeful stems. By this time, we had already transferred Eva's mighty seedlings to our small vegetable garden, where they continued to grow at a randy rate, crowding out my rosemary and eggplants and serrano peppers.

"Fifteen out of sixty," I posed to Wendy. "That's not *so* bad a success rate for my first time." She raised her eyebrows at me, sort of chuckled. I ought to have mentioned by now that Wendy was raised in rural Pennsylvania, that her father, who built his own house, is practically a subsistence farmer and has grown his vegetables from seed for as long as I've known him.

"I mean if it were baseball," I continued.

I might have overwatered most of my poor seeds, it occurred to me, killing them with kindness; or I might have buried them too deep with my clumsy fingers; or I might have simply plucked the berries and depulped the seeds before they were fully ripe. There are a lot of things that could have gone wrong is the thing of it.

My wife's refusal to act impressed didn't dampen my own enthusiasm at my partial (and, by that point, unexpected) success. "Look, Eva!" I exclaimed, "Ta-daaa!" I spritzed my new plants with even greater diligence, moved their card table in and out of their covered spot to afford them optimal sunlight, cooed encouragements toward the new stems and leaves without even a trace of ironic detachment. Then I made a rookie mistake. *Botany for Gardeners* suggested that a seedling becomes autotrophic—an independent organism—once it lifts its first leaves to the light. Reading this, and overestimating my first seedling's independence, I yanked it out of its comfortable cube of soil too soon and must have damaged its few roots, which were far more underdeveloped than I had anticipated. I tried transplanting the poor creature to a pot, but it soon withered and died.

I couldn't just let the seedling be a seedling and do its thing. I had to poke and prod at the soil to hurry it along.

* * *

When Wendy was pregnant with Eva, 3-D sonogram technology was newly available for the purchase. Sample images of fetal faces on that slick photographic paper—images which seemed preternatural and ghoulish to my eyes—were festooned across the wall beside the receptionist's desk of her OB-GYN's office. As these images, in our case and in most cases, were not medically indicated, it struck me at the time as inappropriate, as not-quite-right, somehow. It betrays, I still feel, our unprecedented impatience with the organic order of things. Even the medically indicated tests began to grate against me during Wendy's third pregnancy. It was a "late" pregnancy, a "high-risk" pregnancy, we were constantly reminded, so there were countless batteries of tests to perform, which Wendy hadn't been compelled to undergo during her first two pregnancies, and which struck me as invasive, not so much against Wendy, but against the sprout growing inside her. In due time, we'd be poking and prodding at the poor thing, subjecting her to our smothering love and attention. Her brief time in the womb, her private and self-contained growing medium, seemed special and inviolable to me, something to be respected.

Yet we can't just let seedlings be seedlings.

* * *

We try to teach patience to our children, anyway. The classic *Frog and Toad Together* (1972) by Arnold Lobel, is one of Eva's favorite books. Toad, in one of the chapters, admires Frog's beautiful flowers so Frog gives him a bag of flower seeds so that he might start his own garden. Toad plants his seeds but grows surly when they refuse to sprout right away. He tries all manner of strategies, including harassing the poor seeds: "Toad put his head very close to the ground and shouted 'NOW SEEDS, START GROWING!'" Upon Frog's encouragement, Toad learns that he must simply be patient and allow the sunshine and the rain to do their work. The seeds, in due time, grow into flowers.

* * *

After the mishap with my first seedling, I resolved to practice greater patience with the remaining fourteen plants. Truth is, though, patience is not my virtue. I'm probably every bit as impatient as the septuagenarian in the minivan (if not Lobel's Toad), which is probably why his performance irked me so; it's never nice to witness a display of your own shortcomings. People just getting to know me invariably express surprise to hear that among my favorite hobbies are birdwatching, fishing, and native plant gardening. I'm highly kinetic, which seems to belie such sedate avocations. I walk, for example, at an impossibly fast clip. Colleagues at work often tease me about this. The cadence of my speech is just as fast, so fast that I must expend fierce effort to slow myself down and speak intelligibly. I find it difficult to sit still. "Let's *do* something!" I often exhort my family on sleepy weekend mornings. Yet it's precisely my near-hyper predilections that compel me to pursue hobbies that force me to slow down, to breathe deeply and take life's measure. It may be why I write and read, too.

Life, however—or at least the modern lives to which most of us have accommodated ourselves—tends to discourage, if not altogether quash, our efforts to enact greater thoughtfulness and patience. Staccato bursts of unrelated or loosely related activities, many of them mediated by various technologies, increasingly define the texture of my days, as the very form of this chapter might suggest. It's staggering to contemplate all the sheer stuff I did and the things that happened, most of it fairly banal, in my domestic and workplace spheres during the few months that I nursed my few seeds into tiny plants. I won't bore you with a daily catalog, or even the highlights, such as they were, but take my word for it—it was a lot.

Tending to the flat of seeds each morning for a few moments offered me relief from the low-level chaos that increasingly defines our *now* and never seemed like an additional chore. For weeks, those sleepy seeds didn't seem to be doing *anything* and they expected so little of me. They were in no rush. I could almost feel my pulse abate in their presence. It was nice to be on seed-time.

* * *

There's nothing particularly special or even contemporary about my sense that our felt lives rush past at too dizzying a speed. Such concerns date back at least as far as the pastoral literary tradition of the Greek and Roman poets (Theocritus, Virgil, Horace, et al.) and, in the United States, to the beginning of the Industrial Revolution. *Rural Hours* (1850), Susan Fenimore Cooper's nature diary of Cooperstown, New York, challenges in its very title the quicker rhythms to which her neighbors were adjusting. During her long life, she dutifully worked as her father's secretary, bolstering his more prominent career as a novelist. Yet it's tempting to see *Rural Hours* as a bold challenge to her father's comparatively action-packed Leatherstocking Tales, which both catered to and shaped the temperament of his time. While her father gained quite a large audience through imagining Natty Bumpo's masculine adventures, the younger Cooper offered an audacious alternative in *Rural Hours*, "the simple record of those little events which make up the course of the seasons in rural life," as she writes in her preface. The dispersal of various seeds, incidentally, occupies a fair bit of her attention. "Friday, 12th .—" she writes,

> The aspens are in leaf, and look beautifully on the hill-side, their tremulous foliage being among the very earliest to play in the spring breezes, as their downy seeds are the first of the year to fly abroad; these are as common in the wood at one moment in the spring, as the thistle-down later in the season among the fields; one often sees them lying in little patches along the highway, looking like a powdering of snow-flakes. The birds of some more delicate tribes use this down to line their nests—the humming-bird, for instance.

Stop rolling your eyes, reader. This is important. Slow down. Look. As Cooper looked. "Pleasant day," she writes later in *Rural Hours*:

> Walked some distance along the bank of the river. Gathered handsome berries of the cranberry-tree. Found many vines along the bank in that direction; bitter-sweet, with its red berries; hairy honeysuckle; green-L briars, with their dark-blue berries. . . . Observed several soft maples of a clear gold-color throughout, while others near them were bright crimson; they are not so variegated as the sugar maple.

What have you noticed outside, lately?

* * *

My seed project may have started out as a pecuniary matter, as part of my larger project to propagate native Florida plants, but I kept at it so doggedly, I think, mainly because I liked the way it felt, the way it feels, for those few moments each day when I paid close attention to something so small, so simple, and yet so wondrous. Thoreau, we ought to remember, didn't claim to have "great faith in a seed" to dress up our present-day T-shirts and coffee mugs and backpacks. He wrote these evocative lines in one of his later essays, "The Succession of Forest Trees," to convince a skeptical public that the dispersal of seeds by wind, water, and animals—not spontaneous generation, or God—accounted for the eventual appearance of an oak stand where a stand of pines had recently been cut down, and to convince his neighbors that this scientific fact was something worth marveling over. Thoreau painstakingly tracked the eating and caching habits of jays and squirrels and examined the understory in Concord's established woodlots to demonstrate the symbiotic relationship between trees and animals. Small oak trees "planted" by squirrels permeated the understory of Concord's dense pine forests, Thoreau observed, but withered undetected beneath the dense canopy of the established pines; once the pines were cleared, any surviving oak sprigs flourished under the more favorable conditions to succeed the onetime pine forest. A tree, then, starts from seed. Case closed. "If any one asserts that it sprang from something else, or nothing," Thoreau wryly argued, "the burden of proof lies with him." Thoreau's scientific discoveries, again, amplified his sense of wonder with the natural world. That a tree originated in a small seed was for Thoreau "equally mysterious" to the competing divine or pseudoscientific explanations advanced by his contemporaries.

* * *

As I write these lines, I have yet to transplant my surviving native plant seedlings into larger pots. The young coffee and strongbark and caper plants boast several leaves. They stand several inches tall in their soil cubes and might be root-bound by now. Soon, I tell myself, I'll scoop them out and transplant them into pots. Soon. But I don't want to rush things. It's nice to be on seed-time. Meanwhile, I find myself brooding over the Svalbard Global Seed Vault, or "doomsday vault." It's easy to take the cynical view, the very necessity of the enterprise underscoring our shortsighted industrial agricultural practices and unsustainable living practices, generally, the vault itself a harbinger of, well, doomsday. Still, as I tend my few seedlings on my patio in the cozy warmth of the subtropics, my mind wanders to the Svalbard workers wearing thick parkas in their sub-zero environs, gathering and storing the billion-plus seeds that represent all of the world's crops in a large room down a long concrete tunnel carved into a frozen mountain on a small spit of land at the top of the planet. I think of the Native-Seeds-Search seed banks and seed school in Tucson, the Russian scientists breathing life into those 32,000-year-old seeds of *S. stenophylla*, I think of the Talmudic rabbis and Bartram and Cooper and Thoreau and all the present-day seed-savers out there. But mostly I think of my incorrigible younger daughter looming over her parsley and pea and corn seeds—"ta-daaa!"—and I marvel at our wise and enduring faith in a seed.

2

The Last Patch of Florida Land

People travel to the Florida Keys not so much for the land but for the water. What little land there is jutting just above sea level from Key Largo to Key West has mostly a weary, provisional feel to it, unlikely limestone outcroppings curling southwest just over 100 miles. Most of the Keys aren't even true islands but exposed remnants of onetime reef, the hardened remains of ancient sea creatures and artificial fill, some of it cobbled together by Henry Flagler's laborers in the first decade of the twentieth century so that they could lay track for his doomed railroad. The tracks, stretches of which you can still see, were washed under by the Labor Day Hurricane of 1935 along with hundreds of human victims, roughly half of whom were World War I veterans employed by President Roosevelt's Works Progress Administration to build the present-day highway.

But I'm all about the neglected land of the Keys today. I'm not interested in its lovely aquamarine waters, maybe because so many other people are. I operate under the assumption (highfalutin and obnoxious, I realize) that the most worthwhile places to see are likely those that hold the least general appeal. And so I'm on my way 100 miles south from my Florida home to the Dagny Johnson Key Largo Hammock Botanical State Park. This scruffy, 2,400-acre natural site stretches like a long green finger northward on the island for several miles starting where the U.S. Route 1 crosses Jewfish Creek onto the Keys from the Florida mainland. I peel away from most of the Keys-bound commuters about twenty miles before this intersection, when I turn off the U.S. 1 onto Card Sound Road just south of Florida City, not so much a city proper as a strip of highway festooned by every fast-food franchise you can imagine on either side. The Card Sound route juts eastward across the Card Sound Bridge to northern Key Largo and Country Road 905, which then cuts southward for about ten miles—most of this acreage representing the hammock—before joining back up again with the U.S. 1.

It's about eight miles longer getting to the Keys from Card Sound Road, so commuters generally stick to the more direct route on the U.S. 1 from Florida City, which was the route of Flagler's railroad as well. It's mostly a pleasant, wild stretch of land along Card Sound Road, accented by intermittent expanses of marsh and mangrove-lined creeks. I open my windows to take in the sulfur smell of the mangroves, which sure beats the smell of the automotive exhaust and fried food I've left behind in Florida City. Still, the tension between the wild land and our human designs upon it can't be escaped so quickly. Gargantuan cement power poles on the north side of the road loom like schoolyard bullies over the mangrove-lined creek on the south side. I pass an enormous Cemex cement plant, which surprises me. It doesn't seem like there's enough solid earth around to sustain such an enterprise. Before long, I pay my one-dollar toll, cross the bridge over the open expanse of water, and find myself on the northern end of Key Largo.

A combination of factors has staved off most real estate development here. As Joy Williams documents in her indispensable book, *The Florida Keys: A History & Guide* (1987), speculators bought up much of the land in the 1950s and planned to create a new city of 100,000 people. Thankfully, the Nature Conservancy and the U.S. Fish and Wildlife Service bought the land back and designated it the Crocodile Lake National Wildlife Refuge. In the 1980s, a massive condominium development was well underway on the adjacent site of the present-day Dagny Johnson Key Largo Hammock Botanical State Park, but the developers went bust. Today, the embattled presence of the American alligator, American crocodile, Key Largo cotton mouse, Schaus' swallowtail butterfly, Eastern indigo snake, and Key Largo woodrat—all of which receive some measure of federal protection as threatened or endangered species—represents the strongest bulwark against future development. I haven't yet seen a woodrat in person, one of North America's most endangered mammals, but photos of these nocturnal rodents suggest that they're much comelier than the Norway rat, which most people think of when they think rat. Florida's version is smaller and boasts much larger ears and eyes. They could really use a rebranding campaign.

William Bartram was impressed enough by Florida's woodrats that he contributed one of the earliest accounts of the species in his *Travels* (1791). "The wood-rat," Bartram writes, is a very curious animal, they are not half the size of the domestic rat; of a dark brown or black colour; their tail slender and shorter in proportion, and covered thinly with short hair; they are singular with respect to their ingenuity and great labour in the construction of their habitations, which are conical pyramids about three or four feet high, constructed with dry branches, which they collect with great labour and perseverance, and pile up without any apparent order, yet they are so interwoven with one another, that it would take a bear or wild-cat some time to pull one of these castles to pieces, and allow the animals sufficient time to secure retreat with their young.

The woodrat, along with the manifold Florida plants and animals that Bartram painstakingly describes in his classic work, might be seen as links in a chain that connect Bartram and his contemporaries with those of us living in Florida now. It means something, I think, that the ingenious log structures of the Key Largo woodrat, which I might stumble upon today in the hammock, would closely resemble those pyramids that Bartram gazed upon and described over two hundred years ago. It may be the closest we can get to our American predecessors, these singular moments of shared sight across centuries. These ever-evolving but enduring landscapes are fast disappearing, however—collateral damage, mostly, of our competing human endeavors (e.g., agricultural, residential, and commercial development), which include collecting pressure by orchid, fern, and bromeliad thieves, tree snail and butterfly poachers, and the various environmental depredations that have accompanied our drastically warming planet (incursions of exotic plants and animals, advancing armies of new pests and blights, etc.). Bartram, writing well before the Industrial Revolution, couldn't imagine that humans would represent a threat to woodrat well-being far greater than bears and wildcats, that we would so drastically alter the wild land he so assiduously documented.

I remember how blue it made me feel in 2003 when the movie version of *Cold Mountain* was released, and I heard that it was mostly filmed in the Carpathian Mountains of Romania, not in the American south. One of the major complications of filming the movie in the United States, apparently, was that the landscape of the American south had been so irretrievably altered since the Civil War. Some might call this progress, I suppose, but it seemed almost inexpressibly sad to me that filmmakers seeking to capture an American past not so very distant, really, were now compelled to outsource our forests and meadows and mountains to Eastern Europe.

Most of us, these days, must drive a fair distance in our carbon-spewing automobiles to access shrinking acres of green. We are all the progeny of William Faulkner's multiracial McCaslins and Sartorises and Edmondses in *Go Down, Moses* (1942), who hear the whirring of the sawmills chewing through cypress and gum and oak, who feel at first that the Big Woods and their creatures (ivory-billed woodpeckers and deer and bears) will surely repel this "puny gnawing," but who see the wilderness recede further and further from their homes in the span of their mere human lifetimes.

* * *

I drive on—what choice do I have?—make my way south toward the entrance of the Dagny Johnson Key Largo Hammock Botanical State Park between a high thicket of trees on either side of the narrow two-lane road. I must be buzzing past innumerable tree species in this hammock, and I can make out the rusty bark of a gumbo limbo here, the scythe-shaped leaves of a mahogany there, but nearest the road the trees stand not so much as individuals but as uniform green walls; they've recently been trimmed back with what must have been an enormous vertical mower. Left to their own devices, it wouldn't take long at all, clearly, for these tree walls to converge and erase the highway. Our human encroachment on the land seems fairly modest for the moment, anyway. I lean my elbow out the window, take in the spicier, vegetal aroma that has overtaken the earlier mangrove sulfur.

A few parking spots and a high concrete archway—a remnant from the abandoned real estate development—greets me at the park's mouth. "WELCOME TO . . . *the Real Florida,*" a brown sign against the archway reads. I've been to this park a few times, and my initial impression is always the same as I walk under the archway and enter the hammock, that it's not quite "real" enough and that it's even somewhat creepy, the inharmonious convergence of this wild hammock and the broad asphalt road, originally designed for automotive, rather than pedestrian, traffic. There's a vague *Planet of the Apes* feel to these few accessible acres of the park. It's not only the archway and the asphalt road. As you walk, you glimpse partially buried coral walls amid the green; you reach a circular courtyard, which seems to have been designed as a traffic roundabout; you pass through a dank concrete tunnel beneath an abandoned roadbed. Would a contemporary filmmaker, I wonder, be able to erase the archway, the coral walls, the courtyard, the tunnel and asphalt road from the camera's field of view?

The "real" part of this park, the wild part, isn't too impressive at first glance. The first thought you're likely to have is that it's little more than a bramble. Hardly any of the stately (and mostly non-native) palms that you see on the Florida postcards. The canopy isn't very high, only thirty feet or so. Most individual trees boast only modest, near spindly, trunks. A dense, green understory of shrubs and vines—and, no doubt, the thicker clouds of mosquitoes off the asphalt trail—dispel any notions you might entertain of traversing the hammock itself. There's not much chance I'll glimpse a woodrat's abode through the foliage. It's impolitic to say, but one could see how real estate developers and politicos alike could look at this tangled landscape and figure that it wouldn't be any great crime to clear it for condos.

The trouble, however, is with our eyes, not with the "bramble." When it comes to trees and forests, we tend to celebrate heft. Maybe it's John Muir's fault, whose voice and concerns seem so contemporary compared to his lesser-read predecessor, Bartram. All the hay Muir made over those mighty sequoias out West. Or those Hudson River School artists and their outsized landscape paintings. It takes some concentration to set aside these notions privileging the scale of individual specimens and to see and appreciate the great tree *diversity* standing on either side of the asphalt trail—the tradeoff for size in a subtropical hammock. I'm standing on the site of the greatest tree diversity in the entire United States(!) Bill Pranty's *A Birder's Guide to Florida* (2005) informs me. Taking some time to study the leaves and bark of the trees before me, along with the help of a separate guidebook, I'm able to distinguish pigeon plum from poisonwood from wild tamarind from gumbo limbo from Bahama strongbark from satinleaf from blolly from lancewood. And more! Most of these trees originated in the West Indies and were established here through the digestive tracts of migratory, seed-eating birds: Bahama mockingbirds, summer tanagers, white-crowned pigeons, and mangrove cuckoos, all of which can be seen here if you keep your eyes and ears open and get a bit lucky.

I don't get so lucky today. I'd especially like to glimpse a few white-crowned pigeons, one of the local specialties that John James Audubon painted so beautifully on his 1832 visit after shooting God knows how many of the poor creatures from their perches. I scan the tops of the tallest pigeon plums and poisonwoods for the birds. No dice. I turn my attention once again to the plants themselves. Looking down into the understory, I'm able to recognize the shiny green tongues of Jamaican caper leaves, the broader, flatter, and lighter-green leaves of beauty berry, and the crinkly-looking leaves of wild coffee. I've laid down hefty sums to buy these specimens from Carl and Donna at my native plant nursery. I've spent countless hours babying them with copious doses of water, slow-release fertilizers in various optimal nutrient proportions, and neem oil spritzings to fend off various pests and blights. So it's sort of nice, and oddly surprising, miraculous even, to see that these distinct plants actually do grow all by themselves in their natural environs, this still-wild land. Eventually, I reach a birdy patch. I'm not the most talented birder, but I can make out the telltale song of a white-eyed vireo—*chik-aperweeo-chik*—even though I can't spot it inside the dense canopy. Next, I glimpse a couple northern parulas (one of my favorite warblers) with their chestnut necklaces, and several tiny gray gnatcatchers flitting about in the greenery fifteen feet high hunting countless varieties of insects. I see several small ovenbirds, too, bobbing their Mohawk-striped heads as they walk across the ground, mostly away from me. If it weren't for these precious remaining acres of unfragmented hammock on the Keys, where would these tired creatures go during the winter, or on their migration stopovers to and from the tropics? The hammock offers a respite for me as well. I feel my pulse abate as I stand still here for several minutes and just watch and listen while breathing in the ripe, earthy smell of the trees and shrubs in varying states of composition and decomposition.

This contact with Florida's last bit of land before giving way to the ocean makes my mind wander to a more remote human history, more remote than Bartram. Take away the unwelcome remnants of the failed condominium development, it occurs to me, and this second- and third-growth hammock looks pretty much the same as the first-growth hammock must have looked to Florida's Native Americans, who feasted on the fish- and crustacean-rich waters nearby and, in turn, were surely feasted upon by swarms of mosquitoes, no-see-ums, and sand gnats. A site here on Key Largo has been radiocarbon dated to 1000 B.C. In the 1500s, the first Europeans started to arrive, mostly to plunder the island's resources—which included timber from the hammock—enslave the natives, and/or convert them to Christianity. Small wonder that early encounters in and around this Key Largo Hammock weren't always so peaceable. Not far from the very site on which I stand, on June 23, 1837, Captain John Whalton and four of his crewmen—who were stationed on the vessel *Florida*, a floating light to warn ships off the treacherous Carysfort Reef—paddled ashore on one of the ship's boats to gather wood. Unfortunately for Whalton and his crew, the Second Seminole War was still raging and they were ambushed by Indian musket fire. Captain Whalton and one member of his crew were killed, while the two other crewmen escaped. The floating light *Florida* remained in commission for another fifteen years before it was replaced by the Carysfort Reef Lighthouse, the first of six iron screw-pile lighthouses built between 1852 and 1880 off the Keys, which continue to warn ships off its reef. Manned until 1960, the light atop the Carysfort Reef Lighthouse receives its charge today from a solar panel.

Florida's Indigenous peoples. William Bartram. Captain John Whalton. A solitary lighthouse keeper perched atop Carysfort Reef. One of our prevailing myths, writ large in our literature and at least partly true, is that excursions into the wild represent antidotal escapes from society. Yet my various excursions, as I've already mentioned, never quite fit this description. My short visit to the hammock today, for example, puts me into contact with nature *and* humankind, but a different sort of human contact than I'll experience once I'm back at the office.

I continue on the trail, preoccupied by visions of wooden ships under mast and Native American settlements, until the canopy opens up to a mangrove expanse and the asphalt trail gives way to a narrow, unpaved path. I shield my eyes from the restored sun until they adjust to the new light. I can't see the ocean or the nearby Carysfort Reef Lighthouse, but a briny smell overtakes the spice of the trees behind me. I don't see much wildlife about, but a white pelican on the wing drifts lazily across my field of view in the distance. The path loops for a mile or so around this marshy section before it brings me back to the canopy of hardwoods. Pretty soon, I run into a couple walking their dogs, which are permitted at the park on leash.

"Can you get all the way around now," the woman utters as they near, "or is the tide up?"

"I just did the loop," I say, "so I guess it's low tide." They thank me without breaking stride, keeping up with the dogs bucking against their restraints. I didn't know that I wouldn't have been able to go all the way around the trail had the tide been up. But I love that this is true. Maybe there's no escaping the water here on the Keys, after all. No matter. It feels good to be on this last patch of Florida land that just barely escaped our recent human designs, a place still shaped by the peregrinations and digestive inclinations of white-crowned pigeons, and the timeless pull of the tides.

3

The End of Orange Juice?

There's been no shortage of bad news lately, so you'd be forgiven for overlooking the crisis that has befallen the U.S. citrus industry. Yet it's been harder to ignore for those of us living in Florida, the state which typically produces over 70 percent of the nation's citrus supply but has lately produced some of the smallest crops since the 1940s. Hurricane Irma in 2017 and Ian in 2022 decimated many of the groves after cutting swaths straight through the prime citrus region in the center of the peninsula known as "the Ridge," uprooting mature trees and flooding groves. The latest, post-Ian projections forecast agricultural losses in Florida at $1.5 billion and losses from the citrus industry, specifically, at $304 million.

Yet Hurricanes Irma and Ian only exacerbated long-standing difficulties the citrus industry has been facing. Growers can't seem to catch a break over the twenty-five-plus years that I've lived here. Citrus canker was the first scourge on my radar screen. The airborne bacterial disease, which causes lesions to develop on leaves and fruit, proved almost impossible to contain. In 2002, Governor Jeb Bush made the controversial executive decision both to destroy trees afflicted with canker and healthy trees in close proximity to diseased specimens, which resulted in the destruction of 1.5 million trees in commercial groves and 603,000 trees in private homeowners' yards. Next, came "citrus greening," a bacterial disease spread by a tiny insect, which turns the fruit bitter and unusable, and eventually kills the tree itself, including one of my own treasured Persian limes. All the while, residential and commercial developers have been making purchase offers that embattled citrus growing families can't refuse, turning sweet-smelling groves and their associated fruit-stands into less sweet-smelling strip malls and stucco subdivisions. In the five years *before* Irma, citrus production in Florida had already declined by roughly 50 percent.

Before we consign the industry to its unfortunate fate, it's worth reflecting upon how citrus trees—which originated in China before making their way to North America along with the first Spanish conquistadors—

managed to infiltrate so much Florida acreage and the American family kitchen in the first place. It wasn't easy. The notion of drinking oranges, rather than eating them once in a while, was an alien concept at the beginning of the twentieth century. Then, the Spanish Flu pandemic of 1918 struck, claiming roughly 675,000 American lives. Parents were primed for dietary solutions to stave off future scourges. The general public already knew that citrus somehow prevented scurvy among sailors (hence the term, "limeys"), and so the citrus industry adroitly advanced claims of the manifold tonic effects of orange juice, even before scientists identified ascorbic acid (aka vitamin C) as its principal salubrious ingredient.

Sunkist in California enlisted the services of the now-legendary adman Albert D. Lasker, who initiated the "Drink an Orange" campaign. "Orange juice—a *delicious* beverage—is *healthfulness itself,*" the first line of a vintage print ad reads. To bolster its advertising efforts, Sunkist developed new electric juicers for both commercial and residential use. Demand for orange juice spiked, and the industry did a good job responding to, and even shaping, the capricious demands of consumers. The technological innovation of frozen concentrate orange juice soon after World War II, spearheaded by the Minute Maid Company in Florida, was all the rage. Like many culinary advances of its time, frozen concentrate promised to save housewives hours of domestic labor. Readers of a certain age, like me, will probably remember teasing the gloopy frozen mass out of those cylindrical containers with a wooden spoon before diluting it in a pitcher with three portions of water. When tastes shifted in the late 1980s from laboratory-spawned products to "fresh" foods, Tropicana and other companies simply shifted their production and advertising efforts to "not from concentrate" juice.

That was then and this is now. While disease and weather-related calamities, and the enticements of real estate developers, have struck the industry low, nutritionists and pediatricians today may represent the greater threat. Sugar, rather than fat, is the latest bugaboo in our perennial obsessiveness over what foods we ought not to eat, and orange juice (along with other fruit juices and sodas) finds itself increasingly in the crosshairs. In 2017, the American Academy of Pediatrics issued its updated recommendations, warning parents to limit toddlers' juice consumption to four ounces per day, eight ounces per day for children seven and up, citing the adverse effects of weight gain, gastrointestinal issues, and tooth decay.

I'm not credentialed to dispute these expert recommendations, and many of the health claims advanced by the citrus industry over the years (which range from preventing miscarriage, heart attack, and acne to stimulating the get-up-and-go of football players) have certainly been outsized. Even so, in this era of heavily processed, powdered protein drinks, souped-up "water," and dubiously sourced, frozen concoctions derived from exotic fruits purported to be "superfoods," I still put my faith in actual foods, which include the fresh-squeezed orange juice I've enjoyed since I was a youngster.

While I've lived in Florida for most of my adult life, I was raised in the San Fernando Valley of California, that other orange mecca, in a subdivision that was once, you guessed it, an orange grove. A few select survivors of the defunct grove graced the backyards of our ranch-style homes. Among my family's first household purchases was one of those squat, compact juicers developed by Sunkist, and one of my early childhood memories was the sight of my father in his skivvies first light of day, plying one of our backyard trees with the strange-looking fruit picker. I can still hear the whirring sound of that electric juicer, the pitch shifting as he pressed the orange-halves against the cone-shaped reamer with alternating degrees of force. I can still taste on my tongue the impossibly sweet, sun-warmed juice. Back in those days, a few remnant groves in the Valley remained, and I remember being struck by the distinctive perfume of citrus flowers certain times of the year and the curious geometries of those tree-rows flying past as I leaned my head out the window of my mother's station wagon. (These geometries, incidentally, inspired the father of American ballet, George Balanchine, to arrange his dancers on stage to stand like trees in an orange grove.)

Okay, so I'm not an unbiased party in this tale of our current citrus woes. And, yes, the citrus tree, as I've acknowledged above, is not native to either Florida or California. All the same, since its introduction several hundred years ago, citrus has worked itself so thoroughly into our home soil—literally and figuratively—that its story at the very least complicates the native versus exotic paradigm. Many of us plant-lovers rely upon this paradigm too uncritically, I'd argue, to designate "good" versus "evil" plant specimens. I'll have more to say about this later, but for now the story of citrus in North America impels us to consider, anyway, whether the dichotomy might prove overly reductive in certain instances. I'm willing to offer citrus, a non-invasive specimen (unlike melaleuca and Brazilian pepper, still ravaging the Everglades ecosystem), at least honorary native standing given its fruitful intermingling with our human story in North America. I think it seemed a miracle to both my parents, hailing from a frigid Scranton, PA, that they could raise their own citrus trees and pick their own oranges to juice and enjoy over their breakfast. It sure seemed like a miracle to me during my California childhood, and it still seems like a miracle to me in Florida, today.

4

Slashed

Pity the poor slash pine, a species distinct from the more beloved longleaf pine, aka heart pine or yellow pine or Georgia pine.

Longleaf pine flatwoods—identified as pine "barrens" by William Bartram in his *Travels* (1791)—once dominated the coastal plain in the U.S. South, covering nearly 90 million acres prior to European settlement. Deploying such terms as "sublime," "stately," and "great," these longleaf forests left Bartram fairly besotted. It would take only a hundred years or so for Euro-American settlers to decimate these woods, the timber felled for ship- and housebuilding, flooring, and fuel. Only about 3 percent of the original expanse remains. These mature longleaf patches in national forests and military bases in the South contain one of the world's most diverse plant communities, support nearly 200 species of birds (providing crucial breeding habitat for the endangered red-cockaded woodpecker), and hundreds of other animal species, several of them threatened or endangered, from the indigo snake to the Florida panther. Contemporary botanical books and guides, such as Rufino Osorio's *A Gardener's Guide to Florida's Native Plants* (2001), call the longleaf pine "magnificent" and "majestic." They inspire memoirs, paintings, and odes, including one entire book of recent poetry, *Longleaf* (2017), by John Saad.

Slash pines, by contrast—"the fast-growing off-site species of pine that is replacing longleaf throughout the South because of its greater commercial value," notes Janisse Ray in her *Ecology of a Cracker Childhood* (1999)—have served awfully few as an artistic muse. It is not an ideal landscaping tree too close to roads and sidewalks, a few online sources claim, as its shaded lower branches die and drop as the tree grows taller and might fall on vehicles or people. "Needles seem to fall from the tree all during the year," a fact sheet from the U.S. Forest Service warns, "creating slippery walks." Unlike longleaf pine, the slash pine has inspired few nicknames. Slash pine, most people call slash pine.

* * *

Pinus elliottii. Slash pine. A large, heavily branched, deep-rooted conifer growing up to 100 feet tall, its bark gray-brown to russet, deeply furrowed and scaly. Crown shape: oval; pyramidal. Leaf arrangement: alternate; spiral. Leaf type: simple. Leaf margin: entire. Distinguished from longleaf pine by its much thinner branchlet tips only a half inch in diameter versus branchlet tips an inch or so in diameter for longleaf; needle lengths eight to twelve inches versus twelve-to-eighteen-inch longleaf needles (in bundles of twos and threes on the same tree, whereas longleaf bundles are always in threes); spiny-scaled cones three to five inches long versus six-to-ten-inch longleaf cones. Wild turkeys and squirrels (gray and fox) savor the cones of both species. Natural range: smallest of all major southern pines, extending from southeastern South Carolina to Central, South Florida, and the Keys, and west to Louisiana. "South Florida slash pine ... was the source of dense, resin-free, long-lasting wood, called 'Dade County pine,' used in early homes," according to the authors of *Native Florida Plants* (2004).

* * *

My eight-year-old daughter Eva doesn't know that slash pine needles and cones are much shorter than the gigantic needles and cones of the longleaf, that they lack the longleaf's miraculous fire-resistance, and that they often live out benighted lives crowded in straight rows on tree farms for their timber and (mostly) for their pulp, used to manufacture cellulose, rayon, toilet paper, and other paper products. What she knows is that the frilly, pale-green seedlings bursting just a few inches above the sandy soil beneath the torn canopy of their parent trees are "so cute." She wants to take several home and plant them.

We are touring the grounds of the Morikami Museum and Japanese Gardens in Palm Beach County, Florida, the site of a short-lived agricultural settlement founded by Japanese immigrants in the first decade of the twentieth century. My wife and I tell Eva that it wouldn't be right or even legal to harvest these infant trees from the scrupulously maintained grounds. (What *we* don't know yet is that these frilly, apparently trunkless, seedlings are in the "grass stage" of slash pine life, the first two to five years when these trees forgo upward growth to develop a large tap root instead. During this phase, the vulnerable apical tip, buried at the center of its foliage clump, is fairly well protected from fire. The developing tap root hoards carbohydrates for the energy it will use during the "bolt stage" that comes next, when the tree bolts as high as five feet per year to usher the apical tip above the reach of most ground fires.) We promise our daughter that we will visit a plant nursery soon and buy a young slash pine, preferably one a bit older and taller than these ankle-high seedlings. Eva doesn't seem so happy about this delay in her plan. A band of blue jays holler from high up in the scaffolding of slash pine branches, criticizing each other, or us.

* * *

Slash pines "create a natural bird sanctuary," an online source suggests. They "provide shelter to birds from predators, attract the pileated woodpecker (the big 'Woody Woodpecker'), and are home to owls. Even eagles and egrets will make their nests in the treetops of a large pine." Yes. This morning as I walk the dog, I notice a yellow-crowned night-heron perched about sixty feet up on a thick slash pine branch bathing its pretty plumage in the dawn's molten light. For the past several springs, we have watched a veritable rookery of these handsome herons build their nests and raise their young in the high branches of two slash pines at our neighborhood park. Pine Breeze Park, its name. Eva likes gathering up the rust-colored needles shed by the trees at the park to line the bottom of the screech owl and woodpecker nest boxes we've installed in our oak trees.

* * *

Locating a slash pine tree for sale at the nurseries closest to our home proves to be more of a challenge than I anticipated. The fellow at the largest nursery I frequent in Broward County offers me a perplexed look when I ask him (optimistically) where he keeps the slash pines, as if I had asked after the tennis rackets, unicycles, or unicorns he surely stocks along his neat garden rows. Gathering his wits, he explains that very few people visit the nursery looking for slash pines, which most consider "sloppy."

Small wonder that so few slash pines remain in my neighborhood, named Palm Beach Farms. Once a pine flatwoods, then a pineapple farm (hence the neighborhood name), the slash pines and the understory of palmetto, wiregrass, wax myrtle, and the hundreds of other plants associated with this most extensive terrestrial ecosystem in the state, were first thinned to provide ample sunlight for the pineapples, peppers, and beans grown here and, then, all but cleared by the end of the 1970s as the last homes in my neighborhood were built on small lots of a quarter acre or so. Several large specimens remain here and there, but over the past ten years we've lived in the subdivision I've discovered that neighbors are a heck of lot more likely to remove a slash pine from their property than to plant one. Its "sloppy" needles notwithstanding, Hurricanes Frances, Jeanne, and Wilma of 2004 and 2005, then Irma in 2017, spooked the South Florida citizenry about any large trees planted near rooftops and windows. The slash pine's reputation for dropping its large horizontal branches has made it something of an *arbor non grata* in my suburban environs. "It's a nuisance tree," one neighbor opines when I ask him what he thinks of the slash pine.

* * *

Nuisance tree. Sloppy tree. Cute tree. Commercially valuable tree. The slash pine—perhaps like most trees—can mean multiple things to multiple people. Eva's sudden interest in these trees makes me want to know more about what they have meant to others whose lives have intersected with them in one way or another. Living in Florida for most of my adult life, I've absorbed faint knowledge that slash pines were associated with the turpentine industry. I've heard the phrase "turpentine camps," usually in association with the various atrocities of the Jim Crow era.

The "naval stores" industry, I learn, dates to the colonial era, when it was discovered that resin could be extracted from southern pines and distilled into pitch to seal ships and into turpentine and rosin for a variety of uses. (Vicks VapoRub, for example, originally contained turpentine.) The bark of mature trees was stripped down to the cambium in a V-shape with a scythe-like tool called a hack. A "Herty pot" container, named after its inventor, was placed below the V-shaped wound to collect the resin. The industry migrated southward from the Carolinas to Florida as the forests north of my state were rapidly decimated for their timber and as the Civil War eliminated the readily available labor force of the southern enslaved. To address the perennial shortage of willing and available workers, Florida prisons leased convict labor to the turpentine camps well into the twentieth century. By 1909, the naval stores industry was leasing 90 percent of Florida's Black prisoners, according to an oral history of the turpentine camps prepared by the Florida Humanities Council. The state eventually outlawed convict leasing, but in 1919 the legislature authorized turpentine operators to hold non-convict workers for debt.

As Isabel Wilkerson writes in her Pulitzer Prize–winning study of the Jim Crow period in the U.S. South that prompted the Great Migration, *The Warmth of Other Suns* (2010),

> From the panhandle to the Everglades, Florida authorities were now arresting colored men off the street and in their homes if they were caught not working. Charged with vagrancy, the men were assessed fines of several weeks' pay and made to pick fruit or cut sugarcane to work off the debt if they did not have the money, which few of them did and as the authorities fully anticipated. Those captured were hauled to remote plantations or turpentine camps, held by force, and beaten or shot if they tried to escape.

Wilkerson defines this institutionalized practice as a form of twentieth-century enslavement called "debt peonage." By charging the African American laborers for everything from transportation to housing, food, and clothing (which they could only obtain at the company commissary), camp owners were able essentially to secure a worker's free labor in perpetuity. There was little state oversight on the conditions in these remote outposts of wildest Florida. White overseers called "woods riders" wielded pistols and leather whips on their horses to keep the African American laborers at constant work under the fierce sun. They worked the men from "can't to can't," meaning from can't see in the morning until can't see at night, and beat uncooperative or disruptive laborers severely, sometimes to death. Food was scarce, housing was shoddy, and disease (including malaria, pneumonia, and heat stroke) was rampant, claiming many lives. In the late 1930s, Zora Neale Hurston and Stetson Kennedy, working for the WPA, visited a turpentine camp in northern Florida, recorded the African American laborers' folk songs, and listened to their stories. When Kennedy asked one worker why he didn't just leave the camp, the worker explained that the only way out was to die out, that if you tried to leave they'd kill you because they had folks to bury you out in the woods.

Florida, in 1941, was the last southern state to strike down its debt peonage laws.

I gaze now at a black-and-white photo of a turpentine camp published in Michael Gannon's book *Florida: A Short History* (2003). A white man wearing a cowboy hat, one of the woods riders I presume, sits atop a muscular horse as he oversees six African American laborers within the frame of the shot bent over the trunks of slash (or possibly longleaf) pines. The men look gaunt. Some wear hats to shield their faces from the harsh sun. What could a slash or longleaf pine mean to these men? On the website for the Library of Congress, I pore over the few interview transcriptions from Kennedy and Hurston's visit to a turpentine camp. I listen to the scratchy recordings of the work songs. But I find no allusions to the actual pine trees. I can only imagine that pines to these exploited laborers meant unrelenting work and cruelty and isolation from family and hopelessness.

The story of Florida and slash pines and us gets worse. In 1935, Rubin Stacy, an African American man accused of assaulting a thirty-year-old white woman in her home, is hanged by a mob from a slash pine tree in Davie, Florida—just a half hour or so from my current home—after which the white men take turns firing seventeen shots into his body. The black-and-white photo of the lynching published recently in the *Sun Sentinel* sits beside me now. Stacy's lifeless body droops from the rather slender slash pine trunk. His head tilts rightward. His hands appear to be bound before denim overalls. Several white men and a white woman strike devil-may-care poses in the backdrop. More astonishingly, a girl of about eight years old or so—my daughter's age—wearing a blonde pixie haircut stands in the foreground to the right. She stares at the camera, apparently unfazed.

1935. This may seem like a long time ago. But how long ago is it, really? Fewer than 100 years. A blink of an eye to a slash pine.

A recent report published by the Equal Justice Initiative features a table listing Florida a close second, only to Mississippi, of African Americans lynched annually, per capita, in southern states between 1880 and 1940. Any number of slash pines, I imagine, are conscripted by whites in Florida and throughout the South to enact these racial atrocities.

* * *

What do slash pines mean to some African Americans in Florida today? I wonder if I might draw a reasonable connection between these black-and-white photos documenting racial persecution in the woods and the young African American woman in my recent environmental literature seminar, who shuddered when I reached to touch the leaves of a Jamaican caper shrub on a field trip and warned, her voice quavering with what seemed very much like fear, "Be careful! Don't touch that!" I don't want to make too much of this isolated incident, but I don't want to make too little of it either. In her essay, "Black Women and the Wilderness," Evelyn C. White reflects upon her visceral aversion to the woods and other rural spaces in the United States and associates this wariness to her "genetic memory" of racial violence inflicted upon African Americans in such environments.

Yet White closes the essay by reclaiming a more salubrious ancestral connection to rivers and trees and to the unconstructed landscape generally. It is an act of re-membering that Lauret Savoy, too, takes up more recently, and more substantively, in her book, *Trace: Memory, History, Race, and the American Landscape* (2015). "The American land," she realizes from an early age, "preceded hate." Savoy notes, later in her book, that the enslaved "forced to work Piedmont soil had an intimate, immediate relationship with this land, cultivating and harvesting its yield by hand. Another yield had to be a community geography apart from the planters' lives and imposed bondage. Private and communal meanings, elements of self-autonomy and agency, emerged from endurance and strength grown *in* place." I glimpse something further of this complex and paradoxical relationship between people of color and the American landscape in Dolen Perkins Valdez's historical novel *Balm* (2015), the reflections of one of her enslaved characters, who recognizes "that the greatest irony of their condition was the beauty of the country in which they toiled, and the heartbreak of their lives was the fogged lens through which they gazed upon God's country. . . . This land around them was both the site of their darkness and the source of their light."

All of which makes me wonder what else the slash pine might have meant to those African American laborers in the black-and-white photo propped beside my keyboard, what *else* besides unrelenting work and cruelty and isolation from family and hopelessness. Perhaps slash pines also represented a source of light for most, or some, or a few of them.

* * *

For now, I spare my young daughter a history lesson on slash pines and racial persecution in Florida. But I'm pleased that it turns out to be difficult to locate a tree for sale. The relative scarcity of slash pines predictably ups its appeal to Eva and gives us more time to linger over slash pine-ness in the world. We begin to play a sort of game as we walk our dog through the neighborhood. First one to locate a slash pine gets a point. What's most curious to me during our contests is simply how little I know concerning which trees stand where along these blocks I've traversed on foot and in my car hundreds of times. While I consider myself more environmentally receptive than most, I didn't know, not really, that a rather magnificent specimen can be found a few blocks from my house down Isabel Road Este on the left (its branches favored, apparently, by spot-breasted orioles!), that there's another nice one with a bougainvillea threading its way through the canopy in the backyard of my neighbor's house just a short way down on 17th Street, that the largest slash pines seem to be the cluster of four that have been left to stand on one of the busier throughways three blocks to the west, or that one rare soul actually planted a line of young slash pines on his or her swale six blocks to the east. Now, I had taken vague note of the existence of these slash pines in the neighborhood, but I had no idea how many of them still survived or where, precisely, most of them stood until I started to look for them in earnest. Knowing the locale of particular trees in one's neighborhood either matters or it doesn't matter. As I would like to think that it matters, I've tried to make mental notes of the slash pines that either Eva or I spot while we saunter through the neighborhood with the dog, and even as we drive in the car about town. *There!* Eva will often beat me to the punch from the back seat. *And there!*

* * *

Did the early twentieth-century Japanese settlers in Palm Beach County take such active note of the slash pines looming over their pineapple fields? What did these trees mean to them? I possess about as vague a knowledge of their defunct agricultural settlement as I did of the slash pines gracing my subdivision. The Yamato Colony, I discover, poring over articles and photos in the archives of the Boca Raton Historical Society, is founded in 1905 by Joe Sakai of Miyazu, Japan, who signs an agreement two years earlier with Henry Flagler's Florida East Coast Railway to form a Japanese agricultural settlement in the Boca Raton area. He and about fifteen Japanese men establish the settlement on a forty-acre site of land, actually a few miles farther to the east than the locale of the current Morikami Museum and Japanese Gardens. South Florida's fledgling population mostly welcomes the colony for its promise to introduce new agricultural methods that might stimulate economic growth. The settlement seems to thrive for a short while. During the 1907–08 season, the Yamato farmers ship 10,000 crates of pineapples from the newly erected FEC train station nearby. "Progress and prosperity are said to be everywhere in evidence," a 1906 article in a local newspaper claims, "and a rapid growth for the colony is assured." Some of the men return to Japan to marry and return with their wives. In addition to a wife, Sakai brings back tea and mulberry shrubs and experts in silk worm production. He and others start families. The children attend school in the one-room Yamato schoolhouse. "The Japanese forming the colony of Yamato are adapting themselves to American ideas in their manner of living and dress," a newspaper article from 1908 claims. "They are fully imbued with the American spirit, their highest ambition being to be called Americans and citizens of this country, which they greatly admire."

All the same, the conditions are difficult for the settlers. "Accommodations were simple and consisted of crude shacks built from native pine trees," local historian Geoffrey Lynfield writes. Pineapple farming on rugged uncleared South Florida land proves backbreaking. "No more than one acre a season," Lynfield describes, "could be cleared by even the most hard working settlers using grubbing hoe, rake, and shovel. They had no tractors and all work had to be done by hand. The harsh tropical climate added to the discomfort of the immigrants. Rains flooded the fields and ruined crops. Mosquitoes and flies forced everyone to wear head-nets during the summer months." Competition with Cuban pineapple growers, who could grow pineapples more productively and cheaply, exacerbate these difficulties. Then a blight strikes the pineapple fields, after which the Yamato settlers switch to growing mostly winter vegetables such as tomatoes and beans. A typhoid epidemic claims several lives. Most of the surviving settlers return to Japan or move to California. The Yamato schoolhouse closes in 1922. The Yamato Post Office closes in 1925. The few who stay, and for whom records remain, take up jobs as shopkeepers and cooks, while some continue as farmers, and (lo and behold) successfully so. Hideo Kobayashi acquires more than 500 acres by the outbreak of World War II. After the Pearl Harbor attack, however, Japanese bank accounts are frozen and their movements restricted. In May of 1942, a U.S. District Judge orders that Kobayashi's land and all additional land owned by remaining Japanese settlers be turned over to the United States. Government for the site of the Army airfield. The state university where I teach is located on this parcel of confiscated land, long ago cleared of its slash pines and pineapples and peppers and Japanese farmers.

Yet one original member of the Yamato Colony, George S. Morikami, perseveres well after World War II and eventually owns over 1000 acres of farmland in Palm Beach County. In 1967, at the age of eighty-one, he becomes a U.S. citizen. I marvel at Morikami's endurance and success, which I feel must bespeak his deep connection with the land he acquires. A 1974 interview with Morikami published in the *Miami Herald* confirms this impression. Though a millionaire, he lives in a drab yellow trailer on land infested by sand fleas, surrounded by a tropical garden of pineapples, peaches, mangoes, and other fruits. "I like this," Morikami explains to the perplexed interviewer. "It is simple. The land is all around me. I eat fresh fruits and vegetables I grow myself. No meat. I eat when I am hungry, day or night. If I had to live in town, I couldn't have this." By this time, Morikami has built the beautiful lakes that still grace the gardens he would donate to the county. He plans "to plant Japanese pine trees all around it."

Japanese pine trees. This perks up my ears, of course. The Japanese black pine (*Pinus thunbergii*) and red pine (*Pinus densiflora*) are beautiful conifers native to Japan and surrounding areas, I learn, which vary in appearance from the slash pines that greeted twenty-year-old Morikami upon his arrival to Florida in 1906. I can see why he would have wanted to plant several of them around the lakes he had built on his property. I can only wonder what the slash pines looming over the pineapple fields meant to the Japanese immigrants of the Yamato Colony and to Morikami, himself, who in his final years hoped to plant "Japanese" pines around his lakes. The slash pine served as building material for their first homes. A black-and-white photo of the settlement features Japanese farmers laboring beneath tall well-spaced slash pines. Given the great difficulty of their agricultural enterprise and the ultimate failure of the settlement, I suspect that some of them might have hated everything about Florida pineapples and pines. Yet I also suspect that the slash pines, for some of them, represented one of the more familiar and welcoming natural features of Florida, that the mentholated air from slash pine resin beneath the broken canopy of needles might have reminded them of the outdoors aromas in Japan amid their black and red pines.

* * *

"Why are they called *slash* pines, anyway?" my wife asks me one evening out of the blue, or not so much out of the blue, I suppose, as I'd been going on and on about slash-pine-this and slash-pine-that over dinner. This is the type of talk from her spouse to which my wife has mostly accommodated herself over the years. But I don't have an answer for her question, which surprises her, and surprises me. She raises one of her eyebrows as if to say, *Maybe you should find out.*

Slash pines are called slash pines, I learn, after the "slashes" across its native terrain, swampy land slashed by trees and bushes.

* * *

To locate a slash pine for our yard, I finally do what I might have had the sense to do from the beginning, visit my favorite Florida native plant nursery about a half hour from my house. "Sure," Carl replies when I ask him whether he and Donna have slash pines for sale. He leads Eva and me to a distant patch of their property where three lonely-looking slash pines sit in five-gallon containers. As Carl propagates rows and rows of Jamaican capers and Simpson stoppers and marlberries, and rows and rows of dozens of other native specimens, it's pretty clear to me that he doesn't sell very many slash pines. He confirms as much to me when I ask. I then ask him if there's anything special I should know about cultivating a slash pine. "Not really," he says. "Plant it in a sunny spot and it'll take off." Eva picks out the slash pine she likes (it's somewhat bigger than the other two) and we head home to plant the young tree in the sunniest spot we can find.

Eva joins me to plant the tree in our butterfly garden, pretty much the only area in our front yard unshaded by our oak trees. I dig the hole in the loose sandy earth, add a bit of cow manure and peat moss at the bottom, and lower the slash pine into its new patch of South Florida real estate, adjusting, upon Eva's careful judgment, the precise angle of the trunk and height of the root ball against the adjacent earth. I take care to bank some sandy dirt around the tree's circumference to create a nice well for the water, which I let Eva administer with the hose. As she stands there admiring her new tree, as I stand there admiring her, I feel grateful that unlike the African American debt peonage workers or Japanese settlers of the Yamato Colony she'll be able simply to enjoy this slash pine pretty close to its own terms, unfreighted by human cruelty or duress of any sort. The next instant, however, I realize the hopeless naivete of my fancy—that Eva or anyone can or even should enjoy slash pines as some Platonic ideal. She will develop her own associations with slash pine-ness informed by her own personal role (whatever it might be) in the long and tangled cultural history of slash pines and us. I feel compelled to acknowledge here, too, that despite the folding of the turpentine camps and the halting of once commonplace lynchings from our loveliest trees, environmental racism continues to plague communities of color throughout the nation (e.g., the drinking water crisis in Flint, Michigan) and in Florida, specifically. Consider the sugarcane harvesting practice of field burning in the Everglades Agricultural Area near Lake Okeechobee. As Patrick Ferguson of the Sierra Club reports, the toxic smoke and ash from this practice yields harmful, sometimes catastrophic, health consequences for the nearby communities of color. Antiblack racism, I'd argue, is the red thread connecting Florida's slash pine history with our sugarcane present.

Even so, over these next weeks as we continue to administer daily doses of water to our new slash pine to encourage deep rooting, we linger in the heady throes of slash pine love fairly uncomplicated by racial wrongs, past or present. We pay careful attention to our new slash pine and to the other slash pines in our midst, and isn't this what love is mostly about, paying attention? Living a life as harried as most, I find it's nice just to aim my weary eyes for a while at the curious geometries of slash pine branches when I'm lucky enough to be placed in view of one.

The slash pine outside the tinted window of my doctor's waiting room, looming over the constructed pond, an enormous great blue heron standing on the bank beneath its shade.

The slash pine at our neighborhood park supporting four yellow-crowned night-heron nests constructed with live oak sticks.

The slash pine at the northernmost street of our subdivision looming over the drainage canal.

The slash pine trained as a Bonsai tree in a ceramic pot at the Morikami Japanese Museum and Gardens.

Eva says slash pines "look good with pools." What she means by this, I determine upon probing, is that she enjoys glimpsing the russet bark and pom-pom needle clusters when she turns her head to breathe during her freestyle stroke at her swim practices. She gazes at them between sets, too, when she ought to be paying attention to her coach. She likes the way the needles catch the syrupy orange light of sunset. These mature slash pines, along with some stately live oaks, have been left to grow in the park that houses our municipal swimming pool. In addition to my daughter, red-shouldered hawks particularly appreciate this stand of slash pine.

* * *

Turns out I'm not completely correct that slash pines have served awfully few as an artistic muse. Few, maybe. But not "awfully" few. I discover that the University of Alabama, for example, hosts an annual Slash Pine Poetry Festival in Tuscaloosa. The English Department at the university houses the Slash Pine Press, which publishes poetry chapbooks and mixed-genre work. In his 1986 poem, "Following Pine," Tony Harrison references the "Fresh-felled, lopped slash pine tree trunks," though mostly to lament the earlier destruction of virgin longleaf forests. The poet Jesse Millner of Florida Gulf Coast University writes of slash pines more appreciatively in much of his work. I locate several paintings and photographs online that feature slash pines, although our most famous Florida photographer, Clyde Butcher, clearly favors cypresses and live oaks. Even though there doesn't appear to be a treasure trove of poems and other art works dedicated to slash pines, it's nice to know that these lesser-than-longleaf evergreens nonetheless occupy the imaginations of several poets, painters, and photographers, as well as certain Florida fathers and their young daughters.

5
The Nature of the University

The live oaks gracing a mostly barren campus—small copses and stranded individuals here and there—captured my immediate attention. It was 1996 and I had just arrived at the state university in South Florida kind enough to offer me tenure-track employment. Most of the oaks, I would learn, were planted in the 1970s by a math professor (since deceased) and his large band of student, staff, and faculty volunteers. They had rescued several of the largest, most impressive, specimens from the tree-obliterating path of the rapidly approaching I-95 construction project, where traffic heading to and from Miami, Fort Lauderdale, and West Palm Beach now roars within earshot of campus.

Like most university professors, I've spent an inordinate amount of my time as an adult on college campuses. So I guess it makes sense that my environmental consciousness owes a great deal to the natural spaces showcased across these precious parcels. These groves and gardens, and their often-curious stories, have shaped my perspective toward the constructed and unconstructed landscape, and our proper place amid these places, to at least the same degree as the classes I've taken and taught in the climate-controlled warrens between these canopies of green. If such concerns interest you, too, taking a good hard look at the grounds of your local college or university isn't a bad place to start.

Higher education for me began on the small but leafy campus of Franklin & Marshall College in the urban-ish setting of Lancaster, PA. I was something of an uprooted tree, myself (a "transplant," the saying goes, yes?), having grown up in the San Fernando Valley of Los Angeles. So my eyes were particularly alert to the novelty of the East Coast trees that thrived on the campus, even though it might have behooved me to pay a bit more attention to my calculus textbook too. The umbrella-shaped canopy of a particularly large tree outside the infirmary was the first strange specimen I noticed. What type of tree was that? I asked a classmate. An elm, she told me. Sure. Elm. I'd heard of them. This beautiful tree compelled me to look about at all the other impressive flora. When I took the time to look, I noticed a plethora of giant specimens that I would later identify, through the help of more well-informed peers and professors. Hickories, tulip poplars, and maples, oh my! An old white ash outside Distler House was called the Protest Tree as various university administrations through the years encouraged the exercise of free speech (mostly signage; only the occasional effigy) upon its weathered trunk and branches. It may have been the first tree in which I glimpsed the radical intermingling—though I wouldn't have thought of it in these terms—between the human and nonhuman world near at hand that would inspire the environmental ethic at the heart of this book.

A significantly larger campus awaited me as a graduate student at Penn State University, nestled amid the more rural environs of Happy Valley. Instead of one campus elm, suddenly, there was a phalanx of elms greeting me the moment I crossed onto university property from College Avenue, gargantuan specimens that shaded my walk pretty much all the way to my comparatively bleak graduate teaching assistant cubicle indoors. Here's a story of these elms that will strike readers as incongruous to the current discussion: a violent thunderstorm hit campus during my time there and a bolt of lightning struck one of the heavy elm branches along the path I had just walked hours earlier. The branch crashed down from the tree, struck a student passerby on the head, and killed her. I share this story here partly because it seems somehow wrong to wax elegiac on the Penn State elms without mentioning it, and partly because the episode betrays, however broadly, the complex relationship between trees and us, even on our most pastoral college campuses.

While the green spaces cultivated, or simply left alone, on university property may frequently offer a crucial buffer against the more constructed (and sometimes blighted) suburban and urban blocks beyond the campus borders, it's just as true that universities daily enact the same tortured negotiations between various environmental and human interests that vex our local town councils. It's always been a pet peeve of mine to hear people—both within and without academe—refer to the world outside the university as the "real world." My life on campus certainly seems real enough to me. Regarding the environment, specifically, the same "real-world" pressures that drive unsustainable development and habitat destruction off campus daily threaten the most verdant patches of university property across the country. Student populations grow, as does demand for student housing, parking garages, classroom buildings, recreation centers, and football stadiums. Trees, and their on-campus advocates, often get in the way. To wit: if the splendid live oaks on my South Florida campus rescued from the oak-decimating path of the I-95 construction project might be said to be keeping a dirty little secret, it's that the university administration in the 1970s weren't at all pleased to welcome them onto the grounds.

"They put up all sorts of roadblocks," the retired math professor, Jack Freeman, confided in me a few years ago in the months just before he passed away. "They didn't care about native trees at all." Groves of trees planted here and there, they feared, might get in the way of their ambitious plans for building up their new university. It was only after Freeman wrote to the governor of Florida at the time, Reuben Askew—"Now *he* loved the idea!"—that the university administration was forced to cooperate, or at least get out of his way. I imagine that several readers can share their own campus environmental stories that run the gamut between ecological sensitivity and senselessness.

It might be fairly argued that our nation's colleges and universities have taken the lead when it comes to ecological sustainability, broadly speaking, as well we ought to given our shared mission to prepare the next generation for responsible citizenship in our global economy. The Association for the Advancement of Sustainability in Higher Education vigorously promotes its mission through manifold initiatives; many institutions of higher learning have seized upon the AASHE goals through instituting well-funded sustainability offices charged to envision, plan, and help implement sustainable institutional practices, ranging from its facility designs to its financial investments; curricula and entire degree programs in the arts and sciences devoted to sustainability continue to grow; the Princeton Review publishes an informative online *Guide to 322 Green Colleges*, which, if nothing else, suggests an increasing interest in and commitment to sustainability both on the part of universities and their prospective students; a recent anthology, *The Sustainable University* (2012), lays out best practices, action plans, and emerging trends, while also addressing the special challenges institutions of higher learning face amid shrinking budgets and complex political infrastructures.

Yet, it worries me that the word "green" increasingly morphs into a figurative expression in these campus discussions, discussions between professors and students in the classroom and between presidents and trustees during strategic planning sessions. In our zeal to construct LEED (Leadership in Energy and Environmental Design)–certified dormitories and classroom buildings, to institute trayless cafeterias and reduce the food-miles of the offerings, to tap into renewable energy supplies and develop water-conservation and waste-minimization practices—crucial initiatives all—we shouldn't forget the equally crucial and complementary role that the university landscape, itself, plays in our efforts to model and teach sustainability. The grandest "green" initiatives on campus will stand little chance of gaining the hearts and minds of students (and the larger university community) if we overlook the admittedly less glamorous opportunities to preserve and cultivate parcels of literal green between, within, and, in some cases, *instead of,* our new LEED-certified campus buildings.

Our seventy land-grant colleges and universities (which include Penn State, the University of Florida in Gainesville, and Florida A&M) share a special responsibility, one might argue, to institutionalize sustainable land-management practices on their campuses and across the external acres they may own. What must be said here at the outset is that much of this "granted" land was more accurately seized, first, from various Indigenous peoples living on these North American acres for generations, as "land acknowledgments" finally state on the websites of most of these land-grant colleges and universities. (The campuses of Florida Atlantic University, where I work, stand on Seminole, Tequesta, Taino, Ais, and Jeaga lands, while the main Boca Raton campus, as discussed in the previous chapter, was subsequently seized from a Japanese immigrant farmer during World War II to make way for an Army airfield prior to its repurposing as the current private airport and state university.) In any case, The Land-Grant College Act of 1862, or Morrill Act, granted each state 30,000 acres for each of its congressional seats. The Morrill Act and subsequent legislation initiated the creation of many of our state's flagship public institutions. The intent was to promote branches of learning in the "agricultural and mechanic arts," not land conservation, per se. Still, one cannot begin to pursue the advancement of agricultural and mechanical knowledge in our now postindustrial nation (Willa Cather's native tallgrass prairie having all but ceded to our agricultural and ranching interests, to cite just one example) without an eye toward sustainable land-use practices moving forward. These practices ought to be modeled, especially, across the very acreage managed by land-grant institutions, where contiguous tracts of native flora, and its associated fauna, ought to exist alongside agricultural test-plots and laboratories.

I recently visited the websites of the institutions that hosted my undergraduate and graduate educations to explore their current land-management practices. In both cases, I was pleased to discover a substantial level of commitment to the campus trees that left such a deep impression upon me. Curiously, both Pennsylvania institutions—a small private liberal arts college and the state's flagship public university—have recently fulfilled plans to designate, establish, and maintain arboreta on their campus properties. Recognizing that its 1000+ trees (representing 168 species) play a critical role in preserving the integrity of the Chesapeake Bay watershed—in addition to their historic importance and intrinsic beauty—Franklin & Marshall designated a fifty-two-acre portion of its 202-acre campus the Caroline S. Nunan Arboretum in 2007. Its Campus Landscape Master Plan of 2009 sets forth a thoughtful and detailed vision to preserve and enhance its landscape amid the increasingly urban environment of Lancaster. The inventory and management of campus trees is an important component of its larger Sustainability Master Plan, adopted in 2012.

Efforts to build the 370-acre arboretum at Penn State, immediately adjacent the campus, began and stalled in the 1970s, gained momentum in the 1990s, and currently enjoys vigorous development across its three stages. Importantly, the arboretum features various botanic gardens, a 10,000-square-foot conservatory, a larger education center, agricultural research and demonstration areas, and abundant natural areas, including woodlands and fields. While I haven't enjoyed the privilege of visiting the arboretum in person, these transitions between woodlands and managed gardens, managed gardens and agricultural research areas, agricultural research areas and educational buildings, seem usefully to model the *interdependent*—rather than oppositional—relationship between nature and culture that Wendell Berry advocates in his influential essay, "Getting Along with Nature." Berry writes, "As we return from our visits to the wilderness, it is sometimes possible to imagine a series of fitting and decent transitions from wild nature to the human community and its supports: from forest to woodlot to the 'two-story agriculture' of tree crops and pasture to orchard to meadow to grainfield to garden to household to neighborhood to village to city—so that even when we reached the city we would not be entirely beyond the influence of the nature of that place."

The university campus represents one of the more promising sites upon which we might enact Berry's vision. In the years that I was a graduate student at Penn State, I was particularly captivated by one of its heritage groves, a near-wild woodlot right on campus near the arts buildings called the Hort Woods. There, I glimpsed white oaks, black oaks, pin oaks, hemlocks, pignut hickories, red pines, white pines, red maples, sugar maples, and several trees I never got around to identifying. Even to my novice eyes, it was clear to me that many of these trees must have predated the university. I tended to seek out these trees often during the course of my week. I found, and continue to find, that standing beneath a canopy of big old trees even for a short while usefully puts things in their proper place. As Berry suggests in his essay—but what I didn't fully appreciate at the time—it was the proximity of the woodlot to the various architecturally impressive campus buildings nestled nearby that accounted for part of its power. Here was a "fitting and decent" transition, which allowed the unconstructed natural realm entry into my everyday social realm. To put it another way, I didn't need to "escape" to nature as nature was so close at hand. Glimpsing on Penn State's website the precise locales and names of specific trees I remember gazing upon in the Hort Woods some twenty years ago gave me that fuzzy nostalgic feeling that many people experience after tracking down old high school friends on Facebook.

Closer to my current home, the land-grant Florida institutions—University of Florida and Florida A&M—boast an Office of Sustainability and a Sustainability Institute respectively. The Office of Sustainability at UF, among its other initiatives, oversees the Campus Master Plan, which, according to their website, addresses on-campus development impacting "public facilities and/or natural resources as well as off-campus development that may have an impact on university facilities and/or natural resources." The plan, among other initiatives of the office, "informs sustainability policies and practices when it comes to managing land and natural resources at UF." The Sustainability Institute at Florida A&M, in concert with the School of Environment, "serves as a center for education, practice, and sustainable strategies concerning Energy, Water, and Food," and implements various campus initiatives, including their "Campus SEED Garden." I'm certain that competing human and environmental interests continue to duke it out at these institutions of higher learning. Yet the increasing emergence of sustainability offices and other ecologically minded initiatives at colleges and universities—including certificate programs, majors, minors, and whole schools—reveal a dawning imperative that we imagine, articulate, and enact on our campuses an environmental ethic of sustainability.

To be sure, I see plenty to grouse about at my own Florida state university a good ways down the road from UF and Florida A&M. I've rued over the years, for example, all the live oaks on campus (some of them fine old specimens from the I-95 rescue project) that I've seen felled to make room for new buildings, including, ironically enough, the "Live Oak Pavilion." Yet I also celebrate more hopeful developments, even the small ones. Most recently, the university constructed a walkway connecting my academic building to its newly opened gold-level LEED-certified dormitory, which features a small food court frequented by students, staff, and faculty alike. The cement walkway might have been laid out as a straight-shot, so to speak, yet its designers punctuated the simple sentence with two circular islands, several yards from each other, planted generously with coonties. Coonties are slow-growing plants native to Florida that look something like ferns but are actually members of the distinct order of cycads, which ruled the plant world during the early Permian Period of the dinosaurs. Which makes them living fossils. Florida's Indigenous peoples harvested the plant's large storage root and extracted the edible starch to make bread; later, white settlers more lustily harvested the plants to manufacture arrowroot biscuits. By the 1960s, coonties—and the dazzling blue-and-black Atala butterflies that rely exclusively upon the cycads as their host plant—were nearly extinct. Thanks to recent efforts by private citizens, conservation groups, and various state agencies, coonties and their Atalas currently enjoy a modest comeback.

I love that these two coontie islands were planted smack in the middle of the walkway rather than off to either side; that faculty, staff, and student passersby must follow the cement trail clockwise or counterclockwise as it sharply veers around both islands; that rather than careen thoughtlessly between buildings—on foot, bicycle, or skateboard—the circuitous path forces us to pause before these native plants and take their measure. I make it a point to stop and admire the coonties for a minute or two each time I pass, partly to inspect their spiky leaves for Atala caterpillars and partly to provoke (lamely, perhaps) the curiosity of others. Every once in a precious while, a colleague or fresh-faced undergraduate, scarcely realizing what they're in for, will stop and ask me what those strange plants are called.

6

Macroalgae Matters

Storm, my large black-and-white dog of indeterminate breeding, doesn't let me miss too many weekend afternoons at the beach. So here we are, threading our way through the dune of sea oats, railroad vine, morning glory, and sunflower to reach the shoreline. But something's different this spring day, my nose tells me before I even glimpse the ocean. A rotten-egg funk outmuscles the more pleasant dusty green smells of the dune and saline of the Atlantic. I see where the aroma must come from as soon as we clear the dune, flashing my dog-permit to the park ranger in her ATV. The sand just above the tideline is frosted with an especially thick and wide layer of seaweed I know just enough to know is sargassum. The yellowish-brown matt stretches south and north along the sand as far as my eyes can see. The water's calm surface, too, is corrugated with sargassum thickets and stained the color of a murky tea, steeped as it is in the stuff.

Storm sprints down to the weeds and tears figure eights across the vegetation in its state of fragrant decay, energized by the novelty. I find, however, that it's not so easy to lumber atop the seaweed once I catch up to him. Glancing down, the fronds of this particular sargassum seem less leafy than the sargassum I know, mostly a tangle of filaments and tiny air bladders. Now, I'm used to seeing and smelling seaweed at my local beach. I'm used to feeling okay about it that the park service doesn't "clean" it from the sand, knowing that the sargassum on shore and in the open ocean provides nourishment and protective cover for various creatures, including our embattled sea turtles. Yet the sheer quantity of this stinky stuff lathered over the sand and lolling in the current is of a different order, entirely; it can't be so easily written off as "natural." Plus, flies of some sort loop whirligig about my calves and turns out they bite.

It all seems, in a word, wrong.

While I'm probably more receptive to outdoors phenomena than most, the truth of the matter is that I've never really given much thought to seaweed. My line of sight in this swatch of South Florida I've called home for nearly twenty-eight years has ever tilted above the drifting seaweeds toward the ospreys, terns, and frigatebirds above, or below the skin of the sea toward the snapper and snook. Only after sargassum starts to make such a nuisance of itself on my local beach do I truly begin to *see* it and think about it in earnest. For it shows no sign of abating as the season progresses and the days grow longer and hotter. A rare west wind blessedly pushes the stuff offshore, but on most days nets of the scratchy stuff permeate every liquid ounce in the ocean shallows rendering it virtually impossible to swim. Many of my neighbors, friends I'm used to seeing at the beach regularly with their dogs, stop coming altogether.

Suddenly, I've got sargassum on my mind.

Sargassum, I learn, is a brown macroalgae (i.e., seaweed) comprised of over 100 species worldwide. Certain species of sargassum, including the two species common to my local waters, *natans* and *fluitans*, represent the only seaweeds that don't at least begin their life attached to the ocean floor. Partly on account of their free-floating ways, we're in the midst of the largest sargassum bloom in the world, beaches from Mexico to northern Florida buried under this "algal explosion," as one source puts it, extending some 5,500 miles between West Africa and the Gulf of Mexico and comprised of over 20 million tons of biomass. Scientists suspect multiple human-driven causes for the epic bloom, including deforestation and increased use of chemical fertilizer in Brazil and smoke and dust from massive African fires—many started intentionally to clear land—falling into the ocean and providing additional nutrients to the seaweed. "The ocean's chemistry must have changed in order for the blooms to get so out of hand," Dr. Chuanmin Hu puts it, having participated in a study of the phenomenon recently published in *Science*.

While certain species might benefit from the Great Atlantic Sargassum Belt, as it's now called, scientists worry about its more prevalent, deleterious effects on the environment. The expansive matts in the shallows block light from reaching already-stressed corals, seagrasses, and other organisms; they accumulate heavy metals such as cadmium and arsenic, which may be a source of ground contamination; they may cause elevated levels of the bacteria enterococci in beach waters, associated with gastrointestinal diseases and skin rashes; and they hold jellyfish larvae and other organisms that sting swimmers and leave terrific rashes (I speak from experience on this front). The thick blankets of seaweed on shore produce that hydrogen sulfide gas I smelled, a mere irritant for most people but particularly harmful for those suffering from asthma or other respiratory illnesses, and they may interfere with sea turtle nesting activities and hatchling survival rates.

I continue to read up not only on sargassum but on its seaweed associates. I buy and devour in one sitting Susan Hand Shetterly's excellent *Seaweed Chronicles: A World at the Water's Edge* (2018), which, in turn, leads me to an earlier classic by Rachel Carson, *The Edge of the Sea* (1955). I learn some astonishing facts. That marine algae account for half the oxygen in the earth's atmosphere. That hundreds of organisms across the food web (from isopods and amphipods to fish and birds) rely upon seaweed for food, cover, and reproductive habitat. That Carson called the intertidal zone of seaweeds in Maine an "underwater forest." That most of us consume or otherwise encounter seaweeds during the course of our day, even though we probably don't know it, as various seaweeds constitute a critical ingredient in toothpaste, puddings, makeups, medicines, soaps, pet food, and plant fertilizers. That the worldwide seaweed harvest is a massive and ever-growing industry, particularly as we deplete the other ocean bounties we have long enjoyed. Seaweed may not be as prominent a natural phenomenon to most people as bees, frogs, or polar bears, but the collective health of the manifold macroalgae species betrays even more profoundly, perhaps, how significant our human impacts on the planet continue to be in the Anthropocene.

* * *

Here's where my attention turns from sargassum to rockweed (*Ascophyllum nodosum*), one of the most aggressively and controversially harvested seaweeds in the United States. Rockweed is a brown macroalgae that inhabits and often dominates rocky coastal shorelines from the Canadian Arctic, Greenland, Iceland, and Norway to Portugal and the northeast coast of the United States south to New Jersey. In stark contrast to the sargassum of my shores, rockweed uses a sturdy little foot called a holdfast—which may be up to 400 years old!—to attach itself to rocks and ledges in the intertidal zone. At low tide, rockweed's layers of fronds provide a blanket for various species, protecting them from desiccation. At high tide, the rockweed branches rise and sway in the currents sometimes higher than two meters, like leaves in forest trees, providing habitat to thirty-four species of fish and over 100 invertebrates, many of which constitute critical food sources to fish and birds, perhaps most notably the eider duck.

"Here," Carson writes in *The Edge of the Sea,* "all other life exists within their shelter."

I try to hold in my mind what I learn about sargassum along my sandy southeast coast and what I learn about rockweed along the more hardscrabble northeast coast. If the trouble with sargassum today is its overabundance (a mostly human-driven problem) the trouble with rockweed may be its scarcity (again, a mostly human-driven problem). With the exception of the lobster industry, fisheries in Maine over the past half century have either collapsed (e.g., cod) or face increasingly strict regulations on account of their decline (e.g., eels, urchins, scallops). These facts on the ground have only incentivized the rockweed harvest, particularly since 1999, when the Canadian company, Acadian Seaplants Limited, began its industrial-scale operations in the state. Recognizing the peril of the escalating rockweed harvest to the entire biome, Robin Hadlock Seeley, the leading rockweed scientist, organized the Rockweed Coalition with others in 2009. The coalition has essentially been fighting against proponents of the industrial harvest ever since with varying degrees of success. To ensure the regeneration of harvested rockweed, Seeley and her allies convinced the Maine legislature early on to pass a law that prevents harvesters statewide from cutting blades any closer to the holdfasts than sixteen inches. Prior to that, some harvesters had dragged cutting rakes behind their skiffs to rip the seaweed straight off the rocks, holdfasts and all. The coalition also spearheaded the implementation of the state's strictest regulations in Cobscook Bay on the Canadian border, dividing the area into sectors and prohibiting harvesters from removing more than 17 percent of the rockweed from any given area each year. They would like to see the adoption of these management practices statewide. Yet this seems unlikely.

Exactly who owns the rockweed has been the primary source of contention and litigation between the industry and environmentalists. The answer to the question hinges upon whether rockweed ought to be considered a plant or an animal. If it's a plant, according to laws dating back to colonial times, the upland property owners would own the rights to rockweed in the intertidal zone. If rockweed were considered an animal, however, it could be harvested from the sea at high tide by anyone, just like most fish and crustaceans. The arguments for each position are actually more complex than you might imagine, setting aside whether the very name of Acadian Sea*plants* ought to constitute a concession from the get-go. In any case, Judge Harold Stewart II of Maine's Superior Court sided in 2017 with the landowners and the Rockweed Coalition, noting that the rockweed harvest was "no more a fishing activity . . . than is harvesting a tree the same as hunting or trapping wildlife." Acadian Seaplants appealed, but the state supreme court in March of 2019 affirmed by unanimous decision the lower court's ruling, which means that rockweed statewide cannot be cut without the express permission of the landowners. The Rockweed Coalition, in the meantime, has enlisted hundreds of these landowners to its cause, which will likely limit the harvest moving forward. All the same, sympathies among the citizenry, as expressed through other organizations such as the Downeast Lobsterman's Association and the Maine Seaweed Council, tend to straddle the environmentalist and industry positions.

* * *

Spring in Florida, meanwhile, gradually yields to summer, and a daily riot of sargassum continues to plague my local beach. Storm doesn't seem to mind, but I need an escape from the malodorous seaweed and the scorching temperatures. Plus, all this reading about rockweed from my faraway remove in the subtropics makes me want to see this notorious seaweed. Fortuitously, my sudden interest in macroalgae coincides with our family plans to visit Acadia National Park in Maine. As soon as we arrive at Bar Harbor on Mount Desert Island, I take our nine-year-old daughter to the granite shore so I can check out the rockweed and she can hunt for sea glass. (We all have our hobbies.) It's low tide, so this elbow of coastline in town advertises in full view its ledges and boulders, furred with a brown seaweed that I probably wouldn't have taken much note of a year ago, or taken for mere detritus washed onto the outcroppings, but which I now know to be rockweed secured by holdfasts rather purposively to their rocks.

While my daughter Eva hunts rather successfully for sea glass amid the pebbles, I turn over fronds of the matted brown stuff, upsetting tiny crabs and other creatures which had sought out the shelter of the thickets. I marvel at the specific architecture of this seaweed, the length and shape of the individual blades festooned with rubbery air bladders I squish between my fingers. It's easy to imagine what these patches of rockweed must look like at high tide, lolling in the current. It's easy to imagine how Carson could describe the intertidal zone as an "underwater forest" to render the ecosystem more tangible to landlubbers like me. I look up and notice sharp little seabirds, black-and-white guillemots, skittering between patches of weeds below the tideline, a cormorant diving for its prize, a lobster boat beyond trailing a fizzy wake, and I sort of "get it" in a way I haven't before what Carson's driving at throughout *The Edge of the Sea* with her languorous sentences that tend to sweep in several creatures in a single breath. In this way, she emphasizes the interconnections between all flora and fauna in the rockweed zone. "When covered at high tide," Carson writes, "the rockweeds stand erect, rising and swaying with a life borrowed from the sea.... Down below those floating tips small fishes swim, passing between the weeds as birds fly through a forest, sea snails creep along the fronds, and crabs climb from branch to branch of the swaying plants. It is a fantastic jungle, mad in a Lewis Carroll sort of way."

As Eva and I continue along the shore path, pausing time to time to explore new sections of the intertidal zone, tidal pools populated by periwinkles, green crabs, sea stars, and other creatures I can't be sure of (anemones? urchins?), I read the signage calling our attention to the Gilded Age cottages here and there owned by such and such personage, the site of an aborted seawall construction project, the shoal where a luxury liner ran aground a hundred years ago, the enormous boulder distinct in its chemical composition from the other local boulders and deposited here by a glacier during the last Ice Age (which is pretty cool). But the signage on the whole, what with my newfound appreciation for seaweed, makes me wonder whether we tend to underscore all the wrong things with the signs we post about. There ought to be a sign drawing my lazy eyes toward our more commonplace wonders, such as these perfectly ordinary Maine rocks haired over with tendrils of rockweed.

* * *

Sargassum and rockweed. Rockweed and sargassum. These two very different seaweeds are an interesting thing to contemplate—specifically, the rival strategies by which they go about their life business. Rockweed remains anchored all its days to its tiny patch of terra firma by its holdfast. That harvesters know exactly where they might find it accounts, in part, for its vulnerability. Sargassum, by contrast, refuses to be tied down, seeking its fortune abroad; it possesses the algal equivalent of wanderlust and who can dispute its success? An enormous evolutionary advantage for any plant or animal in the Anthropocene may be its predilection for avoiding us.

Yet between rockweed and sargassum, I find my sympathies squarely favoring rockweed, probably because I feel a certain affinity for it. Like this brown macroalgae, I've hunkered down in one place, South Florida, for most of my adult life. Like rockweed, I've tried to mine whatever riches might be found in staying put. It may seem a lazy or complacent life choice, but it's actually not such an easy thing to do these days in our ever more transient and unstable work culture. It can't be easy for rockweed, either, given the extreme conditions it encounters at its place of residence. In the course of a single day, rockweed must endure four separate tidal pulses, much stronger tides at its northern latitude than the comparatively mild tides in the subtropics. At low tide, fully exposed to the air, rockweed must withstand the unrelenting sun and wind to avoid desiccation. As the surf comes in, rockweed must battle fierce thrashings against the rocks, relying upon its small holdfast to stake its modest claim. How could one not admire the stolidity and stick-to-itiveness of rockweed versus the catch-as-catch-can itineracy of sargassum, flitting off to this and that next best thing?

The preceding lines may say a lot more about my own peccadilloes than they say about rockweed or sargassum, both of which, let's face it, enjoy little conscious agency over their life strategies, at least not in the way we tend to define consciousness and agency. It seems foolish to wade too long in this anthropocentric pool, turn seaweed into mere metaphor to glorify my own life choices. I want to know seaweed better on its own terms. I want to probe further the *thingness* of seaweed, itself.

What better way to do this than to start eating some of it. My local sargassum, unfortunately, represents a poor candidate for my plate as the fronds hold relatively large amounts of heavy metals. Yet the market keeps growing in the United States for other seaweeds as a health food. I peruse the websites of Ironbound Island Seaweed, Maine Seaweed, Maine Coast Sea Vegetables, and Heritage Seaweed. These are all small outfits whose few employees harvest little if any of the embattled rockweed and clip from the rocks and ledges only modest and sustainable amounts of the other seaweeds they dry and sell whole to restaurants, food markets, and home chefs in the United States. (Acadian Seaplants, by contrast, processes its industrial-scale rockweed harvest to a fine powder or liquid, then sells most of it overseas to China as animal feed or plant fertilizer.) I'm fairly astonished by how many edible macroalgae species exist in the

Atlantic Ocean—Irish moss, kombu, laver, *Alaria*, kelp, and dulse—and that I can purchase from one of these companies at the click of a mouse.

But I won't need to mail order my first batch of seaweed. For while we're still on Mount Desert Island in Maine, I notice the Ironbound Island Seaweed products for sale at Beech Hill Farm, a pretty amazing organic farm owned by the nearby College of the Atlantic. I pluck from the bins several large packages of dried kelp, dulse, wakame, and kombu, eliciting a skeptical gaze at the counter from my wife, Wendy, who at this stage of our marriage has gotten used to humoring me for such strange enthusiasms.

As soon as we arrive back home in Florida, I set about preparing a variety of dishes featuring seaweed. There's no shortage of recipes online, many of which are featured on the websites of the seaweed purveyors listed above. I manage to prepare a rather delicious tofu, mushroom, and bok choy stir-fry featuring wakame and a not-so-delicious miso soup featuring kombu. Word to the wise: kombu, tough as leather, ought only to be used as a thickener for soups and removed before serving. Next, I simmer a colorful medley of beans with kelp for hours until the kelp tenderizes the beans and dissolves into the scrumptious stew, to which I add sautéed garlic and onion. But the seaweed I truly fall in love with is the purple- and rose-colored dulse. Dulse (*Palmaria palmate*) is a red macroalgae that grows on cliffs and in shaded crevices and pools in the northern intertidal coastlines of the Pacific and Atlantic Oceans. Its paper-thin, deeply indented fronds, Carson writes, "bear a crude resemblance to the shape of a hand." Rich in potassium, iron, iodine, and trace minerals, farmers in Ireland and Iceland have harvested dulse from their rocky coasts for the past 1,500 years, accenting their otherwise bland meals and even chewing dried dulse leaves whole like tobacco. The supple texture of the dried seaweed proves tempting enough that I plop one small frond directly into my mouth, too, straight out of the bag. I savor the sharp iodine notes against my tongue, which segue to a milder asparagus flavor, then a toasted nut finish. I heat a cup of dulse in a cast iron pan over a high flame for just a few moments until the seaweed begins to smoke, and then I incorporate the toasted fronds into a milk-based seafood and potato chowder. The pan-fried dulse lends a sort of bacony (if not quite bacon) flavor to the chowder, which my whole family loves, especially our college-age son, Henry.

* * *

All the same, it's not so easy to return to South Florida from Maine in the middle of August, as anyone who's ever been to South Florida in the middle of August might imagine. It's not only the stultifying heat or the still-thick mats of sargassum that bring me down. No sooner do we settle in than we must evacuate to Georgia as Hurricane Dorian, a Category 4 storm, bears down upon our coast from the Caribbean Sea. It will largely spare Florida, though it will decimate parts of the Bahamas, killing many people in its path. The hurricane dominates the news on TV for several days given its fearsome power and the ridiculous length of time that it lingers over our Eastern Seaboard, wreaking havoc in the Carolinas and even pounding Maine with rain before finally veering offshore into the North Atlantic. As meteorologists and political pundits debate the extent to which we might attribute our ever-strengthening tropical weather systems to global warming, as my family and I remain holed up in an Atlanta hotel room, I can't help but think about the Great Atlantic Sargassum Belt that awaits me back home.

Specifically, I reflect upon the various possible causes for the sargassum bloom currently under review by scientists (which include the indisputably warming seas), and the cavalier way that many of us nonscientists at the dog beach have tended to dismiss our culpability over the past several months. It's the fertilizer in Brazil, the fires in Africa, all my neighbors and I seem anxious—too anxious—to believe.

"Fucking Brazil," has become a popular refrain at my local beach.

While these faraway scourges may be among the leading sources of the bloom, it's just as true that we in Florida contribute plenty of the nitrogen to our local waters that, at the very least, has exacerbated our global sargassum problem. Land-based nutrients from agricultural fertilizers and the runoff from other industries (e.g., cattle ranching, phosphate mining) flow into the Atlantic and Gulf of Mexico from our lakes, rivers, and canals. We also continue to spew our sewage just offshore in Miami-Dade, Broward, and Palm Beach Counties through leaky septic tanks and various outfall pipes. "People talk about the fertilizer, but no one wants to talk about sewage," says Brian LaPointe, an algal bloom expert at Florida Atlantic University, the school where I also work. "I've been fighting that for a long time in Florida." So yes, it may feel good to blame faraway culprits for the sargassum, but an honest appraisal suggests that we've made a fine mess of the coastline all by ourselves. While these thoughts swim in my brain, I notice on the beach one day for the first time in my twenty-plus years as a resident an exposed sea turtle nest, the eggs errantly laid and buried below the tideline, a few dead would-be hatchlings still partly encased within their eggshells, torn open by the surf. I must shoo Storm away from the fragrant carnage. I can't prove it, of course, but it seems likely that the adult female turtle, discouraged and exhausted by the wide blanket of sargassum just above the tideline, chose to dig her nest and lay her eggs on the open sand within fatal reach of the incoming tide.

It all puts me in a dour mood.

* * *

It's in the midst of this low mood of mine that it happens. I'm in my backyard refilling one of our bird feeders when the first bee collides against my skull with a surprising level of force. A split second later it stings my scalp. Then the bright pain of a second sting blooms just beside my left eye, and I'm sprinting back into the house, flailing at the bee still tangled within the thicket of my curly hair. I manage to shed the creature into the basin of my kitchen sink where it winds down like a toy and finally dies.

The bees that attacked me, I know, come from the large hive that colonized one of my woodpecker nest boxes I built and installed ten feet high in one of our live oaks. We've coexisted with the hive for several months as bees have had a rough go of it, lately, rougher than rockweed, and as a local beekeeper, Adrian, assured us that European honeybees are typically rather docile. True enough, up until today. But I can't risk any further the chance that they might attack my young daughter next. Within minutes of being stung, an icepack still firmly lodged against my eye, I'm on the phone with Adrian and he's on his way to my house to remove the hive. He's young, twenty-something, sports a prodigious beard, and goes by the nickname the Bearded Beekeeper. Eva and I watch from a window inside the safety of our house as Adrian, atop his ladder in a protective suit, plies the hive with calming smoke, then removes the entire nest box from the tree, layers of honeycomb bulging out the entrance.

"The bees that stung me," I ask him just after he shuts the rear hatch and I hand him his check, "they die right after that, right?"

"Right," he says. It had always fascinated me that this might be true.

"Do you think they know they're going to die before they sting you?"

"I do," he says. "I do think that they know." He pauses for a moment as he takes off his gloves. I can tell that he's still thinking about my question, that he's about to say something else, and he does. "It's all about the hive."

It's all about the hive. I marvel over Adrian's words for days, weeks. The selflessness of bees! Such community!

It eventually brings my mind back to seaweed, and to us. It makes me wonder what the manifold creatures in the rockweed zone know of community. If the bees know, in their own bee-way, that it's all about the hive, is it such a stretch to imagine that rockweed and its hundreds of plant and animal associates enjoy (if this is the best word) their own unique sense of community as well (to the extent that we can imagine with our own senses the senses of rockweed and periwinkle and eider duck)? I weigh the ethic of the hive, and the ethic of the rockweed zone, against our presiding human ethic in the world that I know, which is to say South Florida, and to a lesser extent the country as a whole. It's tough not to find us wanting by the standard of bees and seaweeds. While a hive mentality is not something we ought to emulate too closely, I worry that we've careened headlong toward the other extreme of narcissistic individualism and that this might be the source of many of our problems, environmental and otherwise. We've grown ever more atomized and hardly enjoy any sense of community at all.

It's a free country, Americans like to say, typically (these days) to justify life-decisions I find suspect. Yet what if we availed ourselves of this freedom to live differently in the days, months, and years ahead? What if we decided that we wanted to live once again in true community, and what if we extended that notion of community, as Aldo Leopold championed in the middle of the last century, to include the people, plants, and animals within and without our rather arbitrary national borders? Might we look at the Great Atlantic Sargassum Belt differently in this state and country if we considered Brazil and Africa, and the sargassum itself, to be a part of our we, a part of our hive? Might we greet all the approaching plagues more constructively, and humanely? As the Bearded Beekeeper says, "It's all about the hive."

* * *

Summer eventually yields to fall, the broiling heat in Florida subsides, the sargassum thins from my swatch of shoreline (perhaps on account of the cooling ocean), and the water blues up. My neighbors return to the beach, and we can all enjoy a nice swim once again without battling the tangled nets of sargassum, their associated sea pests, or the rotten-egg stench. On one such glorious October day, I exchange chipper hale and hearties with my dog-beach pals Vanessa and Richard and Michelle and Emmanuel, essential members of the human community I've managed to forge in the subtropics. Our dogs reacquaint themselves with one other, and with us. We walk the beach and collect, along with our pets' waste, the plastic refuse that's washed up on shore. In this small way, we feel that we do our part. I watch a flock of sanderlings chase the outgoing surf, then retreat from an incoming wave—chase and retreat, chase and retreat—drilling the wet sand for morsels. Schools of mullet have returned from their northern range and puncture the water's surface in silver commas. I see an osprey dive for its prize, a kite-boarder riding the wind beyond along with a few terns. It's easy to think, if only for this brief spot of time, that everything under the sun is and will always be okay.

7

My Garden Tour

It was a terrific honor. Carl, the owner of my favorite native plant nursery, called my cell to let me know that he'd recommended my home garden to the leaders of the Palm Beach Chapter of the Florida Native Plant Society. The chapter, apparently, hosts native plant garden tours of residential yards. They'd need to come out to inspect the property, of course, but Carl was confident that my yard would pass muster. Someone from the organization would be in touch with me.

"Cool!" I replied. "Thanks!"

What was I thinking?

I started to ask myself this question not too long into our preparations (spoiler alert) for the official tour of the "Furman Garden," as it would be advertised in the native plant society's promo material. Why had I greeted with such alacrity the prospect of opening up my yard to the scrutiny of a multitude of strangers? For starters, my wife, Wendy, and I have labored awfully hard over the past six-plus years on our modest quarter-acre property to get it looking like the kind of yard a native plant nursery owner might recommend to the leaders of a native plant society. The main reason we sold our old place and moved into our current home was that we had just welcomed our third child, Eva, into the world and needed a bit more indoor space. Yet, the outdoor space associated with our properties has always been as important to us as the "square footage under air," to quote real estate parlance. In this sense, our priorities buck the national trend. Home yards are increasingly overlooked, underappreciated, and under-imagined places. Small wonder, given the diminished role that the outdoors plays in most American lives. The Environmental Protection Agency estimates that, on average, Americans spends 93 percent of their lives indoors.

My indoor hours probably hew closer to this percentage than I would like to acknowledge, but Wendy and I have done our best to combat this retreat by creating enticing landscapes just outside our windows. We'd offered Eva's older sister and brother a pretty nice native garden at the old place where they spent their elementary school years. We hoped to offer their younger sister, too, immediate environs replete with native plants for her daily inspection. To their credit, the former owners of our new home had maintained an impressive canopy of nine live oaks and a laurel oak. Beneath the lovely oaks, however, it was pretty much a disaster. Our best guess on the understory was that they bought various house plants at Home Depot and just plopped them into ever-dwindling patches of vacant earth beneath the trees when they outgrew their pots. A non-native ficus hedge, prone to whitefly incursions, framed the entire yard, as well, and would have to go. Daily, a fleet of yard-maintenance trucks rumble through my neighborhood shepherding toxic agents doused across these glossy hedges to keep them alive (hedges which bear neither seed nor berry), poisoning the soil in the bargain.

Okay, so there was a loose biocentric principle guiding our landscaping choices, inspired mostly by Thoreau's various writings, complemented by the land ethics more recently advanced by Aldo Leopold, Rachel Carson, Wendell Berry, and Robin Wall Kimmerer, and further inspired by a soupçon of Barbara Kingsolver and Annie Dillard, particularly Dillard's celebration of the potential richness of non-wild ecologies. "This is, mind you, suburbia," she writes in one of her most compelling essays, "Living like Weasels." We planned our new yard with a special eye toward attracting and sustaining an impressive array of local fauna. If not weasels, then warblers and woodpeckers, butterflies and bees, squirrels and snakes.

Armed with the knowledge gleaned from the well-thumbed books that guided our earlier efforts—principally Rufino Osorio's *A Gardener's Guide to Florida's Native Plants* (2001), Dan Walton and Laurel Schiller's *Natural Florida Landscaping* (2007), Craig N. Huegel's *Native Plant Landscaping for Florida Wildlife* (2010), and Robert G. Haehle and Joan Brookwell's sublime *Native Florida Plants* (2004)—as well as our general experience cultivating our original yard of native plants (word to the wise: firebush rocks!), we spent a good while grubbing out the understory of houseplants, the ficus hedge, and a fair bit of the impossibly coarse St. Augustine grass to make room for a hedge of mixed natives—beauty berry, wild coffee, marlberry, locustberry, white indigoberry, Florida boxwood, bitterbush, snowberry, the stoppers white, red, redberry, and Simpson—plus copses of larger shrubs and small trees, including fiddlewood, Jamaican caper, satinleaf, and Bahama strongbark, and the ground covers dune sunflower and sensitive plant (to replace that pesky St. Augustine grass), their purple fuzzy flowers prized by bees and other pollinators. We also managed to find room for a few larger trees: magnolia, wild tamarind (the ferny leaves protect our west-facing wall from the bully sun), and Geiger (the orange blooms dazzled John James Audubon upon his visit to the Keys, persuading him to use the tree as the backdrop for his painting of the white-crowned pigeon). Perhaps most impressively, our chiggery grape vines now wend dramatically through the scaffolding of two of our live oaks on the east side of the yard, their flowers mobbed by a riot of zebra longwings, gold rim swallowtails, Julia, Atala, dagger longwing, gulf fritillary, and other butterflies, these heady clusters yielding to white berries, which have proven a crucial food source for the red-bellied woodpeckers squatting in the downy woodpecker nest box I built with my teenage son. In short, we've mostly converted a tangled understory of exotic and (worse) invasive plants into an approximation of what this patch of subtropical Florida earth might have looked like when it had expressed itself on its own terms.

So, yeah, it was time to show off this yard of ours.

That our rowdy landscape of native plants has been woefully underappreciated by most observers certainly bolstered my initial enthusiasm to showcase our yard for a more sympathetic audience. It doesn't take many years as a native plant enthusiast in my neighborhood to figure out that your particular sensibilities vis-à-vis home landscapes run counter to the prevailing spirit. Judging from most of the yards up and down my block, it's clear that a rival aesthetic carries the day in Boca Raton. Most neighbors maintain an expansive monoculture of St. Augustine grass accented by a few shrubs and small trees pruned in tidy geometries, plus annual groundcovers boasting Technicolor blooms. Leaf litter (contemplate *that* word for a moment!) must be blown off one's property with gas-powered blowers within moments of descending to earth. Michael Pollan described this preferred outdoors aesthetic of the American suburb over twenty years ago in the "Why Mow?" chapter of his early book, *Second Nature* (1991). Unfortunately, these aesthetic values still obtain in my zip code, and I suspect in most suburban zip codes across the country. To keep one's citizenship as a suburban homeowner in good standing involves acceding to these values, sometimes written explicitly into city codes and HOA (homeowner's association) rules and regulations.

A few anecdotes to illustrate my point:

My neighbor (a firefighter and nice fellow, truly) often holds up his gas-powered blower for my inspection as I walk or jog past his house, offering his none-too-subtle suggestion that I clean up my act rather than allow my live oak leaves to molder where they fall and form their natural mulch. Even less subtly, he sometimes shuts off the screaming machine, removes his noise-dampening earphones, and asks, "Wanna borrow it, Furman?"

A separate neighbor recently asked me about my beauty berry shrubs while she was walking her yipping dogs. She had caught me outside crouching over a new planting (not too difficult to do given the amount of time I spend noodling around out there) and couldn't contain her curiosity. "Do you *mean* to plant those plants with the purple berries?" she asked dubiously, squinting toward one of my largest plants.

"Of course," I answered.

She nodded, taking in my terse reply. Spanish is her first language, so the rest of her words were somewhat difficult to understand, but she went on to explain, essentially, that she'd been wondering, because she'd seen those plants out and about in some of the scruffier places in South Florida that she'd visited. But she'd never seen them planted *on purpose* in a yard. It was fascinating to me, what I took to be the subtext of her remarks, the assumption that one would never seek to plant in one's garden something that grew all on its own in the wild.

Perhaps most heartbreakingly, my mother also can't quite understand that our yard represents an aesthetic choice rather than sheer negligence. At least a half-dozen times she has stepped out of her car in the driveway, looked about at the lusty shrubs and trees that strike her as unkempt, and remarked, "Honest to God, Andrew, your house is so nice. If you would just pay a little money for a gardener!"

The first time she said these words, I tried setting her straight, told her that Wendy and I like the way our shrubs and trees look, that they attract all sorts of wildlife and offer such nice shade, that we prefer the varied foliage of our manifold native plants to the useless blooms of the annuals (e.g., impatiens, begonias) that she and most of our neighbors prefer. Eva, I insisted, spends hours outside observing the goings on: picking select berries and seeds for her artwork or for us to plant in starter-trays, tracing the zig-zag flight of butterflies to and fro, chasing and catching lizards and bugs, et cetera. I stopped well short of mentioning Thoreau's landscaping advice in *Walden* (1854), which might be seen as an exhortation to forgo landscaping in our suburban sense of the term: "No yard! But unfenced

Nature reaching up to your very sills. A young forest growing up under your windows, and wild sumachs and blackberry vines breaking through into your cellar." It would have been fruitless to carry on so. The words I had already managed to articulate in my yard's defense were like seeds scattered across hard earth.

If you would just pay a little money for a gardener!

"Okay, mom," I mostly respond now when she broaches the topic of my unkempt yard. "I'll think about it."

All of which is to say that I was looking forward to meeting my ostensible botanical allies, representatives of the Palm Beach Chapter of the Florida Native Plant Society, one of whom contacted me shortly after my conversation with Carl to arrange a visit to inspect my yard. She and a male companion pulled up my driveway in a small hybrid vehicle the following Sunday. There were two of them, it soon became clear, so that one would ever be available to check the sloppily disclosed enthusiasm of the other. While the fellow (the owner of a native plant nursery) positively beamed over my chiggery grape vines and Jamaican capers, his partner in crime sniffed about the yard with greater circumspection. Let's call her Susan, because that was her name. When she paused extra-long underneath our large laurel oak, rubbing her chin as she surveyed the understory, I was pretty sure I knew what had her so concerned.

"So, those ferns under there aren't the native variety, are they?"

How can I best describe the feeling that welled up inside upon her query? I felt as if I was a teenager and my parents had just stumbled across my stash of marijuana. I looked over toward the friendlier fellow, Jeff was his name, as if he might bail me out, but his face was expressionless.

I admitted that the ferns were not the native variety.

"Because we have a pretty strict rule about invasives," Susan said.

Were those ferns a non-starter? Not quite, apparently: "If we use the yard," she declared, "we'll have to mark those ferns." *If,* I mused.

Without knowing it, Susan had tapped the source of some domestic discord in the Furman abode. For as long as we've lived in the new house, I've been lobbying my wife to let me clear out these invasive ferns, or "these fricking ferns," as I more typically refer to them. Left unchecked, they sprawl across the terrain like a conquering army, choking out my other, more desirable plantings. But Wendy—not quite so caught up in native/non-native distinctions—likes the way our ferns look. Plus, whenever I go rogue and pull out a small patch of them sans spousal approval, she takes note of how quickly my experiment goes south, any number of less attractive weeds sprouting up to replace the uprooted ferns. And so the ferns remained for Susan's jaundiced gaze.

After the awkward interlude over the ferns, the three of us moseyed about the property together for about twenty minutes. I made sure to highlight my most impressive plantings, while Jeff paid compliments and Susan mostly expressed various reservations: there were other exotics and invasives she noticed that I hadn't grubbed out (e.g., crotons, oyster plants, carrotwood), she feared that the unfenced pool in the back might prove a hazard for their guests, wondered whether I'd be willing to move the ladder I'd left lying about, that sort of thing.

"What, exactly, are you looking for?" I finally asked as I led them back to their car.

"This!" Jeff replied, which cheered me, but Susan remained reticent. There were other properties that they needed to examine before they'd make their decision.

"We'll be in touch," she said.

* * *

As I've already suggested, the Furman Yard made the cut, but a distaste over the initial interview lingered, exacerbated by the subsequent emails I received from Susan, festooned with numerous attachments detailing all the sheer stuff we were expected to do to prepare our yard for the tour (e.g., label as many plants as we could, draft copy for their promotional mailings, secure tables and chairs for their volunteers, and police-tape to mark off non-parking areas on the street). "Half of me wishes we could just get out of this whole thing," I complained to Wendy over dinner one night. She smiled and shook her head over her plate, knowing full well that her husband wasn't the kind of person who got out of things.

So there I was, irked by the environmentally unsound landscaping aesthetic of my neighbors (and mother) and grousing over the highfalutin 'tude of my botanical allies. Going around being angry at everyone, thinking that everyone's a jerk, sort of makes you stop and think. Like, that maybe *you're* the jerk. My wife wasn't so bent out of shape over the upcoming tour. Why was I? Specifically, why had Susan's peccadilloes over my plants angered me so? It angered me, I realized, because she offered me a snapshot of how *I* probably come across to my neighbors, and maybe even to my wife when I give her such a hard time about her ferns.

It's never nice to witness someone else demonstrating your less admirable qualities. It occurred to me, further, that while I've registered every little neighborhood barb against my landscaping preferences, I've never truly engaged my neighbors in actual conversation about my plants, or about their plants.

Consider my Spanish-speaking neighbor, who wondered about my beauty berry shrubs. I actually know her better than most of my neighbors. For years, she has worked as the crossing guard at my kids' elementary school. We see her practically every morning when we walk Eva to school and cross the busy street she polices. We always say thank you and good morning. So why had I been so curt with her, so defensive, when she asked about my beauty berry plants? Why had I assumed that she was looking down her nose at my shrubs? Why hadn't I given her the benefit of the doubt, offered her a fuller explanation? Why had I assumed that she just wouldn't "get it"?

Partly, I believe, because it's just so much easier to embrace the role of the neighborhood oddball than to go about the more difficult task of playing well with others. The ethos of the rebel, the outsider, the solitary soul bruised, sickened, or just plain fed up by societal convention is writ large into our national identity, a birthright we sup from any number of classic literary works, including James Fenimore Cooper's *Last of the Mohicans* (1826), Ralph Waldo Emerson's "Self-Reliance" (1841), Thoreau's *Walden*, Herman Melville's *Moby-Dick* (1851), Mark Twain's *Adventures of Huckleberry Finn* (1884), plus any number of children's and young adult works that, earlier, prime us for these classics. While I'm all about self-reliance in its more heroic manifestations, my home gardening ethos had veered off that track into holier-than-thou smugness, I feared. This was wrong.

As the date for our garden tour neared, it seemed more and more to me that the guests I most wished to welcome to my yard weren't the members of the Palm Beach Chapter of the Florida Native Plant Society (who already shared my landscaping values), but my immediate neighbors, most of whom might not realize that there *is* such a thing as a Florida Native Plant Society. My neighbors, after all, might come around to seeing the special beauty of native Florida plants once I welcomed them onto the property, might adopt some of my practices and broaden the native plant and wildlife corridor at our shoulders, and might have some interesting stories to tell me about their own lives with plants. Maybe they would just be good people, who would be nice to know.

Wendy and I decided to write a letter to our neighbors up and down the block, partly to apologize for all the cars that would be parked in front of their houses the date of the garden tour, and mostly to introduce ourselves to the majority whom we still don't know. In the letter, we encouraged them to visit our garden the day of the tour, or to stop by *any* time to say hello and check out our plants. Enlisting Eva's help, we walked up and down the street, slipped the letters into the mailboxes, and hand-delivered a few of them to neighbors who were outside. We enjoyed a nice chat with a seventy-something fellow named Ron, just a few doors up from us, one of the few residents on the block who welcomed us to the home when we moved in, but whom we haven't spoken with in the intervening years. Scanning our letter with interest, he revealed that he had lived here for thirty years and told us the history of our neighborhood. It used to be a pineapple plantation, apparently, once it was cleared of most of its slash pine and live oak. That's why our neighborhood is called Palm Beach Farms. A young mother just up the street from Ron was outside with her daughter, a couple years younger than Eva. Our daughter showed her new friend the multicolor rubber-band bracelets she'd been crafting nonstop of late, while Wendy and the mother talked about how the school year was going, what sports the girls were interested in. How small a gesture it took to puncture the barrier of our social reticence, to make our neighborhood feel like an actual neighborhood.

We finished up preparations for the big day. I completed our plant list for the volunteer docents. I bought police-tape and five orange paint buckets to mark off no-parking areas. I printed plant identification tags, listing common and scientific names, affixed them to eighteen-inch floral card stake-holders (we mail ordered a 100-count bag). The morning of the tour, Wendy, the kids, and I walked about the yard clutching fistfuls of these signs, speared the stakes into patches of soil to label all of the plants. Susan was our point person for these preparations, and I would be remiss not to mention here that she was increasingly helpful and kind, and appreciative of our efforts, as the date of the tour drew near. As I've suggested, my irritation with her was mostly misdirected animus toward myself.

* * *

The garden tour, put simply, was a smashing success. Over 250 people visited our garden that Sunday, a few of whom were neighbors who introduced themselves. I can't claim to have escaped all annoyances. We're talking 250 people, after all. One visitor couldn't help pointing out that my particular necklace pod specimens weren't the Florida native variety (who knew?) and shouldn't have been marked as such. Another visitor noticed the lid to our buried propane tank (which we use to power our oven) and advised that we look into a more sustainable setup sourced from the effluvia of cows. Yet, on the whole, a warm and congenial spirit carried the day. Most all of the guests were friendly and polite, and several expressed their appreciation that we opened up our yard to help inspire their own gardening efforts. The volunteer docents, for their part, were helpful, kind, and interesting. One worked as a field biologist. Another was a nature photographer.

"There's something special about visiting a person's garden," one of the docents, Terry, noted through her rich southern dialect. "It puts people in a good mood." She was right.

It put *me* in a good mood, too. I especially enjoyed walking about amid the visitors, answering questions, receiving their gracious compliments. I pointed out some of the yellow-spotted Atala caterpillars that I located on one of our coonties, the few luminous, white snowberries hidden within the gumbo limbo foliage, the female Florida boxwood teeming with red berries. When I wasn't engaged in direct conversation with visitors, I couldn't help eavesdropping a bit.

"You *see!*" I overheard one woman utter to her companion under our canopy of live oaks, "You don't need to plant grass to have a beautiful garden!"

As I expected, several visitors marveled over the complex latticework of chiggery grape vines across the scaffolding of our two live oaks on the east side of the yard. (A photo of my vines had appeared in an article the local paper published to advertise the tour.) The highlight of the day for me occurred just under the canopy of these vine-festooned oaks. I was prattling on about the vines to a small group but stopped myself short upon hearing the deep and unmistakable gurgling notes of a pileated woodpecker. I looked up and spotted the enormous red crest, obscured somewhat by the thick, leathery leaves of the vine, and pointed the woodpecker out to the few visitors in my company. "There! *See* it?" The creature seemed to be foraging in a particularly dense thicket across one of the oak branches twenty feet up or so. We all got a pretty decent look, anyway, before it flew off. The pileated woodpecker may be a common homeplace sighting for some fortunate readers, but not for me. I think it's safe to say that if you live in downtown Boca Raton and successfully attract pileated woodpeckers to your yard, you're doing something right.

* * *

Once again, those ferns that sprawl betwixt and between our more desirable ground covers. *Nephrolepis cordifolia*. Common name: tuberous sword fern. In the aftermath of our garden tour, and once I caught my breath, I decided that it would behoove me to know these plants better. And so the tuberous sword fern, according to the online Plant Directory of the University of Florida Institute of Food and Agricultural Sciences, is a wood fern with pinnate fronds up to three feet in length and three feet wide. Its subterranean tubers distinguish sword fern from the native fern, *Nephrolepis exaltata*. Its randy dispersal occurs via these tubers and the straw-colored stolons that produce them, through its hairy rhizomes, and through its air- and water-borne spores. The tuberous sword fern has been documented in twenty-three Florida counties from the Gainesville area south. While it may not be considered Public Enemy Number One by advocates of Florida native plants (the Brazilian pepper-tree and melaleuca continue to vie for that honor), the tuberous sword fern, like the Brazilian pepper-tree and melaleuca, is considered a Category I invasive species. Which is pretty bad. "Through its aggressive spread," the Plant Directory warns, "sword fern is able to form dense stands and quickly displace native vegetation."

I was sorely tempted to deploy my research to quash once and for all Wendy's misguided advocacy for these pernicious plants. Yet I've decided, at least for now, to hold my fire. I doubt that our ferns will manage to ford the asphalt boundaries of our small property through their tubers, stolons, rhizomes, or even through their promiscuous spores, to colonize my neighbors' gardens or the more distant patches of precious native Florida earth that remain along our coastal ridge. I can keep these ferns in their place. One more excuse to escape the indoors and get some Florida dirt underneath my fingernails. It will be my half-assed Sisyphean task, crawling hands and knees across my yard time to time, ripping out tuberous sword ferns that dare threaten to suffocate our sensitive plant, our dune sunflower, our coontie. What's more, tolerating some of these plants might serve as a check against my own native plant pieties, which, like all pieties, can sometimes veer into the insufferable and absurd.

The distinctions, after all, between native and non-native, preferred planting and "invasive," plant and weed, are not altogether clear distinctions and never were, as I've suggested elsewhere. These are dynamic categories, subject to constant reinspection, reflection, and revision. Climbing up the same two live oaks on my property as our celebrated native chiggery grape vines are two separate vines—Virginia creeper and Dutchman's pipe—that few of my visitors envied the day of the tour like they envied our chiggery grapes. Few even seemed to notice them. Most consider the native Virginia creeper a weed on account of its, well, creeping proclivities, but any number of birds relish their berries and nest amid their thickets, while squirrels, mice, and raccoons, and probably other animals I haven't observed, eat their stems and leaves. The Dutchman's pipe is a non-native (for shame!), but the plant serves as a crucial host for the lovely native gold rim swallowtail, whose caterpillars, in turn, feed any number of our native cardinals, who feed any number of our native Cooper's hawks and screech owls. Virginia creeper and Dutchman's pipe are Jake by me! Who knows what other singular flora and fauna thrive across the scaffolding of my oaks, which I utterly fail to see?

What I mean to say, I suppose, is that we ought not to get too complacent that we know what we're doing at any given time. Napoleon Broward, the Florida governor for whom we've named our second-most populous county, set about dredging the Everglades in the early 1900s under the banner of "conservation." He and his allies couldn't fathom the thumping heart of the ecosystem, its hydrology. They truly thought they were saving the Everglades. Now, I believe that the University of Florida Institute of Food and Agricultural Sciences and the Palm Beach Chapter of the Florida Native Plant Society are probably correct to decry the threat of the non-native tuberous sword fern to indigenous species. But for as long as I maintain this pesky plant in my yard, it will serve as a useful reminder that competing values ever inform our decisions concerning what the earth under our immediate control ought to look like, and for what, and for whom. It will remind me that these freighted negotiations can yield unforeseen results. Our best laid plans can turn out sloppy, and imperfect. Like us. It strikes me as not such a bad reason to spare a plant with a bad rap sheet. And besides, my wife, as I've mentioned, likes the tuberous sword fern.

Being with Animals

8

The Problem with Pretty Birds

The problem with pretty birds is that they are so hard to ignore.

There we were in our breakfast nook, my wife and I, assailing each other over our oatmeal with our respective workplace obligations, which ought to excuse us from competing childcare duties this afternoon. We hurled the important words of our important professions like stones across the breakfast table. *Mediation. Office hours. Deposition.* I knew pretty early on that I was going to lose this particular battle, mediations and depositions (whatever the heck *they* are, exactly) taking precedence over office hours, which I could cancel. But I wasn't ready to give up so soon. It was a bad mood that I was nursing, which I intended to nurse for at least a few more aggrieved sentences.

But then a painter's palette with wings over my wife's shoulder flashed against the sun outside the glass door, uttering silent sentences of its own. *Here I am!* it cried, alighting on our bird feeder, jutting its cherry chest and throat. *Here I am!* it cried, pivoting on its perch, showing off its emerald backpack now, munching millet between its mighty bunting mandibles. *Here I am!* it cried, dipping its whole royal blue head back inside the feeder's mouth for more millet, seed-hulls flowing from its beak like something molten as it emerged. A male painted bunting, first of the season. Around this time each year, late September, these birds abandon their twiggy, grassy, leafy, cobwebby, horsehairy, and rootlety nests in North Florida, the Carolinas, and Georgia and stay with us in the warmer subtropics until mid-April or so. So we've sort of been expecting him. Yet not now. Not now-now, in the middle of our domestic spat. I wasn't feeling cherry, or emerald, or royal blue. For crying out loud!

Have they no sense of occasion, these painted buntings? The answer, of course, is no. They don't care a fig about us or our moods, which is another problem with pretty birds. It's nicer to imagine, in the spirit of Emerson and Thoreau, perfect sympathy between the realm of nonhuman nature and us. Wallace Stevens, however, probably hews closer to the truth about birds and people in his poem "Of Mere Being" when he writes, "A gold-feathered bird / Sings in the palm, without human meaning, / Without human feeling, a foreign song." Though we eavesdrop, shamelessly, the birds don't sing for us. Our relationships with them, and with most wild creatures, are terribly one-sided. Hardly relationships at all.

Still, it's not like I could exactly ignore this pretty, problematic bird outside, over my wife's shoulder.

"There's a painted bunting at the feeder," I said sharply, joylessly, as if to say, *I'm angry at you*. Which is what my wife might actually have heard, as she continued:

"You know I can't cancel the mediation, honey. My clients are flying in from Omaha."

"Do you fricking hear what I'm saying, Wendy!?" I had the sense, anyway, to constrict my voice through my windpipe to spare our four-year-old from hearing these curses from the family room. "It's a goddamn painted bunting for Christ's sake! At the feeder!"

"A male?" Wendy asked, nonplussed, finally hearing the key words through my ludicrous tone and timbre. She pivoted in her seat, glanced over her shoulder out the glass door. "Oh, he's so pretty," she said, as if to say, *Oh, he's so pretty*, adjusting more seamlessly than I was able or willing to adjust to the morning's shiny new terms.

* * *

The thing is, it's not merely pretty, the painted bunting. It's outlandishly, ludicrously, ridiculously pretty. "The most gaudily colored North American songbird," Roger Tory Peterson writes. "Nonpareil," the French name for the bird, "without equal." Its blue head somehow bluer than blue. Its green back "electric," opines Peterson. The chest and neck not a mere red or even cherry, quite. Vermilion, rather, smacks closer to the truth. And all three of these colors on the same small bird! Colors so vibrant that the winged creatures do seem electrically enhanced. A Christmas-light bird. *Look here!* male buntings seem to say. *This is what blue and green and red ought to look like!*

Hard to fathom that such a bird has evolved over millennia, existed, and exists, alongside scruffier sparrows and finches and flycatchers in North America, alongside scruffier us. A male painted bunting makes you wonder, if you're the wondering type: why this particular, improbable animal form? Why these bold contrasts in hue? Why emerald green here, royal blue there, vermilion here? More ordinary, extraordinary curiosities arise, while you're in a thinking mood: This beak? These wings? These spindly legs and tiny claws? What strange and wondrous forces issue such a creature into being?

* * *

Moments like these, when a pretty bird interrupts an irascible mood, I'm reminded of how poor a watcher I truly am, or have become in my harried adulthood. The greater patience of other writers frequently puts me in my place. Like Annie Dillard, who summons spectacular imaginative resources in *Pilgrim at Tinker Creek* (1974) to engage with the natural world ever more mindfully. "When I lose interest in a given bird," she writes in the "Spring" chapter of her classic, "I try to renew it by looking at the bird in either of two ways. I imagine neutrinos passing through its feathers and into its heart and lungs, or I reverse its evolution and imagine it as a lizard. I see its scaled legs and that naked ring around a shiny eye; I shrink and deplume its feathers to lizard scales, unhorn its lipless mouth, and set it stalking dragonflies, cool-eyed, under a palmetto."

The male painted bunting sports a naked ring around its eye too, a crimson contrast against its royal blue head. Rarely, however, do I look at these birds concertedly enough to really notice this crimson ring. There's the person that we are and the person we'd like to be, and the best we can probably do in this life is nudge ourselves, through conscious Dillard-like effort, ever closer to the latter. The other thing we might do is adjust our expectations for ideal selfhood every once in a while, as I've done (and as the preservation of one's sanity dictates). But I still feel that it would behoove me to exercise more patience, more mindfulness, before the actual outdoor world. I doubt that I'll ever match Dillard's patience—or the patience of so many other writers whom I admire, past and present—yet I can surely do better.

And so . . .

Wendy and I rose from our seats at the table, stood before the glass door and watched the pretty, problematic bird, outside. What else could we do in the presence of such a visitor? I called Eva over from her puzzle on the family-room rug to glimpse the painted bunting, too.

"You see it?" I asked, hoping that her spongy brain would absorb the image before it flitted off into dense cover. She's just at the age when memories begin to stick. Wouldn't it be nice if she were able to summon, years from now, this fleeting, feathered vision?

"I see it," she uttered, nose to the glass, pleased but undazzled. She watched the bird for a few moments, then skittered past my knees back to her puzzle. Okay, maybe. Okay, that for now she felt that it was perfectly ordinary and unremarkable that she shared a world with these bejeweled birds.

Three female buntings—now four!—emerged from the nearby firebush and necklace pod foliage to join the male at the feeder. Pretty in their own way, these females, green ship to stern, a bit darker-dashed here and there, as if these few feathers were dipped in water. If these green and dark-dashed birds were the male painted buntings, say, and female painted buntings were a drab brown, all we'd talk about was the beauty of these small green and dark-dashed birds. But these aren't the male painted buntings, so no one talks about the prettiness of plain-old green and dark-dashed buntingness.

Five females at the feeder now and still this single male. His harem? Why is it, I wondered, that we always see so many females and so few males each year?

* * *

The problem with pretty birds is that that they tend to get eaten by other birds. Cooper's hawks, sharp-shinned hawks, peregrine falcons, merlins. All of whom seem to make a decent living here. Solitary, pugnacious killers. The merlins, especially. I saw one just the other day in coastal scrublands near my home, perched atop a withered sand pine surveying its domain, silencing the nervous warblers and vireos in the canopy below, its slate-gray back and speckled chest puffed up against the salt wind.

It may be that male painted buntings, who surely winter here in equal numbers to the females, are simply more skittish and covert than female birds, given their outlandish, ludicrous, ridiculous prettiness. Their feathers, after all, simultaneously shout *Love me, love me, love me!* to female painted buntings and *Eat me, eat me, eat me!* to most everything else, including merlins, including (come to think of it) the ever-expanding band of feral cats in my neighborhood, which rove about most suburban neighborhoods these days, unfortunately.

The problem with pretty birds is that they tend to get trapped and sold by resourceful humans too. Easy to lure inside wooden cages with "rival" decoys, the ornery painted bunting males. Thousands caught every spring, observed John James Audubon in 1841, shipped from New Orleans to France where they fetched a handsome price. Still taken in large numbers in Mexico, Central America, and the Caribbean, sold at flea markets, some for the cage-bird market, some to compete against one another in underground singing battles. I suppose that such clandestine events are somewhat analogous to cockfights or dogfights, but it's tough for me to imagine these gatherings in quite the same light. A clan of human malfeasants, drinking and smoking and gambling over the singing prowess of pretty birds? Is it possible that a more formal air perfumes such contests, that men and women don their Sunday finest to listen to the sweet warbles of painted bunting competitors?

* * *

Pretty birds, provided they don't get eaten by raptors or feral cats or trapped by nefarious humans, entice mates with greater success, thereby increasing their reproductive fitness. You see the tension. Clearly a balance must be struck between these competing interests. Enticing mates. Eluding predators. Most finches and sparrows seem to have it figured out pretty well. Earth tones. A few stripes here and there, a swatch of color maybe at the crown, lores, or eyebrows. Nothing crazy.

Not so the pretty painted bunting.

It might have been a good idea for painted buntings, before people were around to call them painted buntings, to have convened a Council of Learned Elders within the cover of greenbriar or myrtle. A male bunting might have gazed out at his cohorts across the latticework of branches, offered a proposition to the females, *Listen, we know you like pretty greens and blues and reds, but we live in a world with Cooper's hawks, sharpshinned hawks, peregrine falcons, and merlins. So let's not get carried away.*

But as you say, a female bunting elder might have replied, *we do like our greens and blues and reds.*

Which might have elicited the following response from a separate male elder: *While we cower within these branches, look over at those savannah sparrows frolicking out in the open field there. They didn't get carried away, see? A bit of rust on the wings. A gray stripe at the crown. And so they can play out there in the open. And look at the good times they enjoy gathering coreopsis* and *partridge pea* and *beardtongue* and *goldenrod seed. Because they didn't get carried away with too many flashy colors. You have to be reasonable.*

To which a separate female elder might have replied, *Even so . . .*

* * *

Our pretty, problematic bird, this first painted bunting male of the season, fluttered down off the feeder and alit upon a tall blade of grass, more like a reed, tested its rigidity under its modest bunting weight. Wendy and I watched as it skittered up to the top of the reed, which flexed like a bow, as it munched on the seeds bursting from brown, ferny sheaths. I wondered whether it relished those honest-begotten grass-borne seeds more than my store-bought seeds from the plastic cylinder above, whether it enjoyed the flex of the reed more than the stability of the metal perch, enjoyed feeling the impact of its bunting weight in the actual world. I wondered what species of grass, anyway, grew beneath our feeder to produce that seed bursting from brown, ferny sheaths. Probably millet spilled from the feeder-seed.

When pretty painted buntings don't eat my millet seed—from the feeder or from the feeder-seed-borne grass beneath—they eat pigweed seeds and bristle grass seeds and the seeds of wood sorrel and panic grass and spurge and sedge and St. John's wort and pine and wheat and wild rose.

* * *

It occurs to me that several of the green birds on the feeder that I assumed to be females along with our sole male might actually have been immature males, that the proportion of females to males that I see out the window each season might not be quite so imbalanced. For immature painted buntings, both male and female, sport only the all-green feathers associated with female painted buntings. Gradually, gradually, then all of a sudden, red and blue feathers replace the green on male chests and heads. Even their dull green backpacks turn emerald. Which makes me wonder: do immature male painted buntings know what's in store for them, that in a matter of months their plumage will undertake a rather dramatic, multichromatic transformation? And, if so, how does this bear upon their demeanor with their immature female companions? Do immature males cop attitude as they forage about the pigweed, the bristle grass, the wood sorrel, and panic grass? *Out of my way! We may look the same now, but*

I'm gonna be smokin' hot soon. Do immature females—and here I presume that they too know what's in store for the boys—cow before the imminent loveliness of their male counterparts, offer a wide berth, or do I have this all wrong? It may be that female painted buntings couldn't care less about the ostentatious loveliness of their male counterparts. Perhaps they find all the "peacocking" silly—these outlandish blues and reds and greens. Perhaps it's all they can do to tolerate these puffed-up males. They pair up, perhaps, out of sheer pity or desperation. What else are they to do? It's not like they can choose the more down-to-earth savannah sparrows or palm warblers or house finches. They're painted buntings. What I wonder most generally, I suppose, is whether it creates problems for these pretty, problematic birds, the ocular disparity between the sexes.

After all, it's not like birds are always (or usually) so nice to one another. You don't have to be the keenest of observers to notice that birds do seem to squabble quite a bit for more favorable perches on trees, electric wires, and feeders. Some of the prettiest birds are purportedly among the most aggressive. The dazzling throats and diminutive size of hummingbirds, for example, belies their ferocity. "Little assholes," as a more experienced birder friend of mine refers to hummingbirds. Further, while most birdsong sounds sweet to our human ears, the truth is that ornithologists don't know precisely what birds mean to say through their vocalizations. As a character in David Foster Wallace's *The Pale King* (2011) cannily observes, "the birds, whose twitters and repeated songs sounded so pretty and affirming of nature and the coming day, might actually, in a code known only to other birds, be the birds each saying 'Get away' or 'This branch is mine!' or 'This tree is mine! I'll kill you! Kill, Kill!'" It's probably important to keep in mind that much of what we see and hear as loveliness in birds is of our own willful, imaginative making. It's a problem.

Something there is, anyway, that can't deny this imaginative work, my hopeful vision that male and female painted buntings, immature and adult, interact with one another on mostly amicable terms. I like to think, specifically, that males and females alike enjoy a healthy self-regard untainted by haughtiness, that male birds love themselves for their reds and blues and greens and hold their mates just as dear for their duller green dashed with dark, that female birds love their duller green dashed with dark, too, love their mates just as well, but not more or less well, for their brilliant reds and blues and greens.

I like to think that the birds, anyway, have figured things out.

The evidence mostly suggests that painted buntings have done so, after a fashion. When the days grow longer and hotter in their wintering grounds here in South Florida and elsewhere, they light out for more temperate climes northward, seek out brushy roadsides and streamsides, fallow fields and citrus groves, maritime hammock edges and palmetto thickets in places we humans call North Florida, Georgia, and the Carolinas. A separate breeding population favors Texas, Oklahoma, Arkansas, and Louisiana. The painted bunting male sings its "sweet continuous warble," as David Allen Sibley describes bunting song, bravely from open perches. He courts his mate with great ardor, flashing his bright feathers, bowing and strutting. The female mostly pecks at seeds, unimpressed, or feigning aloofness, but eventually hops toward her suitor to join him in shared purpose. The wings of the male bird quiver with delight. The two set up housekeeping.

Male painted buntings don't cultivate harems evidently. They are mostly monogamous. Like people. I guess.

Both the male and female search out potential nesting sites hidden within dense foliage four or five feet off the ground. Sometimes lower. Sometimes higher. The female gathers material for their twiggy, grassy, leafy, cobwebby, horsehairy, and rootlety nests: mesquite and elm and Osage-orange and greenbriar and oak and Spanish moss. She builds the nest alone. But don't decry the laziness of husbands! He has plenty on his plate. Principally, he defends their turf with great tenacity, showcasing for rival males an exhaustive menu of displays: upright display, bow display, flutter-up display, wing-quiver display, butterfly display. Should such posturing fail, he attacks the intruder, dive-bombing and nipping and pecking. He'll yank out whole feathers between his mighty bunting mandibles. Again, the behavior of birds, even pretty birds—especially pretty birds—often belies their loveliness. It's a jungle out there. They can't afford to be kind to competitors. Enough, maybe, that they are kind to their mates.

The female lays three or four small bluish eggs, speckled with brown and gray. The eggs hatch in less than two weeks. She deposits all manner of buggy food into the ever-gaping maws of the chicks: grasshoppers, weevils, beetles, wasps, spiders, snails, caterpillars, and flies. Unlike most birds—less amorous birds—painted buntings raise as many as three broods per season. Once the female renests, the male will feed their fledged chicks.

Yes, it seems to me that painted buntings have pretty much figured out their love business. So brave these gaudy, lit-up birds, who might have donned drab sparrow colors but chose a more passionate route. *Life! Life! Life!* painted buntings cry with their emerald backpacks, with their flutter-up displays, with their dive-bombing and nipping and pecking, with their cobwebby nests, and (perhaps most of all) with their sweet continuous warble. John Keats, who would die of tuberculosis at age twenty-five, gleaned in birdsong the indomitable life force of which he was sorely deprived. "Thou wast not born for death, immortal Bird!" he writes in "Ode to a Nightingale." In reality, most birds—painted buntings included—live very short lives; Wallace's more earthbound, prose passage on birdsong above (*I'll kill you! Kill, Kill!*) offers a corrective, of sorts, to Keats's unbridled romanticism. Yet I find that my mind seeks out a space somewhere between the romantic and the real when birds flit across my field of view. I'm not willing to give up the notion that these few ounces of feathers and bone and flesh, as Keats' ode suggests, epitomize life lived full bore. *Life! Life! Life!* The problem with pretty birds is that they constantly put me to shame with their bravery, their unwavering self-assuredness, their moxie, their lives lived full bore. Self-doubt doesn't seem to be such a big thing with them. "We're never single-minded, unperplexed, like migratory birds," the poet Rainer Maria Rilke writes in the *Duino Elegies*.

* * *

I'd like to believe that my perfectly ordinary suburban life is a brave life, too, yet most social indicators tell me otherwise. A timid life, my home-centered life, from a certain vantage. We are still a young country that celebrates new beginnings, new journeys, constant reinventions of the self. "A vagabond wind has been blowing here for a long while," Scott Russell Sanders declares in *Staying Put: Making a Home in a Restless World* (1993), "and it grows stronger by the hour." I've watched several close friends and colleagues set sail upon this wind for new jobs, new cities, observed these departures with sadness and, admittedly, a tinge of envy and unbirdlike self-doubt. I'm not completely immune to the spirit of our times. It may be why I'm so antsy and irascible with my family sometimes. I'm not single-minded, unperplexed. It's a problem. Like Sanders, though, I've mostly ducked the vagabond wind, hunkered down for nearly twenty years in the same city, at the same embattled state university. From whence did such stick-to-itiveness arise?

The example of birds probably informed my home-centered inclinations from a very young age. My parents, like many American parents, moved my siblings and me around quite a bit, forsaking the East Coast for the West Coast when I was five. I was just old enough during this uprooting to have felt that it was an uprooting, to have felt that home was something we had left behind, something to recover and hold dear. This may be why I marveled, growing up in Southern California, at the story told by several of my elementary school teachers of the cliff swallows' yearly return to the Mission of San Juan Capistrano. Each year on the same exact day, St. Joseph's Day, March 19th, townspeople would raise their eyes to the sky to welcome back the cliff swallow flocks from their winter home in Argentina. The swallows would immediately set up housekeeping, constructing their tiny mud nests against the crusty ruins of the Great Stone Church. The swallows knew something essential, something strong enough to hold year after year after year, and on the exact same day (!), something about the power of their homeplace.

While I never convinced my parents to take me to the Mission of San Juan Capistrano on St. Joseph's Day to observe the swallows' homecoming, I did somehow (and to my continued amazement) persuade them by seventh grade to let me raise homing pigeons in a backyard coop. I constructed the coop (shoddily) with a few of my pals over several weeks before buying my first two pairs of homing pigeons from a local breeder. The old man, who flicked the ashes of his cigarette into his bare palm, explained that I couldn't release the birds from my coop for their first flight until after they had nested and their first chicks had hatched. If I released them before this time, they would simply fly back to his coop at the other end of the San Fernando Valley, and finders-keepers was the guiding protocol among pigeon fanciers he advised through a mischievous, mottled smile. Fair warning. "Etiquette" aside, it was an interesting fact about homing pigeons, which remains interesting. Home is where they raise their young.

I heeded the fellow's admonition and kept the birds in the coop until their first chicks fledged. I still remember the thrill of that first release. Riding our knobby-tired bicycles, my friends and I transported the bird families in brown grocery bags up into the chaparral hills several miles from our neighborhood. (In the years since, these hills have mostly been paved over and developed, planted with stucco and Spanish tile homes, but back then it was wild land, or near-wild land, teeming with rattlesnakes, coyotes, and red-tailed hawks.) We released the birds and sped back home, the sunbaked trails giving way to a long downhill stretch of asphalt road. The homing pigeons, miraculously, were waiting for us in the coop already, their chests puffed up, strutting and cooing. They knew what the swallows knew. Home is where you raise your young.

    I don't raise homing pigeons anymore. Instead, I keep watch for the reliable winter return of songbirds, especially our painted bunting flock. Despite manifold competing factors that vie for my attention—successfully, more often than not, I'm afraid—I still look toward the buntings, these creatures who I know couldn't care a fig about me, or us, but continue to offer essential instruction, abandoning their twiggy, grassy, leafy, cobwebby, horsehairy, and rootlety nests at roughly the same time each year to make our home their winter home.

* * *

The five female buntings this recent, harried morning skittered off the feeder, eventually, swept up the male below and disappeared into the scruffy firebush and necklace pod foliage. "Guess they're finished," my wife said, then sighed. A curious look painted her face. A furrow between her eyes betrayed mild disorientation. The furrow asked, *What was it we were talking about? What unpleasant domestic business must we complete this morning?* I remembered our business together, our little spat over who would watch Eva this afternoon. I'd like to say that the glimpse of our first painted bunting male of the season put me in my place, immediately, that I stepped up to the rather modest demands of parenthood with alacrity. But I can't quite make this claim. I conceded the argument, but I could have been a whole lot nicer about it. Only now do I wonder whether my insistence on nursing a foul mood over something so small amounted in the end to the vanity I foolishly project sometimes onto pretty birds, whether merlins of my own making loom over all that I hold dear. Only now do I glance back in my mind's eye from the glass door toward the remnants of breakfast on the table, toward our family room, toys strewn all about the rug like leaf litter, toward our small daughter looming over her puzzle—our panic grass and wood sorrel, our cobwebby nest, our fledgling with her ever-gaping maw.

9

Summer Animals

South Florida. Summer. And gloominess descends. I mostly blame the unrelenting heat and my retreat indoors. During these hottest months in the subtropics—ever hotter on account of climate change—we tend to shutter ourselves inside the climate-controlled interiors of our homes, offices, and automobiles. Rarely do we linger outdoors to exchange hail and hearties with our neighbors.

Winter in Henry David Thoreau's Concord. A fairly close analogue to summertime in South Florida, at least insofar as the winter cold and snow during the two seasons Thoreau spends at his cabin beside Walden Pond curtail his outdoor excursions and effectively isolate him from most human neighbors. "At this season, I seldom had a visitor," he writes as winter sets in. While Thoreau greets his solitude with alacrity, it's also true that he isn't immune to loneliness, however fleeting. What seems mostly to combat gloominess for Thoreau is his continued contact with a riot of winter animals—geese, foxes, owls, chickadees, titmice, partridges, mice, rabbits, squirrels—many of which he seeks out, along with some old trees, by tromping through the thick snow.

* * *

It's a very old knowledge. We share the planet with nonhuman animals. We need them. Our fate has ever depended upon this kinship, this radical intermingling, originally realized through a sound, a smell, a glimpse, then through the tip of a spear. But not only through the tip of a spear. The oldest works of human art that we've discovered mostly represent animals. Consider the 25,000-year-old Spotted Horses mural painted across a rock wall inside the Pech Merle cave in France. Even in photographs, there's something awesome about the scale of the equine figures, the bold black manes and spots, the way the artists seem to have shaped one of the horse's heads from the natural outcropping of the stone. Note, too, the stenciled handprints above and below the horse figures, these early artists' version of a signature, maybe? But more. The hands. The horses. The conjoining of a human and nonhuman animal presence across the shared space of the stone. Kinship.

The Pech Merle cave mural was painted during the Ice Age. It may be that these early humans painted murals during their coldest months, when they were mostly sealed inside their Arctic caves, when they were hard-pressed to realize physical encounters with animals, when many humans and animals surely starved to death. It's impossible to know what they were thinking when they produced their art, but painting spotted horses against a rock wall might have been their way of sustaining their kinship with these animals by bringing them inside—images of them anyway—shoring up hope.

* * *

So I've been wondering lately whether it might be the nonhuman animals outside that I truly miss most now. It's sort of quiet animalwise, summertime in South Florida. Our manifold warblers and vireos and buntings that wintertime flit nonstop across the scaffolding of my front-yard oaks, like blinking Christmas lights, are long gone until the fall. Come dog days, the bluefish, manatee, mahi mahi, and various other aquatic creatures mostly drift northward along the Gulf Stream or inside the Intracoastal Waterway and its feeder canals to more temperate waters; the snapper and grouper, year-round residents like us, seem too dazed by the hot sea to venture from their grottoes and tug my line. Even the stalwart burrowing owls and gopher tortoises and raccoons sit out the sweltering daytime heat, nestled inside their subterranean warrens and shaggy sabal palm canopies. Maybe I just don't look hard enough, or long enough. "To see an animal," Craig Childs writes in *Crossing Paths: Uncommon Encounters with Animals in the Wild* (1997), "you must first remain very still. You may have to huddle in the dark of a street culvert for three nights before the raccoon comes. You may have to sit naked on the tundra before the grizzly finds you. Or you will simply have to be there."

* * *

Yesterday, my family and I enjoyed a great animal day in summertime South Florida. I walked outside to retrieve the morning paper, ribbons of almost-cool air wrapping about my neck and arms. I looked up and was greeted by a vision of butterflies—zebra longwings, monarchs, and gold-rimmed swallowtails—fluttering over firebush blooms in the yard. Next, I heard the bleats of a red-bellied woodpecker and walked around to the side of our small property to glimpse the bird scooting inside the nest box I had built with my elder daughter, Sophia, and mounted ten feet up the trunk of one of our live oaks. (We had designed the box for the smaller downy woodpeckers in the neighborhood, but they didn't seem much interested, while these red-bellied woodpeckers, by contrast, spent the better part of a year boring out the downy-sized entrance hole so that they could squeeze their larger bodies inside.) I could hear squeaking inside the box; red-bellied chicks must have hatched. I hurried inside, retrieved my five-year-old daughter, Eva—Sophia was still sleeping—and the two of us traced the efforts of the woodpecker parents as they skittered between the heliotrope vine on a neighboring tree, where they collected its fat white berries, and the nest box, where they fed the berries to their squeaking young. Later that morning, my wife and kids took our skiff out on a broad stretch of the Intracoastal Waterway, where we anchored and swam with goggles to search out additional summertime creatures. My teenage son, Henry, plucked a handsome shell from the sandy bottom, inside of which a hermit crab had claimed squatter's rights. Eva inspected the crunchy claws peeking out the shell on the skiff for a while before dropping it back beneath the skin of the brackish water. Next, Henry spotted a loggerhead sea turtle, not too large, watermelon-sized, an adolescent, swimming lazily to and from the dark patches of seaweed on the sandy bottom, working the patches with its raptor beak, unconcerned by our watchful presence a few yards away. When we finally returned home, we were greeted by the piercing notes of a spot-breasted oriole. Stepping outside our vehicle, we located the egg-yolk throat of the bird, spattered with black as if flicked from a paintbrush. It continued to sing its doleful melody from its perch in our largest front-yard oak. Then Sophia noticed the big green shape of a Cuban anole lizard on a separate branch, motionless against the thickly ridged bark.

"What a great day!" Eva declared on the driveway, gazing up at the oriole, or maybe at the lizard. It was all the animals we'd encountered today that she had in mind, it occurred to me. A great day.

* * *

Around 22,000 years ago, Paleolithic artists painted and carved bison, horses, deer, human hands, and mysterious signs against the limestone walls of the Altamira cave in northern Spain. The multiple representations, which extend over 270 meters into the cave, are renowned not only for their age but for the sophisticated artistic techniques and treatment of the three-dimensional medium, anticipating elements of naturalism, abstraction, and symbolism. Although preservationists have battled an algae-like mold in recent years (attributed to the dewy breath of cave visitors), what's most striking in photographs is the freshness of the red and black pigments. The muscular girth of a bison body in brick red atop spindly legs captures my gaze. The simple loops and dots of black, which demarcate eye and ear, lend life and agency to the creature.

* * *

Our ancient intimacy with wild creatures increasingly slips from our grasp in contemporary suburbia. Coast-to-coast, having displaced most Native American communities, we have mostly uprooted the native placeness of our neighborhoods, too, replaced native trees, shrubs, and vines with lawn monocultures accented by a few meager (and mostly non-native) shrubs and specimen trees. While a few animal species have profited from our peculiar landscaping preferences (particularly blue jays, one of the few animals Thoreau openly derides in *Walden*) most native creatures struggle to make a go of it in the bland new environments we've created.

A sour strain of thought would implicate Thoreau for contemporary suburbia and its ecologically unsustainable footprint. As Bill McKibben writes in a footnote to his recent edition of *Walden*, "Thoreau has done his work too well, perhaps; now most of us live in suburban idylls, 'far from towns.' Usually these subdivisions—Fox Hollow, Partridge Run—are named for whatever was wiped out to make room for them." McKibben's general observation rings true, as I'm sure many suburban readers can attest. But while there may be a loose connection to draw between the enticement of the woods for Thoreau and the rise of modern-day, animal-obliterating suburbia, Thoreau, it must be said, would have been aghast by the sight of our suburban neighborhoods. "Hope and the future for me are not in lawns and cultivated fields, not in towns and cities, but in the impervious and quaking swamps," he proclaims in his essay, "Walking." In *Walden*, he offers his own landscaping plan, which might be seen as a plea to forgo landscaping per se: "No yard! But unfenced Nature reaching up to your very sills. A young forest growing up under your windows, and wild sumachs and blackberry vines breaking through into your cellar."

> Blackberry vines breaking through into your cellar.

This permeable boundary between Thoreau's cabin and the wild outdoors resonates throughout *Walden,* in this case pertaining to flora. But any number of animals also test the border between indoors and out, and to Thoreau's delight, particularly during wintertime when human company is scarce. While Thoreau takes pains to describe his sturdy construction of the cabin and his efforts to winterize it, the utter porousness of his shelter leaves the greatest impression. Chickadees flit in and out his open windows and pick their dinner from his woodpile; wasps "by the thousands" settle on the windows and walls inside the cabin and even bed with Thoreau, not bothering him too much, he claims; red squirrels wake him in the morning, "coursing over the roof and up and down the sides of the house, as if sent out of the woods for this purpose." Thoreau's account of the hares perhaps most charmingly evokes the paper-thin boundary between his cabin and the outdoors. "The hares (*Lepus Americanus*) were very familiar," he writes:

> One had her form under my house all winter, separated from me only by the flooring, and she startled me each morning by her hasty departure when I began to stir,—thump, thump, thump, striking her head against the floor timbers in her hurry. They used to come round my door at dusk to nibble the potato parings which I had thrown out and were so nearly the color of the ground that they could hardly be distinguished when still. Sometimes in the twilight I alternately lost and recovered sight of one sitting motionless under my window. When I opened my door in the evening, off they would go with a squeak and a bounce.

We're much more diligent these days about keeping the outside out and the inside in, particularly in my neck of the woods—our *actual* onetime pine flatwoods mostly grubbed out to make room for us and for our climate-controlled domiciles built with cinderblock to withstand the fierce tropical storms of summertime. When my wife and I purchased our new home, we upgraded it with hurricane-grade storm windows, mostly because it would keep my middle-aged self from having to climb a ladder to install heavy metal shutters in advance of an approaching storm. The "Low-E" glass would also keep our energy costs down, our salesman assured us, as less cool air would escape and less hot air would seep inside. As a final selling point, he added that the windows would keep all the noise out, alluding, I suppose, to the mechanized noise of automobiles, lawnmowers, and leafblowers, fairly pervasive sounds in my environs. The windows have, in fact, shielded us from these unpleasant and incessant suburban sounds.

In the bargain, however, they've also shut out the sounds of the oaks whispering secrets in the salt breeze, the squirrels scrabbling across the branches, the curious twinkling notes of the frogs, the buzzes and clicks of countless insects, and they've blotted out all the birdsong too: the bleats and cackles of red-bellied woodpeckers, the piercing notes of spot-breasted orioles, the bright tweets of cardinals, and the monotone trill and whinnies of our screech owls, nighttime. For some reason, I didn't foresee that I'd lose the natural outdoor sounds along with the mechanized noise; I didn't realize, maybe, how much these outdoor animal sounds meant to me, and still mean; I didn't realize how strange and alienating absolute quiet indoors could feel, nary a wild rabbit in my neighborhood to thump against the undersides of my floor timbers.

* * *

On my writing desk before me rests a small seashell that we collected months ago from a nearby beach and that I brought inside. It looks very much like the shell occupied by the hermit crab that we inspected and released on our recent excursion. Shaped like a vortex up to a pointed spire. Six studded whorls, washed in a caramel and cream swirl. A gastropod shell, I learn through a bit of research. Florida fighting conch. *Strombus alatas.* Up to three inches. Common in shallow grassy bays. The studs are more properly called subsutural spines.

* * *

Turns out it wasn't a loggerhead turtle that we observed feeding underwater the other day. I had only assumed that it was a loggerhead because they're by far our most common sea turtle, and it obviously wasn't a leatherback, and it sort of looked like a loggerhead, and after living in South Florida for nearly twenty years I'm more clueless than I ought to be about sea turtle identification. It was a green sea turtle. Henry took its photograph that day with his underwater camera and showed it to his supervisor at the nature center where he just started to volunteer. "Nice greenie," she observed. Easily distinguished from other sea turtles because they have a single pair of prefrontal scales (the scales in front of their eyes) rather than two pairs found on other sea turtles. Status: Endangered. Only 85,000 to

90,000 nesting females estimated to exist. Hunted into near oblivion for its meat and eggs.

John James Audubon explored the Florida Keys in 1832 to locate and paint our specialty birds (gratuitously shooting thousands) and also offered a dispassionate account of the sea turtle–hunting trade. "To upset a Turtle on shore," he writes in "The Turtlers,"

> one is obliged to fall on his knees, and placing his shoulder behind her fore-arm, gradually raise her up by pushing with great force, and then with a jerk throw her over. Sometimes it requires the united strength of several men to accomplish this; and, if the turtle should be of very great size, as often happens on that coast, even handspikes are employed.... Few Turtles can bite beyond the reach of their fore-legs, and few, when once turned over, can, without assistance, regain their natural position; but, notwithstanding this, their flippers are generally secured by ropes so as to render their escape impossible.

* * *

Sea turtles are currently protected by the Federal Endangered Species Act of 1973 and Florida's Marine Turtle Protection Act. Before these laws were in place, Sid and Roxie's Cannery across from The Green Turtle Inn restaurant on Islamorada in the Florida Keys processed over 1,000 pounds of turtle meat weekly for steaks, soups, and chowders. The Green Turtle Inn restaurant remains a popular dining destination in the Keys, but the only sea turtles you'll find inside are the ones propped in macabre upright poses in vintage hunting glory photographs on the walls.

* * *

The rock art sites at Tadrart Acacus, located in the desert of west Libya, date from 12,000 BCE to AD 100. The paintings reflect various cultural and climactic shifts in this region of the Sahara. Rather than the arid landscape of basalt monoliths that one encounters today, it was once a green savannah evidently. The paintings feature several animals, including giraffes, camels, elephants, ostriches, and horses. Mark the giraffe. There's something about its curlicue tail, its disproportionately large chest spotted with red below its smaller head and neck, and its slight forward tilt, the legs bent just so. All these features combine to suggest forward motion, or maybe a swoon. Personality even. Insouciance. How did the Indigenous artists and their fellow humans see these giant creatures? As food, surely. But not only as food. Not as food, I mean to say, in the diminished sense that we have come to see (or not to see) the creatures avian, aquatic, and terrestrial that we kill and eat.

* * *

Thoreau doesn't hunt in *Walden*. He pretty much gives up fishing too. He renounces animal food, altogether, as "unclean" and "not agreeable" to his imagination. His wintertime sanity depends upon realizing kinship of a different ilk with nonhuman creatures. While most naturalists of his day studied their subjects down the barrel of a rifle, he anticipates the discipline of ethology through his close observation of animal behavior. His mode of bird study "requires so much closer attention to the habits of the birds, that, if for that reason only, I have been willing to omit the gun." During winter, when his excursions are somewhat limited, he listens from his cabin to the owls hooting in the distance, the foxes yelping after game, the geese honking overhead. He thinks long and hard about animals, and plants, and us. "Why do precisely these objects which we behold make a world?" he inquires. It's a good question. We will never know why these precise plants and animals share our world. Or why precisely *we* share the world with these other carbon-based organisms. But that shouldn't deter us from our beholding. It's worth the effort, Childs suggests: "Times that I have seen the animals have been like knife cuts in fabric. Through these stabs I could see a second world. There were stories of evolution and hunger and death. Cross sections of genetic histories and predator-prey relationships, of lives as cryptic as blood paths in snow."

* * *

Again, this empty husk of a Florida fighting conch shell I've brought inside and balance now in the palm of my hand. Why *does* precisely this object exist to comprise a tiny chunk of our world? Its studs and ridges. Its caramel and cream whorls. The studs, or subsutural spines, help to anchor the creature into sandy bottom, holding it fast against incoming and outgoing tides, I imagine, lending at least a modicum of agency to its comings and goings; the caramel and cream whorls offer camouflage to protect the creature from hungry fish, crabs, birds, other mollusks, and me. Other colors and shapes might have performed similar functions. So why *this* precise object? And, again, why *us*? Why these fingers and toes and forearms and hearts and lungs and genitalia and kidneys and crania? These gorgeous bodies we inhabit for a few precious earth years. It may be that the animal realm, this "second world," has always offered us a precious glimpse of ourselves.

* * *

The painting of a fruit-eating pig-deer, or babirusa, in one of the Maros-Pangkep caves in Indonesia, dates to at least 35,400 years ago and seems to be the oldest example of human cave art that we've discovered. Only a fragment of the original painting remains. The artists ground into a powder the natural mineral pigment and mixed the powder with water to create the paint. The faded lines of the pig-deer's torso evoke hair. The head and legs of the pig-deer seem spindly compared to its inflated torso. Its exaggerated proportions, incredibly, resemble those of the Saharan giraffe, the Spanish bison, the French horses. What could these artists have been thinking inside their complex crania, across continents and millennia, when they painted such comparably thick midsections atop spindly legs?

* * *

Here's what we know. Early humans hunted animals to survive, painted versions of their animal likenesses against the rock walls of their shelters. Aristotle wrote *The History of Animals* in the fourth century BCE to catalog the earth's manifold wild creatures based upon their physiological and behavioral differences, a constant eye on humankind's place amid these groupings. One of the more popular books in the Middle Ages was a collection of moralized beast tales, the *Physiologus*, originally written by an unknown Greek author in the third or fourth century CE. Over the years, it would be translated into most of the European languages and served as the model for any number of related bestiaries, which feature increasingly elaborate illustrations and shifting emphases between Christian allegory and natural history:

> The pelican loveth too much her children. For when the children be haught, and begin to wax hoar, they smite the father and the mother in the face, wherefore the mother smiteth them again and slayeth them. And the third day, the mother smiteth herself in her side, that the blood runneth out, and sheddeth that hot blood on the bodies of

her children. And by virtue of that blood, the birds that were before dead quicken again.

That sort of thing.

Flashing forward, Audubon traveled up and down the continent from Labrador to Key West and the Dry Tortugas to collect thousands of birds and painted them in dramatic poses for the engravings that comprised his monumental *Birds of America* project. Thoreau took daily four-hour walks in the woods and fields surrounding Concord, observed the animal and plant goings on with almost unimaginable patience and documented his efforts in thousands of handwritten pages that he mostly collected in his journal, unpublished during his lifetime.

My efforts? Paltry by comparison. I build and install nest boxes, cultivate creature-friendly native plants across my small yard, and explore the outdoors far less often than I would like. My wife and I live out most minutes of our days, especially summertime, within outside-obliterating interiors. Yet we, too, have sought in small ways to puncture the barrier between outdoors and in. We haven't painted our own walls with animal likenesses, but we've decorated them with a simple pencil-sketch of an oak tree, a watercolor of a Florida fish called snook, a color photograph of a fawn, plus that Florida fighting conch shell that sits on my desk, and I shouldn't neglect to mention the wildflower sprigs that Eva plucks from the plants in our yard (usually without permission) and tends to leave strewn all about the house as if marking her trail. Consider the artwork and other knickknacks that adorn your home. To what extent do we all endeavor, however subconsciously, to bring the outdoors inside? To what extent do these efforts resonate, however loosely, in the earliest human art that we've discovered on the walls of prehistoric caves?

* * *

Thoreau would join the ranks of Walden Pond's "former inhabitants" (to borrow from the title of one of his book's chapters) within his own short lifetime. His lungs ravaged by tuberculosis, he lived just long enough to see his "tight shingled and plastered house" by the pond fall into ruin. One wonders what he thought of its sure and steady dilapidation. He likely viewed the sunken roof and shattered windows as emblems of his own mortality, consistent with the way he viewed the moldering remnants of other human domiciles around the pond. Yet he might, too, have perceived the cabin as melting organically into the white pine landscape of which it was largely constructed, not unlike the way he viewed autumn leaves melting into the forest floor to provide the earth its essential muck as he reflects in one of his final essays, "Autumnal Tints." He might have been bolstered by the ever-increasing merge of cabin and woods, of inside and out, which gives the lie to the rigid divide between nature and culture, animal and human, that existed in his day and in ours. Contentment for Thoreau largely depends upon this puncture. When loneliness threatens, "every sight and sound around my house" reminds him of the "sweet and beneficent society in nature."

Thoreau, for all his charms, tends to come off as strange and remote to my students in South Florida, which they often ascribe to the remoteness of New England and the nineteenth century in general. To disarm them of their first impression, I sometimes emphasize that he was perceived as something of a curiosity (by his kinder neighbors) and an oddball (by neighbors less kind) in his own day. Thoreau's contemporaries—even those few who bothered to attend his lectures or read his work—were already spending more and more time indoors, anticipating the way most of us live now. The roar from the newly completed railroad close to the pond, the rise of factory labor, and the manifold shops opening up in Concord signaled an economic revolution that increasingly ripped Americans from the outside. Nothing good would come of it, Thoreau fears. In "Walking," he contemplates the diminished daily lives of the mechanics and shopkeepers in Concord, who "stay in their shops not only all the forenoon, but all the afternoon too," and wonders how they keep themselves from committing suicide. Our indoor lives were making us unhappy. Even so, Thoreau recognizes that few of his neighbors were about to adopt his ritual of four-hour daily walks, so he offers a humbler proposal in "Walking." Says Thoreau, "We might climb a tree, at least." I try to keep the suggestion in mind when various circumstances of my harried life keep me inside for longer than I feel is healthful. For then, as now, we need the wild outdoors.

* * *

To gain intimate knowledge of the sights and sounds of a particular place outdoors—the society *in* nature—is to gain a measure of contentment. For some people, anyway. I've already alluded to the poetry and prose of Mary Oliver in the introduction. Helen Macdonald, too, describes both this intimacy and the contentment it brings in her memoir, *H Is for Hawk* (2015), as she evokes the patch of rural farmland upon which she frequently hunts with her goshawk. Her hawk, Mabel, has flown off ahead of her up the hill. Nonetheless,

> I feel I might be up there, because now the hill is home. I know it intimately. Every hedgerow, every track through dry grass where the hares cut across field-boundaries, each discarded piece of rusted machinery, every earth and warren and tree. . . . Wagtails, pallets, tractors, a broken silo on its side like a fallen rocket stage. Here is the sheep-field, there is the clover ley, now mown and turned to earth. Further up the track are tracts of mugwort: dead now from frost, seeds clinging to stems and branches like a billion musty beads on ragged Christmas trees. . . . Cow parsley. Knapweed. Wild burdock. The argillaceous shimmer of tinder-fine clay. Drifts of chalk beneath. Yellowhammers chipping in the hedges.

Did you notice? The merging of the unconstructed and constructed landscape, the human and nonhuman, this radical intermingling? Hedgerows and hares and rusted machinery and trees and pallets and birds and silos and seeds and, of course, Macdonald. She continues,

> I don't own this land. I've only got permission to fly here. But in walking it over and over again and paying it the greatest attention I've made it mine. I know where its animals live, and how they move about it. Know that larks sleep on the top of the hill, but on sunny mornings they move to warm themselves on eastward slopes. That when the weather is wet but the rain has stopped, the rabbits in the warrens near the ditches move eastward onto the drier fields to graze.

There's more to say, of course, about Macdonald's distinctive brand of engagement with the wild outdoors. Hunting, to be sure—and as she refers to it—yet at a certain remove too. At times, while seeking prey with her goshawk, she slips into hawkish modes of seeing and being. How does she put it? *I've only got permission to fly here.* Macdonald, in a very real sense, takes flight with Mabel. "Yet," she remarks in an earlier moment of her narrative, "every time the hawk caught an animal, it pulled me back from being an animal into being a human again." Macdonald, the human, hates killing things; she pities the poor rabbits. To recall a line from Walt Whitman's "Song of Myself," she seems "Both in and out of the game and watching and wondering at it." The space Macdonald occupies betwixt and between the human and nonhuman animal realms is something that she negotiates throughout her book in searing prose. It's something that we all ought to negotiate on our own terms, across our own terrain, through watching and wondering.

That said, I'll probably never cultivate the outdoors patience of a Macdonald, or an Audubon, or a Thoreau, or a Childs. I may never put in enough watchful hours at a nearby or faraway swamp or pineland or hammock that it feels like home. But I've tried to commit greater effort toward knowing my immediate place, anyway, toward making my actual home feel like home. I'm convinced that it goes some distance toward alleviating these summertime blues in the subtropics. It's ghastly hot here, sure. Still, it's important to get outside, nonetheless. "Joy cometh in the morning," per David's Psalm 30, and per the Hindu Vedas of ancient India, and per Thoreau. But evenings are good too. By seven-thirty p.m. or so, the bully sun finally begins to melt beneath the sawgrass blades and the outside temperature cools, somewhat. Florida creatures, lazy as all get-out midday, pick up their pace. These are crepuscular days in the subtropics. Wendy and I—and any of our children who we can enlist—frequently walk a few blocks to take the evening pulse of the neighborhood. Before our walk, however, I've taken to sitting beneath our largest front yard oak for a while (as my tree-*climbing* days are pretty much done), simply watching and listening as our yard gains curious life. I've suffered a mosquito bite or two. But that's okay. Plenty of light still bleeds from the horizon so that I can see, and smell, and hear. I've paid enough attention to note certain patterns of rising activity—the crickets, for example, start chiming in much earlier than actual nightfall—but there are just as many disruptions strange.

This evening, I sit on my folding chair beneath the tree and listen as the pleasant cricket notes gradually overtake the less pleasant metallic clacking of what I'm pretty sure are cicadas or katydids. I breathe in deeply through my nostrils. The pleasantly pungent aroma of my white stopper plants fairly connotes the Florida outdoors and soothes my nerves at least as much as the cricket melody. A mourning dove issues its plaintive coo from a telephone wire. A red-bellied woodpecker bleats from around the side of the house, probably one of the breeding pair outside its nest box, signaling its presence to the chicks inside. Time for their supper. The automotive roar from a car motoring too fast toward the stop sign on my corner blots out the crickets and birds for a moment; additional vehicles will continue to do so every once in a while. Two squirrels scratch across the tree branches of the laurel oak overhead in a candy-cane swirl as one chases the other, grousing at its rival or would-be mate with cheeky calls. A separate squirrel roots around noisily in the crispy leaf litter just ten yards away; could it be searching for acorns it buried months ago? A curly-tail lizard scrabbles after its arthropod prey on the still-hot driveway cement. A distant helium giggle betrays the presence of a downy woodpecker up the street somewhere. It grows darker. In the absence of birdsong, car traffic on the wane too, the cricket melody rises more fully. Yet a small flock of chimney swifts hasn't yet taken roost. I hear their Morse code twittering fade in and out of earshot as they make several passes high overhead. I glimpse the silhouettes—stubby cigars with wings—through tears in the oak canopy. It's not much, maybe, but it's home and these are some of our summer animals.

10

Yellow-Crowned Night-Heron

2017

The creature does not rush. It creeps with great care along the tattered russet bark of the slash pine limb, a large stick braced between the mandibles of its stout bill like a tightrope walker's pole. The heron's reptilian toes, yellow and scaled, splay to grip the branch as it makes its way toward its mate. A formidable collector of twigs and branches. Broke this large piece from the adjacent live oak with its bill. *Snap!* I didn't know that birds did this thing, snapped nesting material directly from living trees. The creature joins its mate at their rickety redoubt just taking shape, performs a little dance, flashes nuptial plumes above its cobra neck.

* * *

Yellow-crowned night-heron. *Nyctanassa violacea*. Common. Or fairly common, depending upon your source. At twenty-four inches or so, rather stocky for a heron—"chunky," says Roger Tory Peterson—though longer-necked and -legged than its cousin, the black-crowned night-heron. Its smooth, purple-gray plumage, sharp black-and-white face, and long yellow plumes "lend it a touch of elegance," the Cornell Lab of Ornithology website suggests. Breeds from southern New England to Florida and west to the Mississippi River and Texas. Thrives in coastal marshes, barrier islands, bayous, and mangroves. Hunts all hours of the day, despite its name. "Foraging birds walk slowly along mudflats," David Allen Sibley writes, "searching mainly for crabs, or wooded swamps searching for crayfish."

* * *

This isn't a mudflat or a wooded swamp. It's my local park, a modest square patch of grass, oak, and pine (and basketball court, picnic table, swing set, and slides), flanked on all sides by ranch-style houses. The ten-lane I-95 growls nonstop just a few blocks to the west; a few blocks to the east, the

Florida East Coast trains whistle and clack across the rails at regular intervals hauling phosphate. Yet I've observed these wild creatures going about their life business in this same giant slash pine for the past several years I've lived in the neighborhood. Like clockwork, they return each year.

* * *

2007

"These birds, they go to the right / place every day until they die," Anne Pierson Wiese observes in the opening stanza of her poem, "Profile of the Night Heron."

* * *

2017

Yes. I've watched these birds return to their right place. Today, it's not only the usual breeding pair I spot in the slash pine. As I gaze up into the scaffolding of branches, I notice the early efforts of three additional nests, several adults fortifying their twiggy homes, or keeping watch from a nearby perch, batting their big ruby eyes. A mottled juvenile (progeny, likely, from last year's breeding season), slouches its shoulders like a surly teenager. A veritable colony of yellow-crowned night-herons! Several wading bird species breed socially in rookeries and, in this sense, contrast markedly from other birds I know.

The night-herons' social proclivities would seem like a good practice for the species—sharing resources, spreading genes about aplenty, not murdering one another, and so forth. Something, however, checks my enthusiasm for this new colony. This is Florida and after twenty-odd years living here I've learned to greet all environmental current events with a healthy dose of skepticism. The increased nesting in my park may only suggest the further degradation of their historic nesting sites in nearby cypress swamps and mangrove creeks. Exotic snakes and lizards, say, raiding their nests in the wilder outposts; or water levels out of whack on account of untimely Lake Okeechobee releases by the South Florida Water Management District; or saltwater incursions owing to climate change choking out heron prey. And something else gives me pause.

The social proclivities of these birds haven't always boded well for them.

* * *

1832

The naturalist sails aboard the United States revenue cutter *Marion*, skirts the necklace isles of the Florida Keys. His heart swells with "uncontrollable delight" as the ship safely traverses the coral reef and nears the inlet of Indian Key. From the deck, he observes winged creatures almost all new to him arrayed in the most brilliant apparel. The pilot, his host, a great conch-diver, manatee-marauder, fish-spearer, turtle-toppler, and bird-shooter. He promises the naturalist "rare sport" and ushers him onto his small yawl. Two sailors accompany them to row inshore toward the labyrinth of mangroves. The captain orders his men to stop rowing as they near the thicket, orders them to ready their arms as he sculls the boat alone inside the foliage beneath a prodigious rookery of pelicans. The social proclivities of these birds! A discharge of artillery, the naturalist will later report, seldom produced more affect. A multitude of these great birds—the dead, the dying, the wounded—splash down into the water like heavy rain. The more fortunate creatures scream obscenities as they take to the wing. The sailors reach over the gunwales to collect the game, line the undersides bow to stern with dead pelicans.

This is before most scientists glimpse the possible extirpation of many of the American birds that John James Audubon shoots with heady abandon and paints for his monumental *Birds of America* project (first published in London between 1827 and 1838), before binoculars and cameras, before Henry David Thoreau proposes a "finer way of ornithology" that omits the gun and includes "so much closer attention to the habits of the birds." An oddball proposition from an oddball sort. That shiftless Henry. Audubon, seeking an artistic departure from the stilted museum-piece paintings of his contemporaries, requires freshly shot models. He uses wire to shape the birds he kills into dramatic poses. Between 1831 and 1839, he publishes five volumes of his *Ornithological Biography* to complement his paintings. His account of the yellow-crowned heron (as the birds were then called) appears in volume 4 and bespeaks his intimate hunter's relations with the species. "When wounded," Audubon writes, "the Yellow-crowned Heron defends itself vigorously with its claws, the scratches inflicted by which are severe, and also strikes with the bill. If not brought to the ground, in a place where the trees are close and thickly branched, it is difficult to obtain them without a second shot, for they scamper quickly from one twig to another, and are very soon out of reach."

* * *

1886

The Gilded Age. A banker performs a most unusual big-city bird count in Manhattan on two blustery February days. A poor time of year to identify a variety of birds in the temperate zone. Yet Frank M. Chapman, a member of the AOU (American Ornithologists' Union) and officer of the nascent Audubon Society, knows exactly what he's doing. He identifies 160 different birds atop the heads of New York's most fashionable ladies. Feathered hats all the rage. Five hundred and forty-two of the 700 hats Chapman spies and documents boast feathers gleaned from shot birds. The costliest of these hats contain aigrettes, the long, curved plumes of herons and egrets.

Here's the thing of it. Herons, egrets, spoonbills, and ibises typically don't leave their helpless young in a crisis. A rifle's report or a raccoon's wily approach. Same difference to them. These social breeders stick it out till the end. And so it's quite easy for plume hunters in rickety skiffs and canoes to "shoot out" an entire colony within hours, scalp hundreds of dead birds, preserve the feathers in arsenic until they can deliver them to buyers. By 1886, according to the AOU, five million birds per year are being killed for the millinery trade alone. All the large rookeries are soon shot out from New England to central Florida.

A principal challenge remains: locating the remaining colonies in the nearly impenetrable, mosquito-ridden mangrove islands in the Everglades.

* * *

2017

Several neighbors have escaped climate-controlled interiors to enjoy the park with me. They chase after their wards or study their smart phones, or do both, oblivious to this colony of night-herons. I don't call anyone over to see. Such ostentatious displays of animal *hereness* don't often go well for the animals. Even today. The social proclivities of these birds! We like to glimpse wild creatures in the places we inhabit on their lonesome, or paired, fighting the good fight on the margins. A red-tailed hawk nest on a building across the street from New York's Central Park; a weasel caught unawares after slinking from beneath the cover of a wild rose shrub in the Virginia suburbs; a deer stranded, spindly legs splayed, on pond ice (*Save it! Save it!*). Wild animals among us in greater numbers, however, make us nervous, threaten our claim. *Don't Feed the Wildlife!* a sign warns at my park, decorated for clarity with a reproduction of a rapscallion raccoon and sneaky squirrel. We live in the Anthropocene, the Age of the Humans. We've thrown too much carbon up into the atmosphere, cleared the forests, overhunted the game, polluted and overfished the oceans, precipitated mass extinctions.

It's all about us now.

The night-heron pair I'm used to seeing each year seems to know the score. Bashful birds, they've kept to the trees during the briskest park hours. Only after dusk, years past, have I spotted one prancing across the grass and basketball court, bobbing its head after palmetto bugs and lizards (benighted prey for these crayfish and crab-eaters). So the herons have mostly gone unnoticed. How often do people look up? Yet I worry about what my neighbors might think about this colony making too conspicuous a display. *Is it safe?* Those sharp claws and thick bills that Audubon so feared! These are beefy birds. Tall as toddlers. They issue raspy, unmelodious barks when riled. They release prodigious ribbons of milky excrement from the tree tops. What happens when the first child, or her parent, gets splattered by a night-heron dropping in the park?

Careful, I silently caution these social birds.

* * *

1907

HATS FOR EVERY OCCASION, a vintage millinery advertisement reads. ONE PRICE ONLY 30/C. A LARGE STOCK OF NEWEST MODELS ALWAYS ON VIEW. Beneath a pencil-sketch of a woman wearing a feathered hat twice the size of her head, the caption: OF BROWN CRINOLINE STRAW WITH SHADED BIRDS AND ROSETTES OF TULLE UNDER THE BRIM AT THE BACK

* * *

1889

He is young and hungry and anxious to make his mark. The son of an aristocratic southern family from Charleston, South Carolina, their fortune lost during the Civil War. And so he wonders about these birds flitting over his family's Marco Island home on Florida's Gulf Coast. These egrets and herons and spoonbills and ibises. No large rookeries remain in the state's readily accessible wetlands. But the Indians tell stories of a great colony hidden within the uncharted Everglades to the east. He sets out in his sloop for Fort Myers, purchases supplies and acquires a first mate. They sail southeast in the Gulf of Mexico, the Ten Thousand Islands like eyebrows on the near horizon. They slip inside at Ponce de Leon Bay, thread their way east through mangrove channels, anchor near Tarpon Creek. From there, George Elliot Cuthbert goes it alone on a small canoe, alternately paddles, poles, and pulls the vessel through impossible mangrove thickets between blessed stretches of open water. Days pass. He snatches a few hours of sleep at a time within cradles of mangrove legs beneath the outrageous gauze of the Milky Way. Too, the deafening whine of mosquitoes. Too, the oleaginous aroma of the bear fat he rubs across his skin to ward off the pests. Too, the growls and barks of alligators and crocodiles. Too, the silent water moccasins. Too, thirst. His fresh water supply runs low.

He passes several likely mangrove islands, but no colony. Teeming flocks spiral overhead, flash against the sun, offer hope. A white feather floats by his boat in the tea-stained branch the moment before he claws his way through the last thicket, reaches a wide-open lake and glimpses the mangrove island across the water, the foliage festooned with birds upon birds. "A flower, a beautiful white blossom," he reports to his children. Imagine the stench. The mangrove sulfur yields to the even more putrid effluvia of bird excrement, sunbaked feathers, and regurgitated brackish organisms. But it must smell like money to Cuthbert. Aigrettes at $32 an ounce, double the price of gold. He needs only two trips to the rookery with his French rifle to amass a fortune. He purchases half of Marco Island, buys a schooner, farms his land, basks in his glory. His neighbors refer to him as Captain Cuthbert till the end of his days.

And more. Look for it on the map. You'll find it northeast of Flamingo. Cuthbert Lake.

* * *

2017

Some of my birdwatching friends blame Audubon for shooting up so many birds (which I can understand) and criticize his paintings as contrived, hardly lifelike at all (which I can also understand). His painting of the "yellow-crowned heron," however, seems to balance verisimilitude with vitality. A thoughtful student recently gave me a small book containing reproductions of Audubon's *Birds of America* paintings, which I keep in my office. I flip through the pages before teaching today and inspect plate 336. A male in breeding plumage stands on a dead branch, mandibles agape, neck turned about to gaze up at a dusky juvenile, perched contentedly on one leg on a branch just above. Yes, these are the birds that I watch and know at Pine Breeze Park.

* * *

1876

He is a sickly child. So it might not be a good idea for Guy Bradley's father to move the family from Chicago to the mosquito-infested backwater that is southern Florida. The elder Bradley takes a job as keeper of the House of Refuge for wayward sailors in Fort Lauderdale. The pay is meager. To keep from starving, the family cultivates sweet potatoes (poorly) and catches fish (more ably). The cistern leaks. They drink water from a nearby well instead. Guy and his siblings grow increasingly ill. A sister, Flora, dies. It may be the water. Mr. Bradley resigns and moves the family a few miles north to Lake Worth. He becomes one of Florida's legendary barefoot mailmen, walks the beach with his mail sack between Palm Beach and Miami to avoid the panthers, alligators, and Indians, inland. Guy and his remaining siblings slowly regain their health. The lad develops a fondness for the Florida outdoors. At fifteen, Guy and his older brother accompany a French plume hunter on his twenty-eight-foot sloop on an expedition inside the Hillsboro Inlet. They cruise up Cypress Creek—a busy interchange now on I-95—encounter ancient cypress trees draped with Spanish moss and plume birds. Guy and his brother shoot several of the valuable specimens, plus a turkey for dinner.

* * *

1886

Sarah Orne Jewett publishes a story, "A White Heron," the same year as Chapman's unusual big-city bird count. Sylvia, a young girl in rural New England, is tempted by a male hunter to reveal the whereabouts of a pair of little white herons (i.e., snowy egrets). "I mean to get them on my own ground if they can be found," he asserts. There's a lot of money in it for them if she will only tell the hunter where he might find the nest. Sylvia and her grandmother are poor. Jewett's heroine locates the nest (in a pine tree, incidentally), yet she triumphs through not betraying the birds' secret. "The murmur of the pine's green branches is in her ears," Jewett writes, "she remembers how the white heron came flying through the golden air and how they watched the sea and the morning together, and Sylvia cannot speak; she cannot tell the heron's secret and give its life away."

* * *

1900

A new century dawns, and Americans begin to wonder whether it might be best *not* to seek a feather in our caps. Boston socialite, Harriet Hemenway, is aghast to learn of the horrors of the plume trade. Enlisting the help of her cousin, Minna Hall, they distribute pamphlets and hold tea parties to persuade their high-society peers to boycott the trade. They form the Massachusetts Audubon Society, lobby for anti-plume hunting legislation, their efforts culminating in the passage of the Lacey Act, which outlaws the trade of wildlife, fish, and plants that have been illegally taken, possessed, transported, or sold. On Christmas Day, Chapman initiates the "Christmas Bird Census" of living wild birds, a very different bird count from his earlier, sobering survey of ladies' hats. The Florida Legislature passes Chapter 4357 the following year, "An Act for the Protection of Birds and their Nests and Eggs, and Prescribing a Penalty for any Violation Thereof."

* * *

1903

Paul Kroegel, sans legal authority, fends off the plume hunters from the deck of his sailboat with his 10-gauge shotgun. The unofficial protector of this lovely little undeveloped island in the Indian River Lagoon along Florida's east coast near Sebastian. Members of the AOU visit the island while lobbying for the passage of Chapter 4357 and learn about the plight of the pelicans from Kroegel. He convinces Chapman and his colleagues to inveigh upon President Theodore Roosevelt to protect the island. Roosevelt has an even bigger idea. He establishes Pelican Island as the nation's first National Wildlife Refuge. Kroegel is named warden.

* * *

1904

Even so. Cuthbert's Rookery is shot out. By which I mean snowy egret and great blue heron and little blue heron and roseate spoonbill and white ibis and glossy ibis and limpkin and pelican and tricolored heron and great egret and, of course, yellow-crowned night-heron. Gone. Shot from their low nests just overhead. Crowns scalped. Aigrettes preserved in arsenic. The worthless nestlings bleating above, left to the ants and the raccoons and the vultures. Crocodiles and alligators consume what the birds and mammals leave behind. This, despite the Lacey Act, despite Chapter 4357, despite Roosevelt and Chapman and Kroegel and Hemenway and Jewett, and despite the vigilance of the Monroe County game warden and deputy sheriff. His name is Guy Bradley.

"You could'a walked right around the ruk'ry on them birds' bodies, between four and five hundred of 'em," he reports, having arrived too late at the scene.

* * *

2017

"I see you looking at those birds," a lady at the park, roughly my age, accosts me. She calls from the road that squares this small patch. I've noticed her before. This is her exercise, walking square after square around the tiny park.

"Yeah," I admit, sheepishly raising a palm. "I guess I am." I'm not sure how to take her comment, what she thinks of my looking, what she thinks of "those birds." It's been impressed upon me by my neighbors in ways subtle and not-so-subtle that I'm something of an oddball, what with my unkempt yard of native shrubs and untrimmed oaks rather than stiff St. Augustine grass, my multiple bird feeders and nest boxes and whatnot. I wait for her next words.

"They nest in my slash pines every year." She lifts her chin toward what I gather is her house on the corner, the stucco stained with rust from the sprinklers. It's a boast, birds in her pines. She likes the herons. *Phew.* I amble over to the road so we won't have to shout to continue the conversation. Her name is Marilyn. She's lived here far longer than I have, nearly twenty-five years. The birds come back to her slash pine to nest year after year, keep building up the same nests with twigs. A marvel they never come down in a storm, precarious as they look. She and her husband start looking for the birds in February. The creatures don't finish up and disperse until June. Some mornings they wake her up with their carrying on.

"*Squawk-squawk-squawk,*" she mimics their call, shrugging her shoulders under the effort.

"I can only imagine," I say. "Yellow-crowned night-herons sure are loud."

"Yellow-crowned night-herons," she tastes the words on her tongue. "That's what they're called?"

* * *

1885

As a young man, Guy works various jobs in Lake Worth. He is a farmer, a boatman, a mailman, and the occasional hunter of plumes. The Bradleys move to the frontier outpost of Flamingo deep in the Everglades, the southernmost settlement on the Florida mainland, not least of all to purchase land while it's still cheap. Word has it that Henry Flagler plans to extend his rail line to Key West from Flamingo's Cape Sable area. The family does pretty well, biding their time. At twenty-seven, Guy owns a quarter mile of waterfront land, farms vegetables and sugarcane and fruit trees, owns his own ship, a forty-foot sharpie, *The Pearl,* runs cargo to the Keys, surveys land for the Flagler Model Land company, marries Sophonia Vickers Kirvin, fathers two boys.

Shortly after the passage of Chapter 4357, Guy is named Monroe County game warden and deputy sheriff. Law enforcement runs in the Bradley family, and the regular salary appeals to him, and Guy seems to have changed his views about the ethics of his onetime bloody pursuit. "I will certainly do all I can to find out who are the N.Y. buyers," he writes an official of the AOU. "I believe Stern Bros. are still in the business. They used to buy heavily some years ago when I used to hunt plume birds, but since the Game laws were passed I have not killed a plume bird for it is a cruel and hard calling notwithstanding being unlawful."

Upon the advice of his engineers, Flagler decides against the more direct Cape Sable railroad route to Key West. He'll lay track south-westerly from Miami along the necklace of Keys islands instead. So it's a good thing that Guy has a steady paycheck. A skilled boatman, he apprehends several plume hunters. In 1905, he makes three arrests involving the family of Flamingo neighbor and rival, Captain Walter Smith, including Smith's seventeen-year-old son. "You ever arrest one of my sons again, I'll kill you," Smith threatens Guy. Later that year, the captain makes good on his threat. Guy sees Smith's boys shooting into a rookery on Oyster Keys, sees them make their way back to their father's larger sloop. When he demands to board the vessel to arrest them, Smith shoots and kills Guy with his rifle and turns himself into the authorities in Key West. A grand jury sees it as self-defense and the captain goes free.

* * *

2017

Formerly a pine flatwoods—replete with slash pine towering above the fans of saw palmetto thickets—few slash pines remain in my neighborhood today. First they were chopped down in the early twentieth century to make room for a pineapple farm. Then, most of the remaining pines and palmettos, along with the pineapples, were gradually cleared to make room for my subdivision. Hurricanes take a fair share as well, including the recent hurricanes Frances, Jeanne, and Wilma. A few trees remain at the park and accent the landscape surrounding our homes, but most neighbors don't seem to like these native trees. They're "messy," I hear people complain. They drop prodigious drifts of russet needles, which carpet driveways, clog up roof gutters, choke the grass. Park your car under them wrong time of year and it'll get coated by a layer of sticky sap. So neighbors often have their pines removed. But not Marilyn, who likes the herons.

Palm Beach Farms, the name of our subdivision, harkening back to its pineapple, rather than pine, days.

* * *

1908

The birds return. Only a few. Nothing like before. But they return. Because it's a perfect spot for a colony, Cuthbert Rookery, the two-acre island protected from the raccoons (if not from humans anymore) by the crocodile and alligator-infested moat. So the birds return. Only a few at first. Then more. If nothing like before.

He needs to see this famous island. After numerous failed attempts—a shootout one year, a storm the next—Chapman finally reaches Cuthbert Lake. He hides until sundown beneath an umbrella draped in green denim, observes thousands of birds, more than he dared to hope. They descend from the skies in complicated vortices and settle in for the night on their nests. He approaches at nightfall, takes only a single nest and its eggs for the Cuthbert Rookery Diorama he hopes to stage among his other dioramas at the American Museum of Natural History in New York City. He leaves the living birds alone.

* * *

2017

For spring break, I fly with my family on metal wings to New York City. We see the Statue of Liberty and the Freedom Tower from the deck of a boat, walk the High Line, visit the Guggenheim, the Metropolitan Museum of Art and, of course, the American Museum of Natural History. The main draws for our sixteen- and seven-year-old daughters are The Milstein Family Hall of Ocean Life (that gargantuan model of a blue whale suspended from the ceiling) and the space show in the Hayden Planetarium, narrated by Neil DeGrasse Tyson. But first things first. I make a beeline to Chapman's diorama of Cuthbert's Rookery in the Sanford Hall of North American Birds, drag my wife and the girls behind. It's pretty impressive. A wide variety of herons, ibises, egrets, and spoonbills in various lifelike poses across the scaffolding of mangrove branches, chicks poking their fluffy heads from Chapman's nest close to the glass. I'm drawn mostly to the small details he captured, the yellow and yellowing leaves of a few failing mangrove leaves, the white flecks of guano on some of the greener leaves and the mangrove legs below.

I can't say that my wife or daughters are blown away by the exhibit, and I can't say that I'm surprised. It's been over 100 years since the museum first staged this and many of its other dioramas. Given the heady visual enticements of the virtual realm at our fingertips, there's something quaint about all these stuffed animals, the simulated water, the synthetic tree branches and leaves, the earnest verisimilitude of the painted backdrop. But I like to think that there's another reason for the tepid reaction. We aren't Chapman's intended audience of northeastern urbanites. We live in the subtropics among these creatures that still exist, thanks in no small part to his efforts. This static replica pales in comparison to their vital presence. Several mornings we wake to the scene of a white ibis flock in our front yard drilling their scarlet bills into the sandy earth for grubs. Solitary great egrets prowl the neighborhood searching for lizards within the shrubbery. Tricolored and little blue herons squawk overhead to and from their foraging and nesting grounds.

Plus, yellow-crowned night-herons nest every year at Pine Breeze Park.

* * *

2015

You can still go to Cuthbert Lake. Sort of. Outboard motors are restricted in the area, which is closed to the general public in any case. But if you're lucky you might be able to find a government employee with a permit and a poling vessel who's willing to make the trek. Laura Allen secures the services of biologist Paul Frezza and documents the journey in a brief essay for the National Parks Conservation Association. Since Cuthbert's time, mangrove roots have been chopped back to clear a passage along the creek branches. They pass an old "Do Not Enter" sign and reach the lake. The island, on account of various hurricanes over the years, is only a fraction of the two acres that Cuthbert glimpsed. Allen counts several birds roosting there, about fifty wood storks among them, but it's nothing like the rookery it once was. Park biologist Lori Oberhofer tells her that a record from 1937 notes over 1,000 birds on Cuthbert Rookery. She's counted roughly 200 nests each season for the past decade, making it around the tenth most prolific rookery in the park today.

* * *

2007

Again, Wiese's "Profile of the Night Heron"—these birds who "go to the right / place every day until they die." In the two stanzas that follow the first, the poet makes an imaginative leap from herons to humans. "There are people like that in the city," the second stanza begins. She goes on to evoke the fierce attachment that our most disenfranchised citizens forge with certain city places: storefronts, stoops, corners, benches. "Even when surfaces change," the third stanza begins,

> . . . when the Mom & Pop
> store becomes a coffee bar, when the park
> benches are replaced with dainty chairs and a pebble
> border, they stay, noticing what will never change:
> the heartprick of longitude and latitude
> to home in on. . . .

* * *

Oh, I realize, a metaphor, these herons. It's an apt comparison between herons and humans, and a beautifully wrought poem on its own terms. But something in me resists the metaphor; or, more precisely, something in me resists the anthropocentric impulse that necessitates metaphor to begin with. Don't get me wrong. I've certainly looked toward the animals to glean insight on my sad old self. I typically relish these correspondences, central to the environmental ethic of this book. Yet the mood I'm in, I want these herons to be enough. These birds of Cuthbert Rookery, and the birds of all the other right places, places to which they too return—coastal marshes, barrier islands, bayous, and mangroves—only to discover erasure, either by hurricanes or human meddling. Surely, these wild creatures feel the heartprick of longitude and latitude as well. How long do night-herons languish amid the ruins?

* * *

2017

I have no immediate plans to make my way to Cuthbert Lake and its diminished rookery. Yet I've become a devoted watcher of the more modest yellow-crowned night-heron colony at Pine Breeze Park—this right enough place, anyway. "You sure do like the birds," Marilyn greets me from the road without breaking stride each time she sees me craning my neck, staring up into the pine, by which she means hello. "Yep, they're pretty neat," I say hello back. The birds are quite something to look at, once you commit yourself to staying put for a time.

They don't seem to do a great many things, but what yellow-crowned night-herons do they do with almost mesmerizing deliberation and care. They snap twigs and branches from live oak trees. They walk gingerly across the russet bark and present the twig or branch to their mate, who accepts it, weaves it into the nest. They stand side-by-side to face the evening sun. They preen one another with languorous swipes of their chunky bills, flash their nuptial plumes. They seem so dippy in love, canoodling as they do, that I'm sometimes compelled to avert my eyes. At dusk, they take to the wing in threes and fours, *squawk* over the basketball court as they make their way east toward foraging grounds, which I suspect might be along a rare stretch of mangrove shoreline nearby in the canal beside Flagler's railroad tracks. These night-herons seem to have a good handle on their life business. They know exactly what they're about. With luck, their eggs—protein and calcium-carbonate stuff of wildest night-heron dreams—will soon hatch.

*　*　*

Note: I consulted several sources to learn about the plume trade and its principal actors but wish to express my special indebtedness to Stuart B. McIver's *Death in the Everglades: The Murder of Guy Bradley, America's First Martyr to Environmentalism* (2003).

11
Gone, Fishing

When my city's mayor in South Florida issued a local state of emergency on March 18th, 2020, closing our local boat ramp used by commercial and recreational anglers, the first thought I expressed to my wife was, "Well, at least this'll help the local fish stocks!" Call me an optimist. The various quarantines, worldwide, as we now know, did alleviate some human pressures upon wildlife. Once the gravest threat passed, we mostly returned to business as usual, regarding everything from airline travel to commercial and recreational fishing. Yet that brief window of time, when we lived more modestly across the earth—when animals terrestrial and aquatic seemed to appreciate it—offers us the occasion to reexamine our relationship with the animals we raise, hunt, or harvest for food, including fish.

Fish stocks, globally, have been in dangerous decline for several years. According to the United Nations Food and Agriculture Organization's report, "The State of World Fisheries and Aquaculture 2018," "The fraction of fish stocks that are within biologically sustainable levels has exhibited a decreasing trend, from 90.0 percent in 1974 to 66.9 percent in 2015," while "the percentage of stocks fished at biologically unsustainable levels increased from 10 percent in 1974 to 33.1 percent in 2015, with the largest increases in the late 1970s and 1980s." U.S. fisheries are among the most strictly monitored and regulated in the world. Yet to what extent we are part of the solution or the problem to our global fishery crisis might be debated. It's unclear whether the utter collapse of the cod fishery off our northeast coast in the early 1990s, precipitated by overfishing, has taught us anything. NOAA designates a species "overfished" if its stock has "a population size that is too low and that jeopardizes the stock's ability to produce its maximum sustainable yield." In its "2018 Report to Congress on the Status of U.S. Fisheries," the overfished list in our waters included forty-three stocks, up from thirty-five in 2017.

In addition to overfishing, specifically, the degradation of the environment, generally, continues to ravage global fish stocks. Habitat decline, for example, has all but decimated the venerable wild oyster fishery in Apalachicola Bay on the Gulf Coast of Florida, once the source of 90 percent of Florida's oyster harvest. As Laura Reiley and others have reported, various human-induced factors precipitated NOAA's declaration of a fishery disaster in the bay in 2013. These factors include the increased salinity of the bay water ravaging oyster reefs—caused not only by climate change but by unrestrained freshwater usage for agriculture in Georgia—and the oil and oil-dispersant pollution from the 2010 BP Deepwater Horizon disaster. The wild oyster population had declined so precipitously by 2020 that the Florida Fish and Wildlife Conservation Commission instituted a five-year moratorium on the wild harvest. The state has hired former oystermen to restore the reefs with limestone rock and continues to monitor the hopeful comeback of our beloved wild bivalve. Meanwhile, the aquaculture industry has stepped in to farm oysters in the bay, which, at least, promises a sustainable harvest of cultivated Apalachicola oysters. Still, an oyster farm isn't quite the same thing, culturally or environmentally, as a thriving wild oyster fishery.

Returning to my southeast Florida waters, NOAA's overfished list today includes several species of snapper and grouper targeted by recreational anglers, and targeted over the past fifteen years by, well, me. I don't need an exhaustive U.N. or NOAA report to tell me that fishing practices among recreational anglers contribute more significantly to fish scarcity than we like to admit. My friends and I fish for yellowtail, mangrove, and mutton snapper mostly at night from one of our small boats over the shallow reef just outside our local inlet. We tend to fish long hours into that fuzzy borderland between night and morning, long enough to watch the stars slide across the sky and to fill our coolers with up to ten snappers per person, the snapper aggregate bag limit in my environs regulated by the Florida Fish and Wildlife Conservation Commission. While the minimum size limit for mutton snapper has increased recently from sixteen to eighteen inches (a source of some frustration among local anglers), the aggregate bag limit for snapper hasn't changed in the fifteen years I've been fishing.

"Limit your catch, don't catch your limit," is one of the more popular expressions among our charter captains in the Sunshine State, bless their souls. Even so, few anglers that I've chewed the fat with at my local dock hew closely to this sustainable ethic, and it shows. When I started fishing here as a younger man, we used to catch several large mangrove snappers. No more. If we're lucky, we'll now catch maybe one keeper mangrove on a given night. Small wonder that mangrove snapper has been added to NOAA's "overfishing" list as of its 2018 report, an "overfished stock" defined as "a stock having a harvest rate higher than the rate that produces its maximum sustainable yield." So, yes, I was downright pleased about the boat ramp closure that accompanied our quarantine, which would give our local snappers something of a break from most anglers, not least of all me.

Then, my city's boat ramp reopened to commercial fishermen on April 22nd and reopened to recreational fishermen shortly thereafter. On May 11th, my home county of Palm Beach entered phase one of Florida's reopening plan. The chatter all about at the dock those days, and on local social media, was how great it is that things were finally starting to return to normal. But it filled me with something closer to dread when I gazed across a broad stretch of our Intracoastal Waterway from the road shortly after quarantine to see it overcrowded with vessels. I felt this way mostly on account of the renewed danger that COVID-19 might spread hull to hull, but partly on account of what the renewed boat traffic portended for our local fishery. Count me among the many Americans who weren't so enthusiastic about this creeping return to normalcy. Normal is what got us into this mess in the first place. Both the COVID-19 pandemic and the depletion of finfish from our oceans, after all, can be traced to our toxic relationship with the planet and with other animals that call this planet home. Before Rachel Carson called attention to the impact of DDT on North American bird populations, and long before the collapse of the wild oyster fishery in Apalachicola, Aldo Leopold realized in *A Sand County Almanac* (1949) that our American version of outdoor recreation was causing what he called "biotic pain." Rather than return doggedly to the old ways, it's high time to embrace a new normal regarding the way in which we live, and fish, and cultivate all animal food in this world. If ever there was a time to heed Leopold, to heed Florida's wisest charter captains in the most holistic sense, to limit our catch rather than catch our limit, that time is now.

12

Stingray

We mostly worry about the sharks. Bull. Spinner. Nurse. Lemon. Tiger. Great hammerhead. Dusky. Atlantic sharpnose. Reef. Blacktip. But what are we swimmers to do in South Florida? The COVID-19 pandemic has just reached our shores and all municipal aquatic facilities have closed, indefinitely; U.S. Masters Swim programs nationwide, comprised of over 1,500 clubs, have suspended operations. To preserve our health and sanity, members of my own local club—after hunkering down inside our homes for weeks—coordinate unofficial meetups at the nearby Atlantic Ocean to swim open-water while keeping our social distance. Most of us aren't accustomed to ocean swimming for exercise, which exposes us to manifold new variables: unpredictable chop and currents, impenetrable nets of sargassum lolling at the surface, Portuguese man o' war, and microscopic sea lice (the larvae of jellyfish) and, again, those marine fish of a higher order I've mentioned, which thrive in our coastal waters.

We don caps and goggles. Some of us (not me) wear wetsuits. Some of us (me) trail fluorescent orange buoys attached to our waists by a belt, mostly to keep the boaters and jet-skiers from running us over, partly to serve as a flotation device in case we suffer a cramp or something. Thankfully, we don't see any sharks as weeks of open-water swimming turn into months. The creatures we see most often during our immersions turn out to be the stingrays gliding across the bottom some six to ten feet below the surface, camouflaged to match the earthen hue of the sand. Upon spotting a stingray beneath our swim goggles, we halt our strokes and summon one another's attention to make sure it hasn't escaped anyone's noticing. Our small group develops a feeling close to affection for these marine animals with whom we share a spot of time most mornings. It's usually just one we'll glimpse, flitting in and out of our field of view. No, flit is the wrong word entirely. Birds flit. These aquatic creatures enact no such maneuver that might smack of nervous evasiveness. They hardly seem aware of us at all. Glide seems the most apt word to describe their movement, but this is wrong too as something must be powering them, so swiftly do they sometimes escape from sight. *Advance* might be the best word to describe their steady movement. Capturing a good look at a large specimen crossing below my stroking arms one morning, I notice the undulations at the edges of its disc, like the ruffles of a skirt in the breeze. Can these mildest of movements account for its swimming proficiency? All I really know about these creatures, it occurs to me, is that they have barbed tails you wouldn't want to step on, which is why Floridians do the "stingray shuffle" while we walk in the ocean shallows. Which is to say that I know practically nothing about our local stingrays.

* * *

It's not so easy to figure out which species of stingray we've been encountering, once I decide that it would be nice to know. Florida waters, I discover online, host a panoply of "ray" species. Southern. Cownose. Spotted eagle. Manta. Lesser electric. Atlantic. Bluntnose. Roughtail. Smooth butterfly. Yellow. Devil. Some I can rule out immediately, but that I can't narrow down the list of possibilities to two or three likely suspects through summoning to mind particular features of these stingrays I've been seeing regularly for weeks now (the shape of its disc and eyes, its proportions, even its precise color) gives me pause. We don't (or at least *I* don't) look at things as carefully as I think that I look. I *spot* a lot of things out there in the world, I suppose I'm saying, but rarely do I enact the watchful patience to truly see them.

It's a good thing that one of my swimming partners, Vanessa, totes a small underwater camera with her most days and this morning captures some terrific footage of a large stingray. The creature lingers in our presence longer than most tend to linger, lingers long enough for me to unclip my swim buoy, hold my breath on a few dives to hover from above within six feet or so, hang with it as it advances slowly across the sandy bottom, the edges of its disc barely rippling. Back at home, I return to various stingray resources on the web while I scrutinize on my smartphone the photographs Vanessa sent to me of our stingray. It doesn't take too long for me now to identify our swimming companion. Southern stingray (*Dasyatis americana*), aka the kit, stingaree, or whip stingray. Because its olive-brown disc is about twenty inches wide and diamond-shaped, its tail is almost twice as long as its body, and, enlarging the image on my smartphone's screen, I can clearly see that irregular row of short spines trailing down its back, plus a longitudinal flap on the underside of its tail that resembles a ship's keel. I must admit that those spines along its back and the keel beneath its tail hadn't truly registered with me in the ocean while I thought I was watching the stingray so closely.

It takes more than patience to see something. There's skill involved, too. You have to learn how to find something and look at something, and every *something* has its own set of rules, I've figured out from my encounters over the years with so many other creatures, terrestrial and aquatic. What I've learned about southern stingrays, specifically, is that when they aren't swimming and feeding, they like to bury themselves beneath a thin layer of sand and take in water to their gills through raised openings called spiracles. I've figured out how to locate stingrays, then, by looking for these spiracles, and for the eyes atop stingray heads, protruding darkly from the sand while I perform my freestyle stroke above them. Apparently, I've been swimming above countless camouflaged stingrays for weeks without knowing it. It makes me wonder what other wild creatures are down there, which I just haven't yet learned how to see.

I want to learn how to look at the southern stingray even more deliberately and concertedly. Heaven knows I have the time as spring bleeds into summer. I'm not teaching, or doing much of anything else, on account of the pandemic and my downright privileged status as a nonessential worker. Though I'm usually as harried as most between my workplace and domestic obligations, suddenly there's no place that I really need to go most days, and nothing that I really need to do. My swim companions and I take to the ocean several days a week, where I begin to contemplate the thirteen ways and more of looking at a stingray. The world on fire, such as it is, watching stingrays in the water, thinking and learning about them when I'm on dry land, doesn't seem like such a poor use of my time.

* * *

Stingrays, like their close relatives the sharks, are Elasmobranchs, a class of animals characterized by their boneless, cartilaginous skeletons. Most of the 200 species of stingrays, worldwide, live in coastal saltwater ecosystems, though the pelagic stingray lives in the open ocean. Stingrays, manta rays, and eagle rays belong to the same animal order, Myliobatiformes, but hail from different families. Eagle rays sport a distinct snout, rounded pelvic fins, and angular wing flaps, which help them to leap out of the water to avoid predators (i.e., sharks). The two species of manta rays also sport angular wing flaps, but they have horn-shaped fins on either side of their mouths and swim with their mouths open to filter feed. Stingrays and eagle rays, by contrast, hunt bottom-dwelling prey, such as small fish, crustaceans, mollusks, teleosts, stomatopods, and annelids, using sensory organs near their mouths to detect their bioelectrical signals. Once they secure prey in their mouths, located on the underside of their disc, stingrays use their strong teeth to crush the shells of their prey. Unlike most aquatic predators, they chew their food with molar-like teeth before swallowing.

Here's a fun fact: the mostly flat teeth of male stingrays become sharper each year during mating season to help them hold on to slippery females, and their amorous enthusiasms often leave a mark on the poor females. The gestation period for stingrays can be quite long, ranging from six months to two years (four to eleven months for southern stingrays), before fully functioning live young are born. Females, interestingly, do not connect to their young through a placenta. Rather, embryos, in what scientists call aplacental viviparity, subsist off the yolk sacs, and then off uterine milk through secretions, until they are large enough to survive on their own. Southern stingrays, at this point, give birth to up to ten "pups," about the size of a human hand.

How long will these pups live out there in their watery realm? Who knows? Lifespans vary greatly between stingray species, and we don't have reliable data for southern stingrays. Some freshwater species in Asia may live for up to twenty-five years, while others, perhaps most, might live for seven years or so. But it's rough going for most stingrays in the Anthropocene, just as it's rough going for their close relatives, the sharks. According to a global analysis conducted by the IUCN (International Union for Conservation of Nature), one quarter of our stingrays and sharks are in danger of extinction, mostly on account of overfishing. Asian consumers, unfortunately, prize the beautiful patterns on the disc of reticulate whiprays, or honeycomb stingrays, for their shoes, handbags, and wallets. While most other stingrays are not intentionally targeted by commercial operations, many die as bycatch after being scooped up by trawling nets. Rays, the IUCN researchers discovered, were generally worse off than sharks, with five out of the seven most threatened Elasmobranch families made up of rays. A more recent study by Nathan Pacoureau and his colleagues, published on January 27, 2021, in the prestigious journal *Nature*, concludes that "since 1970, the global abundance of oceanic sharks and rays has declined by 71 percent owing to an 18-fold increase in relative fishing pressure," a depletion that has "increased the global extinction risk to the point at which three-quarters of the species comprising this functionally important assemblage are threatened with extinction."

The IUCN lists the conservation status of the southern stingray as "data deficient."

* * *

The endangered devil ray (*Mobula mobular*), is one of the earth's largest rays, and one of the most reclusive. It mostly inhabits the deep pelagic waters of the Mediterranean Sea, where it filter feeds off plankton. While you're unlikely to find a devil ray along the Florida coast, this didn't keep the Major League Baseball expansion team in Tampa Bay from adopting the name Devil Rays, during its inaugural season in 1998. In 2008, however, the team shortened its name to the Rays, ostensibly to reference the more prevalent Florida phenomenon of the sun's "rays," as indicated by the twinkling sun inside the "R" of its logo. I count this marketing shift from ocean-ray to sun-ray as a significant downgrade. Yet the team hasn't completely abandoned its devil ray origins and, during its 2020 World Series appearance, they sported stylish caps adorned with the multicolor likeness of a devil ray.

* * *

I know a lot more about stingrays, and southern stingrays, specifically, the next time I spot one beneath my swim goggles in eight feet of water. I know, for example, that those ripples at the edges of its disc truly do account for its propulsion. Scientists at Harvard University and the University of Buffalo applied algorithms of computational fluid dynamics to map the flow-field of water around live stingrays, the leading-edge vortex, specifically. (A vortex, essentially, is the mass of whirling fluid created by a stingray's oscillations.) What they discovered—which might impact the future design of automobiles, airplanes, and submarines—is that the vortices created by stingrays' unique movements cause favorable pressure fields (low pressure at the leading edge and high pressure at the trailing edge) to propel stingrays forward with maximum efficiency. Of particular interest to me, the stingray's flatness enhances its overall efficiency as well, through reducing negative drag, which informs our understanding of optimal body positioning for human swimmers too. Today's swim coaches may not use the terms of fluid dynamics, yet they do spend a good bit of time encouraging their swimmers to achieve the flattest position possible in the water, often referred to as the "streamline" position. Small wonder that so many swim teams throughout the country—including my own daughter's swim team, the Mantas—have adopted one ray or the other as its team name and mascot. Stingrays just make swimming look so darned easy.

I know, too, that the southern stingray's barbed and venomous tail just several feet below me includes serrated teeth up and down each side. I know that while most stingrays are nonaggressive, they will use their tails to defend themselves from threats, or perceived threats. On September 4, 2006, the wildlife expert, conservationist, and television personality, Steve Irwin, the "Crocodile Hunter," was killed while filming in Australia's Great Barrier Reef when a short-tail stingray pierced the thoracic wall protecting his heart with the barb of its tail. I also know what this large ray is probably doing down there as it swims across the bottom. As its eyes are located at the top of its disc to locate predators (like me, this ray might be gauging), it must be using its ampullae of Lorenzini, these tiny sense organs around its mouth that I can't quite discern through the silty water, to pick up the bioelectrical field of a shrimp or clam snack skittering across the sandy bottom. I keep a greater social distance today, because my own bioelectrical signals might be screwing up its hunt.

If I worry now that my swim pals and I might be interfering with the finely calibrated hunting technique of this stingray with our sloppy strokes from above, I worry too that our constant disruption of the coastal bottom I've been staring down at so often, lately, has upset the ecosystem upon which the southern stingray, and countless other vertebrate and invertebrate marine species, depend. As sea levels rise on account of climate change, my city has outsourced several beach renourishment projects over recent years to maintain the current boundaries between the terrestrial and aquatic realms, thereby protecting our high-rise condos looming over the ocean. The first thing I notice when I look into this a bit is that proponents of the practice insist rather stridently upon using the term "nourishment," not "renourishment," which arouses my suspicion. Renourishment, in any case, seems the more accurate term to me, not least of all because my own local beach has been re-"nourished" at least three times that I can remember. I feel it bears repeating that climate change, for which we humans (particularly in the developed world) are culpable, is the root cause of this escalating problem. During each renourishment project, an enormous dredge collects massive amounts of sand over several weeks in nearshore waters, forming large borrow pits, and pipes the gathered sand onto the shore in a slurry to extend the beach seaward. While such efforts temporarily stave off erosion and protect our human population from potential storm surges in the (increasingly likely) event of a major hurricane, beach renourishment also changes the natural pitch of the tideline and the sediment size composition of the onshore and nearshore sand, smothers live rock bottom, and reduces densities of prey for stingrays and other species. "The beach and nearshore coastal habitats are substantially disturbed by and can be functionally degraded through the process of nourishment," the scientist Charles H. Peterson and his colleague conclude in their article published in *BioScience*. Knowing this gives me pause as I linger in the stingray's sphere today. As John Muir once said, "When we try to pick out anything by itself, we find it hitched to everything else in the universe."

"We are not wholly involved in nature," Henry David Thoreau lamented in his most famous work, *Walden* (1854). Nearly 200 years later, we increasingly realize that we *are* wholly and inextricably "involved" in nature, even if it's not the sort of reciprocal, appreciative, and spiritual involvement that Thoreau had in mind. Most of my neighbors in South Florida will never see a southern stingray up close, or at all, but it's just as true that southern stingrays can't truly escape them, or us. I'm reminded of our inextricable involvement in their lives several days a week as I gaze down at them while I swim in the open ocean and, especially, as I widen my gaze to take in the corrugated patterns across the distinct dredged-and-filled sand all about these creatures, and, finally, as I struggle to exercise in our overheated ocean as its temperature rises through the summer to the upper-80-degree-Fahrenheit range. My enhanced awareness of our inescapable presence in the lives of southern stingrays, and everything else, only makes me more interested in them.

* * *

Stingrays have occupied our headspace more than I've been aware once I start to research them in earnest. In addition to inspiring the name of a Major League Baseball expansion team, and any number of youth swim teams, the ever-popular Corvette Stingray was first introduced by Chevrolet as a concept car for the racetrack in 1959. In 1963, a version of this model was released to the public. The progressively streamlined, flattened shape of Corvette Stingray models over the years suggests that the designers at Chevrolet work tirelessly toward emulating the Platonic ideal of stingray-ness on four wheels.

I've never owned a Corvette Stingray, but one of my first bicycles, maybe my actual first bike (I can't remember), was an apple-red Schwinn Stingray. The Schwinn Stingray, originally released in 1963 as well, had high-rise handles and a banana seat. If you're of a certain age, you might know precisely the bike of which I speak. You may have owned one. If you still have it, and it's in good condition, you could sell it on eBay for several thousand dollars.

* * *

A "stingray" is a simulated cell phone tower that law enforcement agencies in the United States sometimes set up to gather information from a suspect's mobile device, thus obviating the need to gain a court order to obtain phone records from a wireless carrier.

* * *

We see a spotted eagle ray one day for only a moment. It's much larger than our southern stingrays and easy to identify with its white spots against the dark background of its body. Not long after we notice it, the ray glides offshore through the silty blue water beyond our sightline. But not before I notice how it manipulates its "flow-field" differently than our southern stingrays. Rather than oscillate the edges of its disc, this eagle ray flaps its more butterfly-shaped "wings" like, yes, a butterfly. It makes me wonder whether the precise fluid dynamics of its movements might have something to teach me about my own, rather inefficient, butterfly stroke. I wonder, too, what eagle rays think of these balmy coastal waters, the density and diversity of prey possibilities, the composition of the dredged sand and those strange borrow-pit hollows, one of which it might be lurking over just now.

* * *

Although I've learned a fair bit about stingrays through poking around at the research online, I still feel like I hardly know anything. I'd like to know more. As luck would have it, one of the leading scientists studying Elasmobranch fishes (i.e., stingrays and sharks), Dr. Stephen Kajiura, happens to work at Florida Atlantic University, my own place of employ.

His lab, I read on its website, is "primarily interested in the integration of sensory biology and behavior with functional morphology." Uh, okay. I don't know Dr. Kajiura, but I contact him over email, tell him about my ocean swims and my increased interest in stingrays, and ask if he'd be willing to chat a bit about his research and about stingrays, generally, all the while sort of angling for an invite to his lab, or maybe on one of his field work outings. He promptly replies to my email, and confirms, as I've sent him one of our stingray photos, that the Elasmobranchs I've been seeing are, indeed, southern stingrays. While the COVID-19 pandemic precludes any face-to-face meetings for now, he describes the current research focus of his lab, which mostly involves tracking the local blacktip shark migration via airplane, aerial drones, fixed underwater cameras, and acoustical bottom monitors. Stingrays, however, remain "near and dear to his heart," he writes. He tells me a bit more about them in the few subsequent emails that we exchange. There's still much to learn about movement and habitat use apparently, how stingrays use magnetic cues to navigate. The increased development of offshore power generators and their associated "anthropogenic magnetic noise," Kajiura writes, may disrupt the stingrays' natural navigation. A study published on February 5, 2021, in *Science*, "The Soundscape of the Anthropocene Ocean," affirms my colleague's suspicions. "Anthropogenic noise," Carlos M. Duarte and his coresearchers argue—referring to vessels, active sonar, acoustic deterrent devices, energy and construction infrastructure, and seismic surveys—"is a stressor for marine animals."

Kajiura, however, seems even more concerned about beach renourishment. "Beach renourishment," he suggests (I note that he uses the term "renourishment," not "nourishment"), "has the potential to really mess up the nearshore environment." He goes on to describe how the rapid influx of huge volumes of sand smothers and buries all the fauna established along the nearshore bottom, the primary prey of stingrays, which include crabs, worms, and bivalves. It can take months, he worries, for the new sand to be recolonized by these vital benthic creatures. "It would be really interesting," Kajiura writes, "to do a tagging study of stingrays in an area before and after beach renourishment." His reflections only increase my concern for stingrays, who have become near and dear to my heart too.

* * *

Meanwhile, a film on Netflix about a separate marine animal, *My Octopus Teacher*, takes the country by storm. It's all anyone can talk about on social media, it seems. I watch the film, which documents the relationship that develops between Craig Foster and a specific common octopus. Hoping to stir himself from a midlife malaise, Foster seeks out the bracingly cold waters of a shallow kelp forest near his home at the tip of South Africa, a biome teeming with marine life. This is where he encounters the octopus, which captivates him, and us. We watch as Foster gradually gains the creature's trust through freediving every day to visit her (spoiler alert: the octopus turns out, definitively, to be a *her*) for nearly a year. Through these daily immersions, Foster realizes something close to intimacy with this cephalopod, which sets him on a path toward healing back on land.

I'm as gobsmacked by the film as everyone else. What most accounts for its emotional power, I believe—above and beyond the gorgeous footage of the creature and its underwater environment—is the narrative thread, delivered in Foster's voice, which transforms this strange cephalopod into an animal a good bit more familiar. The first words we hear in the film, in fact, offer a sort of thesis statement that an octopus, believe it or not, is a lot like us. "A lot of people say that an octopus is like an alien," Foster intones as we watch footage of an undoubtedly alien-like creature gliding above the camera, "but the strange thing is, as you get closer to them you realize that we're very similar in a lot of ways." Indeed, the octopus we come to know over the next ninety minutes is, in turn, curious, fearful, playful, mischievous, ingenious, resourceful, resilient, and affectionate. She seems genuinely to seek out a friendship with other creatures, such as Foster. She suffers a near-mortal injury but summons her resources and manages to overcome her wounds. She seeks out a mate, ushers the next generation into the world, and cares for her progeny (i.e., thousands of eggs) fiercely before finally perishing, as cephalopods—and we—do.

So, yeah, *My Octopus Teacher* enchants me.

All the same, the longer I think about the film while I continue my own forays to commune with the ocean and our stingrays, the more I find myself chafing against something in it, something inchoate at first that slowly becomes clearer. What bothers me, I eventually figure out, are the terms the movie implicitly reinforces regarding our engagement with the nonhuman natural world. We must identify with a creature to be interested in it, much less enchanted. More, we must reach out and touch them, as Foster does, presenting his hands, arms, and even his face for his octopus' tender, tentacular inspection. Without realizing such contact—physical and emotional—we have a tough time ascribing value to nonhuman creatures.

Not that I begrudge Foster his contact with his octopus teacher. The relationship seems reciprocal, for one thing—and quite beautiful for another. Yet, while the documentary might have inspired me to reach out and touch these stingrays I'm encountering, it weirdly has the opposite effect. There's enough of this sort of thing going around already, I learn, vis-à-vis stingrays specifically. Stingray encounter programs are all the rage among tourists at various locales, worldwide, and this may not be a good thing for the stingrays. Scientist Mark Corcoran and his colleagues, studying "Stingray City Sandbar" in the Cayman Islands, have expressed concern over the possible negative impacts of such sites on the behavior and general ecology of stingrays. Through tagging them and tracking their movements with automated acoustic bottom monitors, Corcoran and his team concluded that "supplemental feeding is likely altering the movements and spatial distribution of elasmobranchs and other marine organisms at many sites worldwide."

I find myself wondering about this impulse of ours to gain familiarity with wild creatures by imposing ourselves on their world. "We seek contacts with nature," Aldo Leopold wrote in his classic work, *A Sand County Almanac* (1949), "because we derive pleasure from them." He shared this impulse, and imbibed it, as Foster does, and as I do, yet Leopold cautions against its coarsest manifestation in the "trophy-recreationalist," who must "possess, invade, appropriate." Leopold challenges us, instead, to deploy our imaginations a bit and learn to value, especially, those wild places and creatures we may never touch or even see, much less possess. And so I find myself more and more keeping my respectful distance from the stingrays I encounter while I swim in the ocean—cringing, even, at a few underwater photos my swim pal has taken of my big hominid form crowding a poor creature one morning. The stingrays I observe do not seem familiar to me—not really—and that's okay. While I never touch one or realize the sort of contact that Foster realizes with a common octopus, just swimming in their general sphere, watching them enact their stingray-ness for these brief moments a few times a week (more, just knowing that they're out here even when I *don't* see them) puts me in a different place. It's a good place to be, swimming in this silent ocean.

* * *

Summer yields to fall, the COVID-19 pandemic worsens, and the ocean water temps decrease into the comparatively chilly 70s. Even so, my most stalwart swim companions and I continue to enjoy our open-water swims. One day, over a stretch of rocky bottom close to shore, I notice an especially small stingray and halt my stroke to point it out to the three swim pals with me. "Aw, it's a baby stingray," Vanessa says as we catch our breath above the water. Maybe, I think. Yet I've learned enough by this time about how to look at stingrays to know that its small size doesn't necessarily mean that it's a baby. I take a series of breath-holds to hover a respectful distance above the small creature and take in the unusually round shape of its disc, the shortness of its tail-length compared to its disc-length, and its pretty pattern of dark spherical blotches, which I'd never noticed on the discs of southern stingrays. It takes one of our other swim companions several breath-holds to actually see the stingray, which suggests how effectively this pattern of blotches camouflages the creature against the rocky bottom. I sear these visual details onto my memory and look up images of various Florida stingrays online as soon as I return home. Yellow stingray. We had just shared some swim time with a yellow stingray.

Swimming amid yellow stingrays and southern stingrays, and amid so many other marine creatures these plague months, offers me a glimpse of the wider living world carrying on more or less as it's carried on for millennia. I come to see myself, and my primate pals plying the ocean waters with me, as a small part of this living world, yet still a part. Contemporary Native American voices I encounter reinforce this essential worldview. "Imagine walking through a richly inhabited world of Birch people, Bear people, Rock people," Robin Wall Kimmerer poses in *Braiding Sweetgrass* (2013), "beings we think of and therefore speak of as persons worthy of our respect, of inclusion in a peopled world. . . . Imagine how much less lonely the world would be." During this difficult year, my contact with human people necessarily diminished, I do feel less lonely on my open-water swims on account of my increased—though socially distant—contact with the stingray people.

13

This Is Not a Chapter on Manatees

45–50 million years ago. The fossil record shows that the ancestor of the manatee, genus *Dugong*, appears in Florida. The modern manatee, genus *Trichechus*, lives in Florida during the Pliocene, some three million years ago, their rib fragments among the most abundant fossils in shallow-water marine and estuarine deposits dating from this epoch.

But this is not a chapter on manatees. Because I wasn't going to write a chapter on manatees. For the same reason, I haven't written a chapter about alligators or palm trees. Because when most people think about Florida, they already think about manatees, and alligators, and palm trees. Plus, I suppose, Walt Disney World, Florida Men (and Women), horrific acts of gun violence, and fantastically—as opposed to normatively—corrupt politicians. I've managed not to write about any of these topics in my writings about Florida, because that's not the kind of Florida writer I want to be. I want to write about the wild Florida close at hand that most people—even those living in Florida—may not realize exists. I want to write about all the ways in which we might participate, meaningfully, in this one world.

* * *

But then I was swimming in the Atlantic Ocean a few miles from my home with a few of my open-water swim pals along our typical two-mile route back and forth between the Palmetto Pavilion and Red Reef Beach and we encountered a family of manatees, or they might have encountered us first. I'm still not sure if we saw the manatees first and decided to linger in their presence, or if they glimpsed us first and decided to linger in our presence.

Glimpse. I'd assumed eyesight as the manatee's dominant sensory perception, as it's my dominant sensory perception. Yet I was wrong about this. A nictating membrane protects the small eyes of manatees from salt water but significantly impedes sight. They mostly rely upon touch (and also hear quite well) to navigate their aquatic surroundings. Stiff, sensitive whiskers, or vibrissae, adorn their mouths, while finer hairs are distributed across their bodies. The whiskers sense tactile cues, help manatees to grasp food and channel the plants into their mouths. Their finer hairs help manatees detect even subtle shifts in temperature, current, and pressure wakes. If the manatees spotted, or, rather, detected us before we spotted them, I imagine that they felt with their fine hairs the pressure wakes stirred up by our sloppy hominid strokes.

* * *

10,000–20,000 years ago. Middens—the fancy word for aboriginal trash heaps—suggest that Florida's first humans hunted manatees for food.

* * *

Here's what I'm sure happened during my recent manatee encounter. At some point, both the manatees and humans decided that we'd all linger for some time in one another's presence. My swim companions and I had just turned back from our halfway point at Red Reef Beach. We were swimming at a pretty fast clip, towing our inflatable fluorescent safety buoys; Vanessa and I were training hard for an upcoming 12.5-mile open-water race around the island of Key West. The water couldn't have been deeper than ten feet or so. We hang tight to the coastline during our ocean swims, more to avoid collisions with reckless boaters and jet-skiers than out of any fear of sharks. The water was calm, clear, and very blue, hardly silted up at all on account of the light winds and current. I could see the corrugated bottom of pale sand as I stroked, strands of sunken sargassum, shells, and, yes, random pieces of discarded plastic, which I sometimes (though not always) retrieve from the ocean bottom and stuff into the pouch of my swim buoy to discard later. Then I heard Vanessa's shriek so dropped my legs to lift my head out of the water. Was she okay? I thought she might have gotten wrapped up in the toxic tentacles of a Portuguese man o' war, which happens to us too often, regrettably, to be considered an uncommon occurrence. But no.

* * *

1492. Forget (for a moment) all the other stuff you associate with Christopher Columbus and this date. For in addition to all the violence, disease, plunder, and enslavement he visited upon the Indigenous peoples of the

Caribbean, he also noted in his journals that "they must have cows or other cattle," as he chanced upon what were most likely manatee skulls. During his fourth and last voyage to the New World some ten years later, Columbus brought his teenage son, Ferdinand. By this time the European explorers were more familiar with manatees, referring to them as mermaids or sirens. Ferdinand thought that the meat looked and tasted like veal, though the Roman Catholic Church would later define the manatee (incorrectly) as a fish, permitted for consumption during Lent and other abstinence days.

* * *

"Manatees!" Vanessa cried, probably for the second or third time. Our other friends, Mike and Margaux, had stopped by this point too.

"Yeah, I see them," Mike said, then dived below after unclipping his safety buoy. I lowered my head back into the salt water and then I saw them for the first time, hovering there just a few feet away from us, these enormous brown sausages. I'm afraid that that's the image my brain conjured to familiarize these strange and wondrous creatures. Sausages. They seemed to be rotating slightly on their axes as they floated beside us. Three of them. One was about half the size of the other two. A manatee family!

Curious that I assumed it was a nuclear family—a father, mother, and manatee-child. How American! How middle-aged and male of me! I didn't yet know that the Florida manatee is a subspecies of the West Indian manatee, that mothers (cows) reach sexual maturity in three to five years, fathers (bulls) in five to seven years, that calves stay with their mothers for up to two years, according to the Florida Fish and Wildlife Conservation Commission (FWC), but that male manatees *do not* stick around after the breeding period expires, that they "leave a cow alone" after the breeding period, which is an interesting way of putting it.

I suppose I didn't know much at all about manatees at the time of our encounter.

The two larger manatees might have been the mother and another adult female, tagging along for the ride, which was somewhat unusual as manatees (excepting cows and their calves) do not typically travel together. However, they will congregate in warm-water sites during winter—power-plant discharge canals and artesian springs—and socialize at other times when they chance across each other, so I suppose that's what these adult females were doing, socializing, which wasn't so very different than what my human friends and I were doing in these nearshore, subtropical waters.

* * *

1774. William Bartram, during his travels through Florida to explore the region's plants, animals, and Indigenous peoples, observed along the banks of what we now call Manatee Springs State Park the bones of a manatee killed, he writes, by the Indians. "The grinding teeth," Bartram documents, "were about an inch in diameter; the ribs eighteen inches in length, and two and an [sic] half in thickness, bending with a gentle curve, this bone is esteemed equal to ivory; the flesh of the creature is counted wholesome and pleasant food; the Indians call them by a name which signifies the big beaver. My companion, who was a trader in Talahasochte last winter, saw three of them at one time in this spring; they feed chiefly on aquatic grass and weeds."

* * *

Here's some more of what I now know about manatees in the United States. Adults typically grow between nine and ten feet long, snout to tail, and weigh roughly 1,000 pounds. They are aquatic herbivores, feeding solely on seagrass, algae, and other vegetation in freshwater and estuarine systems in the southeastern United States. When active, these marine mammals surface to breathe every thirty seconds or so but might remain submerged for up to twenty minutes while resting. Congregating exclusively in Florida during the winter, manatees have been found as far west as Texas and as far north as Massachusetts during the summer. They can hold vegetation in their flippers thanks to their jointed, finger-like bones, and, like elephants—their nearest relative—can use their prehensile upper lips to secure their plant food and draw it into their mouths, eating from 4 to 9 percent of their body weight daily. Their mouths contain only molars (which grind rather than bite). These molars constantly shift forward and fall out, only to be replaced by new molars from the rear, an adaptation which accounts in part for the relatively long lives that luckier manatees enjoy. They may live over sixty-five years in captivity. A manatee named "Snooty," born in Miami in 1948, lived until July 23, 2017, at the Bishop Museum of Science and Nature in Bradenton, Florida, where he was moved. He was sixty-nine. Still, only about half of the wild manatees that reach adulthood survive into their early twenties.

* * *

1832. John James Audubon, who had no qualms about shooting scores of birds and most other fauna, expresses at least a modicum of concern over the manatee hunting practices of his guide on Indian Key, James Egan, in "The Florida Keys" section of his journal: "The pilot, besides being a first-rate shot, possessed a most intimate acquaintance with the country.... For years his employment had been to hunt those singular animals called Sea Cows or Manatees, and he had conquered hundreds of them, 'merely,' as he said, because the flesh and hide bring 'a fair price' at Havannah."

* * *

What I noticed most about the manatees while we basked in their presence was not their small eyes, or those stiff whiskers at their snouts, or their flippers, or their mottled, grayish-brown, leathery-looking skin, free from algae in our saltwater environs, but the slow way they seemed to roll about. They seemed so easeful in the water the way they lolled, which I might have noticed on account of the greater effort it took me to dive, swim, and tread water amid the manatees. It was hard not to see something joyful in it, manatee lolling.

The way the manatees rotated their bodies about, however, might have had something to do with their inability to move their heads sideways. While most mammals have seven cervical vertebrae, the manatee sports only six. Consequently, it takes some effort for manatees to see what's behind them. To catch better glimpses of what the four of us primates were up to swimming in their sphere, the manatees would have had to shift their entire bodies, which is pretty much what they were doing.

* * *

1885. It's clear by this time that the Florida manatee is in trouble. "Ten years ago," an observer noted, "the meat (of a manatee) could be bought at fifty cents a pound. The animals are becoming far too scarce to admit of its being sold at all. There is no doubt that the manatee is fast becoming an extinct animal."

* * *

I want to think about hunting for a moment. An important distinction must be drawn between hunting for sport or profit and subsistence hunting, hunting simply to keep from starving. The Native Americans whom Bartram encountered, and the earlier Paleo-Indians—who descended upon the Florida peninsula approximately 12,000 years ago—surely hunted manatees to stay alive. This hunting practice would continue among the Seminoles into the 1960s according to a recent article in *The Seminole Tribune* by Damon Scott. The article features an archival photograph of a Seminole man dressing a recently killed manatee, slash pines looming in the background. Big Cypress councilman Mondo Tiger reflects in the piece, "You could live on the amount of meat it provided for weeks. They were part of our diet." Other early Florida settlers, too, Scott's article suggests, relied upon the manatee for food. Fair enough. But this isn't the sort of hunting that decimated manatee populations before protections were put into place.

* * *

1893. Manatees are finally placed under protection under Florida state law, chapter 4208.94, which expressly prohibits the hunting of manatees.

* * *

The few other times over the past twenty-five years that I'd been lucky enough to glimpse a manatee while swimming had only been brief encounters. Hardly encounters at all. A single manatee on each occasion, a dark shadow I glimpsed from above, gliding off beyond my field of view. (Manatees, typically slow-moving, can swim at bursts of up to twenty miles an hour.) These manatees, as I've said, seemed every bit as interested in us as we were in them. They might have found something curious about the pressure wakes created by our laborious freestyle strokes, or maybe just something curious about the whole notion of us—mostly hairless animals sharing their more familiar waters.

"They're not dangerous, right?" Vanessa asked as we rose to the surface, treading water to gather our breath. I'd sort of been wondering the same thing. I knew that manatees weren't dangerous in a general sort of way. But they were hanging so close to us, and the two larger ones were so big; it was difficult not to ponder the possibility that they might be dangerous. They were clearly checking us out with their small, dark eyes, circling us, or if not circling us, exactly, floating themselves about us within easy reach. I didn't yet know about their grinding, rather than biting, teeth, or that there has *never* been a report of a manatee attacking humans, or any other animals for that matter, although there have been reports of hapless humans—spring-breakers, typically—freaking out in fear of an attack when chancing upon manatees. I would not freak out.

"No," I answered, "they're not dangerous." I must have sounded semiconvincing, because Mike and Margaux dived down again to loll beside the manatees some more, while Vanessa unclipped her buoy from her waist and began unfolding its almost-watertight compartment to retrieve her cell phone, secured in an actually watertight plastic pouch. Twisting open the fasteners to the pouch, she asked me if she should use the cell phone beneath the water to take a video, whereupon I tried to advise her that she ought to start the video above the water, then stuff the cell phone back into the clear pouch before lowering it into the salt water. But in her excitement she must not have heard me. Or in my excitement my words might not have matched my thoughts, because she just lowered her phone into the salt water, sans pouch, her head and feet following after.

It was fiercely tempting to reach out and touch these extraordinary animals, who looked both cumbersome and lithe at the same time. But I didn't touch them. "I don't think we're supposed to touch them," I told Mike at the surface, after I thought I saw him place a palm on the side of one of the adults under the water. As much as I craved contact with these wild creatures, I'm wary of all such precious moments when I'm lucky enough to puncture the veil between the human and nonhuman animal worlds, as I've suggested earlier. I didn't really know anything about manatees. We lived mostly in alien worlds. What germs might be communicated between us? How dangerous might it be for manatees to think that a human touch might be a kind touch? Plus, it just seemed wrong, if not illegal, to assume greater familiarity with these sea cows than we already enjoyed simply basking in their presence. Sea cows. Even this unscientific moniker for the creatures emphasized how alien they were to us, so alien that we needed to rope in the name of a terrestrial, domesticated creature to describe the manatee.

* * *

1969. Manatees are listed as an endangered species under the Federal Endangered Species Conservation Act, which supersedes the 1966 Federal Endangered Species Preservation Act. Increased federal protections occur in 1972 (the Marine Mammal Protection Act) and 1973 (the Endangered Species Act). At the state level, the Florida Manatee Sanctuary Act of 1978 stipulates that "It is unlawful for any person, at any time, intentionally or negligently, to annoy, molest, harass, or disturb any manatee." Conviction for violating the law may be punishable by fine up to $50,000 and/or one year in prison.

* * *

Look, but don't touch manatees. The FWC is actually quite clear about this in the "Viewing Guidelines" section of their website. The danger, as I'd suspected, is that too much familiarity with humans might alter their behavior in the wild, making them less fearful of humans and more susceptible to dangerous human encounters, specifically boat strikes. Due to the manatees' buoyancy and slow speed, they have been susceptible to fatal injury incurred by boat propellors for as long as we have been motoring vessels in Florida's abundant waterways. "The largest cause of human-related manatee mortality in Florida is watercraft collision," according to the FWC's "A Boater's Guide to Living with Florida Manatees." The report goes on to emphasize, somewhat weirdly, that injuries from propeller cuts or from the impact of the vessels, themselves, are not always lethal, that "most manatees have scars or a pattern of scars on their backs or tails after surviving collisions with boats."

Do they truly mean "most manatees," as if a population of propeller-scarred manatees were something normal that we should just wrap our heads around? Or, more hopefully, do they mean to say that most manatees, *who have survived collisions with boats,* have scars or a pattern of scars on their backs or tails? Either way, it's sort of messed up, right?

* * *

1981. Governor Bob Graham and singer/songwriter Jimmy Buffett found the nonprofit Save the Manatee Committee with a mission to protect endangered manatees and their habitat, and the Adopt-A-Manatee program begins.

* * *

We stayed amid the manatees in the nearshore waters of the ocean for over half an hour, and they stayed with us. It wasn't an encounter you wanted to hurry past, and the manatees seemed to feel the same way. Yet we, by which I mean we humans, started to shiver eventually. It was April of 2021 and the water was still cold, at least by Florida standards, by which I mean somewhere in the low 70s. Our lips blued, we finally decided to swim away from the manatees toward the Palmetto Pavilion a half-mile or so to our south. What didn't occur to me as we swam from them, as they remained, was that they might have associated us with food, and that they might have expected us to feed them. I knew that manatees were having a harder time of it in Florida over the past few years—habitat loss, boat strikes, a spate of red tides that attack the central nervous system of manatees and other creatures, fierce winter cold snaps on account of the polar vortex—but this was just before the local and national print media and TV broadcasts began featuring reportage on the mass starvation event imperiling manatees across the Sunshine State.

Beginning in December 2020, according to the Marine Mammal Commission, the state witnessed "a drastic uptick in carcasses and manatees requiring rescue along the Atlantic coast of Florida." Starvation—rather than the more typical culprits of cold stress and vessel strikes—accounted for most of these casualties. In all of 2021, 1,101 Florida manatees died, nearly twice the number of fatalities recorded in 2020 and a new record. (The old record of 830 deaths was set back in 2013.) As I write these lines in the early months of 2022, we have already seen over 300 manatee deaths. Experts attribute the current catastrophe to poor nearshore water quality, which has led to the widespread die-off of the seagrass beds on which manatees rely. More specifically, pollution from farm and residential fertilizers, leaky residential septic systems and sewage lines has spewed too many nutrients into the waters, fueling algal blooms that have blocked the sunlight from reaching the seagrass below.

So it was very possible that the three manatees I encountered while swimming in the ocean, who seemed so healthy to me, were not so much frolicking with us as exploring whether the novelty of our presence might indicate the possibility of food. The upshot: it's not really true anymore that "The largest cause of human-related manatee mortality in Florida is watercraft collision," as claimed by the FWC's "A Boater's Guide to Living with Florida Manatees." Humans, after all, created the conditions that gave rise to the algal blooms choking off the sea grasses, which have sustained manatees for millions of years. We own this crisis.

Just as we have been forced to own our earlier manatee crises.

* * *

1991. Aerial surveys report only 1,268 manatees in Florida waters. Over the next several years, various Florida county and state manatee protection plans are implemented. These plans include the addition of protection zones and refuges for manatees, increased and enhanced boating regulations and law enforcement, manatee education, and increased manatee research and monitoring.

* * *

1996. The estimated number of manatees in Florida waters climbs to 2,639.

* * *

2001. Then 3,276.

* * *

I decide to seek out manatees more concertedly, rather than leaving it to chance encounters during my open-water swims in the ocean. Toward this end, I set out with my wife, Wendy, and our younger daughter, Eva, for Florida's Gulf Coast and—where else?—Manatee County. We rent a log cabin in Palmetto, a town clearly losing the battle against commercial and residential overdevelopment. Yet the property where our cabin sits, replete with old cypresses and live oaks shaggy with Spanish moss, represents something of a countryish haven smack in the middle of the sprawl. Sitting on one of the handcrafted rocking chairs outside our door, I listen to the rising calls of northern parulas in the trees, the *tea-kettle, tea-kettle, tea-kettle!* song of what I'm pretty sure must be a Carolina wren. I glimpse overhead a small flock of strange-looking birds flying eastward fast, which I see just well enough to identify as roseate spoonbills. Eva spots chickens in a coop and donkeys in a pasture just beyond and dashes off to visit these creatures. But none of these animals are the ones we're primarily here to see.

We drive the next morning for the nearby city of Bradenton and the Bishop Museum of Science and Nature to pay homage to the longtime home of Snooty, and to see what other manatees might be in residence today. Even before arriving at the museum, it's clear to me that Gulf Coast residents of my home state have manatees on their mind to an even greater extent than we do on the Atlantic side. I spot manatee likenesses everywhere. License plates. Mailboxes. Billboards. Bumper stickers. In

Bradenton proper, there's a beautiful bronze sculpture of a manatee and its calf near the riverwalk overlooking the Manatee River. There's a Manatee Avenue, a Manatee Performing Arts Center, not to be confused with ArtCenter Manatee, a Manatee Players Theater, a Manatee Memorial Hospital (for humans). True, it's the county name and all. You'd expect to see it on signage, but maybe not so ubiquitously.

The small but modern Bishop Museum impresses us immediately with its well-organized display of Florida fossils, including an enormous mastodon and other archaeological material representing Paleo-Indian, Archaic, and precontact cultures. There's a planetarium show too, which we'll check out later, for we pretty much make a beeline through the fossil display to the Parker Manatee Rehabilitation Habitat, a 60,000-gallon habitat modeled after a cypress spring. We're the only visitors at the aboveground viewing area and we've arrived just in time to watch one of the manatee scientists stuffing a rather gorgeous assortment of lettuces—endive, romaine, red leaf, hyacinth—into a white tube. The tube, the young woman tells us, is designed to sink to the bottom, thus replicating the locale of the aquatic vegetation in the manatees' natural habitat. We don't talk about this, but state and federal wildlife officials, I know, are in the midst of a momentous manatee feeding experiment in the wild to address the mass starvation event, distributing thousands of pounds of lettuces at various sites on both coasts. The program seems to be helping some, yet everyone knows that it's not a viable long-term solution. Manatees need healthy seagrass beds to forage at creek and river bottoms, not the frilly leaves of romaine lettuce strewn across the surface by human feeders.

The museum manatee scientist tells me that the three healthy-looking juvenile manatees floating in the tank now had suffered cold stress, that Aria—she points to one of the creatures—had also suffered a boat strike. I can see the white propeller scars across its back. She adds that they hope to release all three manatees into the wild in a few months' time. The quick way she works into the conversation their imminent release makes me wonder if she's used to having to bat back guests' concerns over the appropriateness of housing manatees in captivity. Probably so, I imagine.

I tell her about my magical ocean encounter with three wild manatees while open-water swimming, and she tells me that I was right that they probably didn't see us swimming so much as they sensed our presence. Manatees see twice as poorly as a legally blind human person, she explains, and only see in blues and greens. She tells me that I was probably wrong, however, to think that the two larger manatees were unrelated adult females. Chances were greater that one of the larger ones was the older calf of the mother, as sometimes the calves hang around their mothers past their seasons.

"Like human children," I reply, nudging Eva, who doesn't laugh.

"Yeah, I guess," the woman says, not quite laughing either.

"So is this where Snooty lived?" I hear myself ask.

"Yes," she says, tersely. I don't say anything further, and probably oughtn't to have said anything at all. It's a sore subject, I learned just before visiting the museum, Snooty having died not of old age—as I'd assumed—but of drowning after the underwater hatch door leading to a small plumbing area was mistakenly left open. The juvenile manatees in the habitat were able to enter and exit the space, but Snooty, on account of his size, was unable to negotiate his way out of the small area to reach the surface for air.

We watch from above for a while as the three smallish gray creatures (much grayer than the mostly beige creatures I saw in the ocean) nibble on their lettuces, rising to the surface intermittently. We head out the door and down a set of stairs to watch the manatees underwater through the thick glass. We can see the manatees much better from this vantage. I'm struck by the slow speed but impressive range of motion of their front flippers, which propel them quite agilely about. We can also clearly see the fine hairs across their backs and sides billowing in the current as they paddle about, hairs that enable these practically blind mammals to navigate their environment. I hadn't noticed these hairs during all the time I spent with the three wild manatees in the ocean. Funny what you don't notice.

* * *

2006. Manatee numbers continue to rise in three out of four state regions.

* * *

2008. The Florida Manatee Management Plan is implemented with the following goal: "To remove the manatee from the state imperiled species list and effectively manage the population in perpetuity throughout Florida by securing habitat and minimizing threats."

* * *

2011. 4,834 manatees are estimated to live in Florida waters.

* * *

2016. The number of Florida manatees climbs to an estimated 6,250 individuals. The federal government reclassifies the species from endangered to threatened.

* * *

Sure, we've made a mess of the planet in the Anthropocene. That's why we call it the Anthropocene in the first place. Yet, our well-justified cynicism about all that we're doing wrong tends to overshadow one crucial thing we ought to remember. When we decide, collectively, to make a positive impact upon the environment, we have done so with great success. When Rachel Carson's *Silent Spring* (1962) and her powerful statement before Congress in 1963 demonstrated how the commonly used pesticide, DDT, imperiled countless animals and contaminated the world's food supply, the United States and other countries banned its use, which led to the remarkable comeback of bald eagles, ospreys, pelicans, and other wildlife. When it became clear in the 1970s that chlorofluorocarbons were depleting the ozone layer in the stratosphere, which protects the earth from the sun's harmful ultraviolet rays, the United States and other countries banned CFC-containing aerosol propellants, which dramatically curtailed the level of ozone depletion.

We were doing much better by the manatees, too, until our current crisis.

* * *

Our next day on the Gulf Coast, we drive north some hundred miles or so to Weeki Wachee Springs State Park. Most famous for its live mermaid shows (i.e., young women in mermaid costumes performing impressive underwater acrobatics), the 538-acre park has been entertaining visitors since 1947. In the days before Walt Disney World, roadside attractions like Weeki Wachee were *the* places off the highway for northern tourists to visit. Many of these quirky Florida attractions have since closed, yet Weeki Wachee has managed to hold on, largely on account of the talented and attractive mermaids, who work as state employees. Yet we're not here for the live mermaid show or for the animal show, the river boat cruise, or the waterslides in the swimming area. We bypass the long line for admissions at the main entrance and drive straight to the Weeki Wachee River, where we've rented two kayaks and a standup paddleboard (for me). Today, we hope to encounter wild manatees! This river, thanks to the mild water temperature on account of its artesian springs, is one of the more likely places that we might encounter a manatee, or, with luck, might see more than one creature. The warm-water outfalls of various Florida power plants, including one canal very close to our home on the east coast, would constitute a sure thing this time of year, but this isn't the sort of "wild" manatee sighting we have in mind.

"Any manatees out there today?" I ask the young woman at the rental counter as she checks her computer to see that we've signed our waivers.

"No reports of any yet," she says, "but it's definitely possible."

"Great," I reply.

A young man hands us our lifejackets and points our way under a canopy of live oaks toward the marina at the riverbank, where separate team members help us put in. I am by no means a confident standup paddleboarder. I had wanted to rent a kayak, but a third kayak wasn't available by the time I got around to booking our rental online. Wendy and Eva head off in their orange vessels and I follow after them best I can on my knees, then manage after a few strokes with the long paddle to rise to my feet. A few more precarious strokes and I gather my balance enough to look about. The narrow river and its tree-lined bank is, in a word, gorgeous. But maybe not so gorgeous as it once was and should still be. The water below my paddleboard is powder blue and clear all the way to the sandy bottom, but I take special note (of course) of the seagrass beds. They should be greener, I suspect, but the beds are coated with dark algae, isolated tendrils of greener, algae-free grass here and there. The dark algae, I'll confirm later, betrays the excess nutrients polluting the river. The algae smother the native seagrass and provide no nutritional benefit for manatees or other creatures. Volunteers and park employees, in fact, have been using rakes and special vacuums for years to clear as much of the gunk as possible.

"Keep your eyes peeled for manatees," I call to Wendy and Eva nonetheless. The downstream current is a blessing, but it pretty much scoots inexperienced paddlers (read: us) where it will along its winding path, including directly into the low-hanging thickets of foliage either side of the river. Eva manages once to get hopelessly stuck in an overhanging bramble and doesn't appreciate our help as we paddle over to try to free her.

"I'm fine," she says, the foliage having forced her into leaning almost fully backward, her arms crossed over her face, her paddle balanced precariously across the kayak. "I'm not stuck," she ludicrously insists. Tweens!

"You *are* stuck," I declare from my knees on the paddleboard. Wendy and I shift and lift various offending branches about. It takes some time, but we finally manage to extricate our daughter and set her aright down the middle of the waterway.

Despite the complication of the current, the three of us enjoy a fairly easeful adventure. The day will grow hot, yet the cool waters of the river and the shade from the overhanging canopy of bald cypresses, live oaks, cabbage palms, magnolia, sweetgum, and other trees keeps the temperature comfortable. I hear the unmistakable scream of a limpkin, then spot the handsome, brown-and-white speckled wading bird on an island around which the river forks. I hear the repetitive, interrogative notes of red-eyed vireos and the *zheeps* of great-crested flycatchers, one of which I also spot with my eyes. Wendy and Eva see a small alligator scooting from the bank into the water to elude them. I see something large and dark thwacking through the overhanging foliage ahead, which turns out to be a barred owl, still in its fluffy juvenile plumage. I take several decent photographs of the owl with my smartphone, somehow without losing my balance and tipping into the drink.

What we don't see on this two-hour paddle are manatees. But that's okay.

* * *

Depleted by our excursion, we lumber back into our car and settle in for the long drive across the peninsula to our home. Until we get to the six-lane surface streets and big box stores of Orlando's outskirts, it's a pretty drive through rural stretches of Florida's interior: rolling green landscape dotted with lakes, old live oak trees, and (it must be acknowledged) too many competing dollar-store franchises in the single-traffic-light towns beaded along the road's necklace. The whole way back I can't stop thinking about the thing that the young woman at the rental counter had said about the prospect of us encountering wild manatees. *It's definitely possible.* Sure, there might have been something of the saleswoman in her encouragement. Yet, she wasn't wrong about the possibility of us locating manatees along the Weeki Wachee River. This possibility, itself, added to the thrill of our paddling adventure. When I think of all my adventures in wild Florida over the nearly thirty years I've lived here, it's the possibility of an encounter with some phenomenon of the Florida spectacular—as much as the encounters, themselves—that continues to propel me outdoors. We didn't see manatees on our paddle down the river, but we *might* have seen them, and that made all the difference.

As we consider the terrific struggles of the manatee in my home state today, and our own culpability for these struggles, I can only hope that we recognize what's truly at stake, not only for the manatee, but for us. Do we really want to live in a place where it's no longer even possible to see manatees, as it's now impossible to see, say, Carolina parakeets and ivory-billed woodpeckers? It's a hopelessly anthropocentric slant on the current crisis, I realize, but I'll make no apologies. As I've said, this is not a chapter about manatees. It's a chapter about us. Manatees, after all, are only trying to do their manatee-thing in Florida that they've been doing with dazzling success over the past three million years. The question is whether we newcomers to the peninsula will make the small sacrifices necessary to let their, and our, Florida story continue.

* * *

Note: I am indebted to the comprehensive FWC Manatee Timeline for many of the chronological factoids in this essay.

14

Fox

The thing about seeing a fox is that a fox doesn't want to be seen. It took me a long time to see a fox in my asphalt-frosted region of South Florida. I knew that a small number of foxes eked out a living along some of the scruffier acres of my county, because signage at my local parks warn against feeding foxes and other wildlife, and because the sea turtle scientists and volunteers whom I chat up at the beach time to time have bemoaned the presence of foxes, who prize sea turtle eggs, and because, yeah, I finally managed to catch a precious glimpse of ginger fur and bottlebrush tail one evening at Yamato Scrub, a 217-acre natural center at the north end of my city. The sun was melting in the west while the fox melted into the shrubbery. This was a long time ago. So I've known that foxes were, in a general sense, here. Yet I never imagined that foxes might be seen in my neighborhood subdivision until my wife burst in the front door one recent evening, our daughter and our dog trailing behind, and shouted, "Guess what we saw?"

I guessed owl. Screech owls are the wild creatures in our neighborhood that typically excite Wendy when they make their appearances.

"Fox!" she corrected me, unclipping Storm's leash from his collar. "We saw a fox."

"No way."

"Way," Eva replied, unsarcastically. Our eleven-year-old daughter, the youngest of our three children, seemed interested by their sighting, if not quite as excited as my wife.

* * *

Gray fox. *Urocyon cinereoargenteus*. A Florida native weighing only between seven and thirteen pounds. Found throughout the state, though more abundant in the north. Nocturnal. Relishes small prey in the Rodentia family—rats, mice, moles, voles, gophers—though will eat pretty much anything from which they can extract calories: nuts, berries, fish, frogs, lizards, insects, birds, trash. One of the few members of the Canid (dog) family to climb trees, so watch out lizards, insects, and birds! Gray foxes mate in January, February, and March. Both male (dog) and female (vixen) feed and care for their pups—also called kits or cubs—usually between three and five pups per litter.

* * *

It qualified as a big deal that Eva had seen the fox, as getting our daughter to join one or both of us on our twice-daily dog walks, or even to leave her room, had been something of a trial of late. We were still in the early throes of the COVID-19 pandemic, and the local schools had all shifted to remote-learning formats for the remainder of the academic year. Eva's recreational swim league had canceled the rest of its season, and pretty much all public facilities had closed indefinitely. When Eva wasn't grousing through one of her online school sessions at the kitchen bar, she was holed away in her upstairs bedroom for what seemed like an unhealthy amount of time, playing Roblox or scrolling through TikTok, and rarely reading. We floated any number of enticements to lure her out of her lair. A swim in the backyard pool. A jigsaw puzzle. A dog walk. Dessert. Eva greeted each one of these overtures with a disarmingly sunny no thank you from behind her closed bedroom door. *No thank you!* Given our strange and frightening current circumstances, it was difficult to determine whether, or to what extent, her withdrawal betrayed her possible anomie that ought to be addressed, or whether, or to what extent, it was just the normal business of adolescence, Eva forging her own identity independent of her parents. That sort of thing. As I've mentioned, she's our third child and much younger than her siblings, by which I mean to say that we were pretty tired, parentingwise, and probably let too much go. Did I mention TikTok? Sometimes, we forced her during the first spring and summer of the pandemic to join us downstairs or outside; mostly, we took the path of least resistance, left her to herself, honored her no thank yous.

No thank you! . . . No thank you! . . . No thank you!

But she'd gone on that nighttime walk with Wendy. They'd seen a fox. We hoped that such a spectacular vision might encourage her to get out of her room and off her electronics more often to explore with us once again the immediate outdoors, the real-world wonders close at hand. Fox!

* * *

A family of foxes is called a skulk, a leash, or an earth, though Catherine Raven in *Fox & I* (2021), her winning memoir on the relationship she forges with a fox in the Montana backcountry, refers to a group of foxes as a "cozy," which I like best of all.

* * *

It's not easy being a dog or vixen to a cozy of kits. Foxes, while fierce hunters themselves, are preyed upon—particularly while still kits—by dogs, coyotes, bobcats, owls, and hawks. Dangers are everywhere, Adele Brand writes in *The Hidden World of the Fox* (2019). "She [the vixen] may move them [the kits] if disturbed, or bluff-charge predators, even dangerous ones. . . . By early summer, the vixen looks bedraggled. The exhaustion of motherhood results in a tattered coat and battered brush, and householders dismiss her as scruffy. As a human who has fostered ten fox cubs, I have a lot of respect for wild vixens."

* * *

The prospect of fox-spotting, as we had hoped, worked in our favor for a time to lure Eva out of her room. "Evaaa!" I'd call upstairs from the landing, "Time to find our fox!" (I already thought of the creature as *our* fox.) I'd hear the latch to her door clicking open, then I'd retreat to the kitchen for fear of spooking Eva with my physical presence bottom of the stairs. Wendy and Eva led us each time to the very spot they'd seen the fox, only a few blocks from our house, not too far from the narrow one-way street bordering a thicket of tall grasses, cacti, and large non-native trees with spherical leaves the size of dinner plates. A soupy drainage canal just beyond the thicket separates our subdivision from the next one to the north. It made sense that our fox would hunt dusk till dawn hereabouts, then hunker down during the day, maybe within the thicket's dense cover. But a week of unsuccessful scouts turned into two weeks, then three weeks. No fox. Eva's enthusiasm waned. The odds were low, she realized, that we'd ever see our fox again. She mostly took to her room.

"What do you say, Eva?" I'd call up the stairs, the tenor of my voice tinged already with defeat. "Help us find our fox?"

"No thank you!"

"Please!"

"No thank you!"

"Eva, please come out of your room!"
"No thank you!"

* * *

Please come out of your den! I silently pleaded with our fox each time I set out on one of my fruitless searches throughout the neighborhood that whole year. Discouraged, I began to query the neighbors I'd see out and about taking in their own exercise, while keeping a safe social distance (Florida rules: one full-sized alligator between us, tail to snout). Our neighborhood was trending the way of most suburban neighborhoods in the country, even before the plague, which is to say that few people spent much time outside their climate-controlled homes and few neighbors truly knew one another. Yet owning a dog that demands walks has put us into contact with a fairly wide number of our neighbors, mostly neighbors who also own dogs. Nonetheless, I wasn't getting any great intel, foxwise. No one else had seen the fox, though a few suspected that it was foxes toppling over their garbage bins. I found this unlikely, given the small size of foxes and the gargantuan proportions of the covered trash receptacles distributed by the city.

What's more likely, it occurred to me, though it ought to have occurred to me earlier, was that our neighborhood fox or foxes were the ones digging up the snapper carcasses from my frequent saltwater fishing jaunts, carcasses I bury in various locales about my front and back yards after stripping them of their fillets. I'd assumed all this time that it was raccoons sniffing out the burial sites. Raccoons are Jake by me, but I felt better about the stinking carcasses and fish scale strewn across my yard some mornings knowing that they might be nourishing our neighborhood foxes instead of, or maybe in addition to, the raccoons.

* * *

The way Wendy and Eva described the fox they saw—smallish with a lot of red on it, bushy tail, crossed the street right in front of them and skittered into someone's backyard without looking their way—made me certain that our fox was a red fox. But it took only a bit of research to figure out that it was probably a gray fox they glimpsed. Gray foxes are often confused with red foxes, because gray foxes can have a good bit of red on them too, while red foxes—distributed throughout Florida, though not native—often advertise patches of gray or grayish white, especially at the throat, chin, and belly. Gray foxes tend to be a bit smaller, their heads rounder with shorter snouts, but, yeah, it's confusing. The tail-tips are the true tell between species. Red foxes sport white tail-tips while gray foxes have black-tipped tails. I asked Wendy after figuring all this out if she and Eva had noticed the color at the tip of the fox's tail—was it black or white?—and watched my wife's placid expression tilt toward one of benign consternation, a look I've sort of grown used to seeing over the past thirty years, before she finally uttered, "The tail-tip? Are you nuts?"

* * *

Brand marvels over the evolutionary processes that over millennia have resulted in the physical creature we know as fox, which live on every continent except Antarctica. "In a very real way," she writes, "foxes are built around mice." She proceeds to describe those preposterously large tails that help them keep their balance, their light bones, their ultrasensitive hearing, the layer of tissue behind their retinas, *tapetum lucidum,* that enables them to see at night (vertical pupils also help), their suspected use of the magnetic field together with auditory cues to gauge the angle and distance of their predatory leaps.

That foxes have a yen for rodents must be one reason they live in, or at least pass through, my neighborhood. In addition to the few other wild animals I see out and about at the crepuscular times I walk Storm to evade the Florida heat—raccoons, opossums, owls, bats, iguanas, nighthawks—I see plenty of plump rats crawling across telephone wires, creeping up sabal palm trunks into the dense cover of their shaggy crowns, and skittering across live oak branches, animal sightings I tend not to share with my wife. The presence of foxes on the ground, perhaps, is why the rats travel up high across the wires and trees in the first place. Mice, moles, and voles, too, evidenced by the castings of our owls I sometimes find and my embattled vegetable garden every winter, also carry on their prodigious life business in my neighborhood. The "mousing" prowess of Raven's fox friend in *Fox & I* constitutes one of the more enchanting episodes in her memoir. The small stomach of Fox, as she calls him, can't possibly keep up with his kills, so he buries caches of his mutilated, sometimes half-devoured, prey all about Raven's property, including the area where she likes to read *The Little Prince* to the attentive Fox from her camp chair. This compels Raven to build a cobblestone wall to mark a mouse-free zone, or MFZ, which she hopes Fox will abide. The effort pretty much fails.

* * *

I wondered some more about the digging proclivities of foxes, specifically the prospect of our mystery fox digging up my fish carcasses, shearing raw flesh from frame with its sharp carnassial pairs—an upper premolar and lower first molar—to glean the precious proteins left behind after I'd taken my fillets. I wondered about their ostensible digging up of sea turtle nests. While I was doing all this wondering, I spotted one of the sea turtle volunteers I didn't know at the beach, digging up on hands and knees one of the post-hatch turtle nests to survey how successful the nest seems to have been, depositing shards of spent eggshell into a white bucket. He was a hale fellow in his sixties, a cloud of gray hair parted loosely over his forehead, rosy and wet from his efforts. He seemed pleased that I'd approached him, interrupting his labors on a hot summer day. I asked him if foxes were still digging up turtle nests along the beach and he replied from his knees, "All the time," arching his back, resting his hands now on his thighs. "They're pretty good at sniffing them out," he continued. As he talked, a pair of migrating willets flitted southward over the nearshore water, flashed their big black-and-white wings. He pointed toward a disturbed nest nearby. "See how that nest's all dug out?" I nodded. "Raccoons don't make such a mess when they raid a nest. But the foxes dig up the whole thing. They're smart, too. They wait until the turtles are nearly hatched to snap them up." This last detail made me cringe. I knew about nature red in tooth and claw and all, but it sounded rather macabre, foxes waiting about for baby turtles in their shells to grow large enough to make a tasty meal, a turtle nest buried in the hot Florida sand their microwave oven for all intents and purposes. He must have recognized the squeamish look on my face, because he told me that the sea turtles had enjoyed a remarkably successful nesting season this year, despite the foxes and other predators, that what I really ought to worry about is global warming. The sex of sea turtles and several other reptiles, he explained, is determined by temperature. The hotter the temperature during incubation, the greater the likelihood of hatchlings turning out female. "Hot chicks and cool dudes," he said. "It's been so darn hot this year that most all the hatchlings this season have been females, hot chicks."

* * *

To call a pretty woman a fox used to be a thing, too, and might still be a thing, which is odd, as foxes, technically, are dogs. Yet foxes share various qualities with cats. Gray foxes can retract their claws, like cats. They use the whiskers on their faces and legs to navigate, like cats. The light way they amble on the balls of their feet is also quite catlike. Though seldom heard, foxes issue up to forty varieties of more doglike yaps, yelps, and howls, including a guttural chattering called gekkering.

* * *

The yelp that jolted me awake in the predawn darkness, I was fairly certain, came from Wendy, though in our many years together I'd never heard quite this utterance from her throat. I bolted toward the sound in my underwear to discover in Eva's bathroom that our daughter had located a pair of scissors on Wendy's work-desk and cut off practically all her hair, her beautiful auburn shock of tight, shoulder-length curls shorn now above her small ears. She stood there with Wendy before the mirror, an inscrutable look on her face, one that I'd identify as awe if I were hard-pressed to tag an emotion to the blank stare.

Here was one of those times as a parent when you're called upon to remain calm. The damage, after all, had already been done. Yet it was impossible for me, being me, to remain calm. I didn't yell. Not exactly. But I fired a dizzying series of questions and comments toward Eva. *Why did you do this to yourself? If you want to cut your hair you have to ask us. Are you trying to tell us something? Did you see this on TikTok? Did one of your friends put you up to this? Do you not like being a girl? Speak!*

Eva couldn't possibly process the barrage.

"Andy," my wife said, silencing me. Wendy, per usual, performed calm with much greater expertise. She stroked Eva's back, spoke to her in soothing sentences. We weren't angry, she assured our daughter. Only concerned. We only wanted to understand why she did this, what she was feeling. Eva claimed not to know why she chopped off all her hair. It wasn't something she planned on doing or even thought about. She just did it. Her eyes seemed full, though she wasn't crying. I couldn't tell whether she was upset by what she'd impulsively done, the dramatic results she could see in the mirror—stray ribbons of unevenly shorn curls flying every which way—or only upset by the interrogation, all the unwanted attention raining down on her now from her parents, attention she'd grown so good at avoiding behind her closed bedroom door. *No thank you!*

Our daughter didn't understand why we were making such a big deal out of it. I knew enough not to rile Eva further. Maybe it wasn't such a big deal. I didn't wish to argue. Yet, it was hard for me at the time not to see her predawn act as a self-inflicted violence.

* * *

Sarcoptes scabiei. A microscopic parasite that infects foxes and other wild mammals with mange. Mange is a devastating affliction that causes intense skin irritation, patchy, and sometimes complete, hair loss. A fox will do nearly anything to relieve itself of the itching. A fox will bite off its own tail. A mange-afflicted fox, without treatment, will surely die, typically from starvation or hypothermia. The U.S. federal government, to protect the interests of ranchers, intentionally inflicted mange upon the foxes, wolves, and coyotes in the western states up through the mid-1900s. "Land managers," Raven writes, "collected sheep and cattle carcasses and infected them with mange-carrying mites—*Sarcoptes scabiei*. They left the infected carcasses near dens. Foxes, wolves, and coyotes fed on the infected carcasses. Mites jumped off the carcasses and onto the living animals. Wrapping their six dirty legs around as many hairs on as many wolves, foxes, and coyotes as they could reach, mites injected *Sarcoptes* bacteria into the predators' bloodstreams."

* * *

Foxes have been around for millions of years the fossil record suggests, since the late Miocene in North America and the Old World. They've only had to deal with us for a fraction of this time. Our early years together weren't so bad. Some 16,000 years ago, a fox was laid carefully in a grave beside a Paleolithic woman in what is now Jordan. Scholars speculate that foxes might have been partly domesticated by these ancient peoples. Our forebears might have appreciated that foxes killed and ate rodents. It might have been nice to have them around the cave, nice enough to feed them tastier scraps from the larger animals we hunted. Foxes play important roles in Aesop's tales, Old English literature, and the oral tales of Indigenous peoples from North America to Japan. Foxes, in these tales, range from wise and benevolent figures to tricksters. The Blackfoot and Apache tribes associate Fox with fire and the sun, while the Arapaho associate Fox with the sacred pipe.

Still, the more recent track record of our human relations with foxes hasn't been so hot. Our rapacious agricultural and ranching pursuits across the globe the past 10,000 years or so have put us at odds with the various species of fox. One would suppose that a culture with a long-standing adage about foxes and henhouses isn't likely to be a culture that treats foxes very well. In the United States and United Kingdom alone, they have been shot, poisoned, trapped, and bludgeoned to death as nuisances, bred and slaughtered for their fur, hunted for "sport." The traditional British foxhunt involving horses, hounds, and men in fancy black and red apparel is probably the type of foxhunting most familiar to readers. During these hunts over the past 300 years, foxes are often ripped to shreds by the hounds, disemboweled while still alive, doomed to experience a most brutal, cruel death. While the Hunting Act of 2004 banned the chasing and killing of wild animals by packs of dogs in England, various exemptions exist, and illegal foxhunting continues as well. In the United States, "penning" is the even crueler practice of setting dogs against foxes or coyotes in enclosures from which they can't escape and deriving pleasure (I suppose) from watching the dogs maul their victims to death. While animal welfare organizations work to pass legislation outlawing the practice, there are still nineteen U.S. states in which penning is legal.

Small wonder that the foxes in my neighborhood, and elsewhere, don't much like to be seen by us.

* * *

I pretty much gave up on seeing a fox in my neighborhood. Then I ran into a neighbor roughly my age, Dale, at the side of his house. He was just getting back from walking his golden retriever. I know Dale. He's a nice guy, an arborist who's given me some tips on how I might prune, though not butcher, my live oaks to help the hurricane-force winds pass through them. He lives close to where Wendy and Eva claimed to have seen the fox months ago. I'm not sure why I hadn't asked him earlier about foxes in our neighborhood, but I asked him now if he'd ever seen foxes here.

"Oh yeah, sure," he said, our impatient dogs bucking against their leashes. "They have a nest or den or whatever in the Millers' backyard behind ours, under their wooden deck."

"Wait, what?" I asked, flabbergasted by the matter-of-factness of Dale's report.

"They raise a new litter every season," he continued. He told me that he'd seen one of the adults darting across the street at night any number of times. Pretty small, he said. Pretty scruffy looking. He thought, as I'd suspected, too, that they probably hunted for frogs and rats and whatnot in the drainage canal just a half-block away from where we were standing. The Millers' house fronts the one-way street, the thicket of tall grasses, cacti, and non-native trees, and the canal, I realized, gazing behind Dale's backyard into the general vicinity of what must be the Millers' backyard.

We talked for a while longer about the foxes. Dale agreed that it was pretty cool that foxes lived here. He liked seeing them when he saw them. Some neighbors, however, worried about their cats, he said. Some neighbors worried about rabies. Some neighbors worried about their young children. Some neighbors, he said, don't like the fact that wild foxes lived in our midst.

* * *

Foxes are about the same size as cats and don't prey upon them. It's coyotes cat-owners should worry about. (Cats shouldn't be let outdoors, anyway, given the ravages they inflict upon wild birds.) It's true that foxes occasionally succumb to rabies, but they account for only about 7 percent of cases reported to the CDC. Of the twenty-three rabies-related pet deaths reported between 2009 and 2018, none were attributed to foxes, while eight were attributed to dogs. Rabid foxes will, on very rare occasions, attack unsuspecting humans, as a quick search on YouTube reveals. In April of 2022, occasioning perhaps the worst recent bit of PR for foxes, authorities were forced to euthanize a rabid red fox and her kits in Washington, D.C., after she bit nine people around Capitol Hill and exhibited generally aggressive and odd behavior toward countless other tourists and politicos.

All the same, the more I talked with people about foxes and read about foxes—from recent memoirs to classic children's books (e.g., Roald Dahl's *Fantastic Mr. Fox*, Colin Dann's multibook series, *The Animals of Farthing Wood*)—the more I shamelessly scrolled through post after post on fox-themed Instagram and other social media platforms, the clearer it became that we mostly marvel over the presence of these wild creatures across the bruised and battered environments we occupy in the Anthropocene. The wild animals native to Florida—from manatees to seaside sparrows—have had a particularly rough go of it, thanks largely to our encroachment, the manifold deleterious ways in which we've altered the landscapes and waterscapes up and down the peninsula. How wondrous that gray foxes still make a go of it here. They evoke for us the wildness near at hand that we still hope to retain. A color photo of a wild gray fox bounding across the wild grasses of Yamato Scrub just a few miles from my home graces the Palm Beach County Natural Areas home page.

What's more, three rescued gray fox orphans were recently released at the Okeeheelee Nature Center in the western part of my county, a small patch of green surrounded by strip malls and stucco developments. The goal, a news article in the *Sun Sentinel* reveals, was for the foxes to reestablish a small population in the pine flatwoods here, joining the small population of bobcats and other small mammals. "There's no reason to think these guys won't do well," the manager of the Okeeheelee Nature Center tells the reporter. Most of us are clearly rooting for the foxes, in my county and elsewhere.

* * *

Wendy and I were rooting for Eva, of course, as all parents root for their children. It just wasn't so easy to know how best to extend our love toward her. Clearly, she was going through a confusing time. Like many tween girls today, she was launched into puberty at an age that seemed to me impossibly young, impossibly cruel. We discussed privately whether gender confusion and/or body dysmorphia accounted for her rash act with the scissors in the predawn darkness. Comically, at least in retrospect, we brainstormed the manifold things we ought to say and do, and the things we ought not to say or do—hip progressive parents that we were—to support our youngest child in her (or his, or their) journey of self-exploration and self-actualization.

Was Eva a hot chick or a cool dude?

As Eva only expressed her feelings verbally to us under great duress, we floated to her the idea of seeing a therapist. "Just to have someone you can talk to besides us," Wendy exhorted. "Ugh," Eva replied. She didn't want to see a therapist. She was fine, she insisted. And, well, she might have been fine, it occurred to us as the months passed, as she decided to let her curly hair grow. "You sure you don't want to keep your hair short?" I asked. "No," she said. "Because if you want to keep your hair short, it's totally up to you," I said, because that's the sort of father I wanted to be. "Cool," Eva replied. "Mom can take you to Curls Rock," I continued. "It's your hair," I said, "your decision." "Cool," she replied again. She'd started to say "cool" an awful lot, suddenly, which I never knew quite how to interpret. There was something dismissive in it maybe. Something not-cool.

Life marched on. Eva turned twelve. She started a new year at a new public middle school, in person. She wouldn't wear skirts to school, or even shorts, but she developed a fondness for eyeliner and lip gloss and ludicrously expensive facial moisturizers. Her swim league started back up and she surprised us by joining without resistance. She seemed to enjoy her practices and meets and, mostly, seeing her old swim friends again. She asked us to take her ice skating at a local rink, so we took her ice skating, which she liked enough that we signed her up for lessons. She seemed reasonably happy. She didn't excel at school, but she did okay. Okay, we decided, was okay. For now.

* * *

I continued, though half-assedly, to look for our neighborhood foxes. I began burying my snapper carcasses a bit shallower, making it easier on them to make their nighttime raids. It was no big deal, really, to rebury their leavings the next morning. Curiously enough, Eva about this time developed the rather infuriating fox-like habit of raiding our food-stores and leaving the evidence sloppily strewn about, too—empty Hershey bar wrappers, lava cake boxes, and ice cream cartons left behind in the freezer rather than thrown in the trash the sure mark of her midnight mischief. In any case, I ought to have installed a night-vision camera in the yard to check out the goings on, foxwise, while we slept. I ought to have headed over to the Millers to ask them all about their foxes, see if they'd mind if I poked around a bit for foxes in their backyard. But I didn't do either of these things, partly because I didn't know the Millers, partly out of laziness, partly because parenting and worrying over Eva, plus my university job, plus the business of my other children and my aging parents—all of which is to say, life—left me fully occupied.

I did manage to pick up the phone and speak with Dirck Aumiller, the Palm Beach County Parks district manager headquartered at Okeeheelee, as he happens to be an old friend of mine. I was curious as to whether the effort from a few years ago to rewild Okeeheelee with gray foxes, according to the report in the *Sun Sentinel,* had been successful. "Oh, yeah, they're definitely here now," Dirck told me. He'd only seen one once, trotting across one of the service roads at the park early in the morning. But one of his coworkers, who walked for exercise at Okeeheelee in the predawn darkness to beat the heat, saw them pretty much every day. Other coworkers, he said, also saw them on occasion, usually at dusk or dawn. Such sightings, while common, were special enough to merit mention in the snack room or out and about on the park grounds. "They're pretty cool animals," Dirck said.

* * *

I finally saw one of our neighborhood foxes early one morning while I was walking alone with Storm. The day's first light was just starting to bleed into the sky. He, or she, appeared for only an instant, trotting onto the asphalt road from an easement of overgrown shrubbery and a couple nice slash pines on the left side of the road some twenty yards ahead of Storm and me. Just as quickly, the creature disappeared into an easement on the right side of the road, heading in the general direction of the Millers' backyard it occurred to me. I'd like to say that this wild animal and I exchanged a meaningful glance, something like the gaze exchanged between Raven and Fox in *Fox & I*, which sears Fox's face into Raven's memory, or something at least like the shorter gaze Annie Dillard shares with a weasel in one of her most famous essays. But the wild creature in my neighborhood didn't seem to notice me at all, or glance even to the left or right to check for traffic as it trotted quickly onto and across the asphalt street. Neither did Storm seem to notice the fox. All I really noticed about it was the red-tinged gray of its fur, the outrageously thick tail, and the way its back hardly seemed to undulate as it moved. It's hard to describe, but something about its ambulation seemed undoglike and, yes, wild.

* * *

Foxes, to Thoreau, epitomized wildness. He sought them out throughout his short lifetime, traced their tracks in the snow to glean what they had to teach. Foxes dig their own burrows, he notes in an early journal entry, which offers him further encouragement to build his own house beside Walden Pond. He laments the senseless brutality of a fox hunt in the "Winter Animals" chapter of his most famous book, which documents his two-years' and two-month residence on the pond's shore. Prior to his habitation at the pond, while on a two-week boating excursion with his elder brother on the Concord and Merrimack Rivers, an encounter with a fox reaffirms his longing to establish a more harmonious, reciprocal relationship with these wild creatures as he recounts in his journal: "While I write here, I hear the foxes trotting about me over the dead leaves, and now gently over the grass, as if not to disturb the dew which is falling. Why should we not cultivate neighborly relations with the foxes? As if to improve upon our seeming advances, comes one to greet us nosewise under our tent-curtain. Nor do we rudely repulse him. Is man powder and the fox flint and steel? Has not the time come when men and foxes shall lie down together?"

* * *

Flash forward to the present and Raven in the backwoods of Montana, a place wilder than both present-day Palm Beach County, Florida, and mid-nineteenth-century Concord, Massachusetts. Raven, like Thoreau, wonders why we don't cultivate more neighborly relations with wild (what she calls "unboxed") animals. "Maybe," she speculates, "we like pretending that they are not very human. Or that we are not very wild." I love this passage from *Fox & I*, which crystallizes the sentiment that seems to propel her narrative into being. Throughout, Raven implores us to reconsider the impermeable boundaries we've invested so much energy in upholding between the human and animal realms, encourages, instead, the radical intermingling at the heart of *this* book too. Indeed, I'm probably Raven's perfect audience, as I seek constant contact with what wildness I might access near at hand.

Even so, my decidedly more constructed environs, the embattled lives that foxes (and other "unboxed" animals) bravely pursue on my coastal ridge crammed with people, compels me to wonder, too, whether the problem between foxes and us isn't so much the impermeable barrier we've upheld between the wild and human realms but that no barrier exists now at all. City and suburban foxes, anyway, have had too much of us. "We are redesigning the fox," Brand observes. She alludes here mostly to their behaviors—their diet, territories, lifespan, and social interactions—but recent research suggests that we may be changing their very anatomy. The snouts of city foxes in London, specifically, seem to have been selected to be broader and shorter than the snouts of rural foxes, presumably on account of the advantage such snouts offer for rooting through trash bins. Just as we unintentionally cultivate weeds through our gardening, as Michael Pollan has suggested, we may be in the process of cultivating *Vulpes domesticus*. I find this terrifying. Sure, I've read Bill McKibben's classic, *The End of Nature* (1989). I know that from a zero-sum perspective there *is* no "wild" anymore, no parcel of land or drop of sea or carbon-based organism that has eluded our human touch. Something there is, however, that wants what was once-wild to remain as wild as possible. At the end of Mary Oliver's poem, "October," the poet sees a fox, who doesn't see her, and she relishes rather than laments this moment of noncontact. Here's the final stanza: "so this is the world. / I'm not in it. / It is beautiful." How wild is a fox that digs its burrow beneath the wooden deck in a Boca Raton backyard, a fox that digs up snapper carcasses I've buried in my front yard? As wild as we can let it be.

* * *

I didn't see our wild or semiwild neighborhood fox again over the following weeks, and months, though I was plenty busy observing the feral creature living under my own roof. Eva, that whole first year of middle school, still stayed in her room and on her electronics more than we preferred, but when it wasn't too hot, she could be coaxed into the occasional walk around the neighborhood. Sometimes on these walks we enjoyed what might be called an actual conversation. She'd decided that she didn't like the heat of Florida and probably wouldn't live here when she grew up. She'd decided that she didn't like Chipotle anymore (thank heavens!), but tacos were still her favorite food. She'd decided (largely on account of her hair) that she might be biracial and subjected her mother and me, repeatedly, to complicated genealogical queries. She'd decided to wear oversized, nonprescription eyeglasses each day to school. I found the twelve-year-old Eva more mysterious than our neighborhood foxes by far, and endlessly fascinating. Often, while I was driving her to her bus stop in the morning, while she listened through earbuds to the playlist she'd carefully curated on her smartphone, she'd catch me glancing her way for just a second or two too long.

"What?" she'd say, turning to face me, staring me down through the clear lenses of her clunky eyeglasses. "Nothing," I'd say, returning my eyes to the road. I'd lift a fist between us, inviting a fist-bump to wish her a good day at school. She'd rebuff the gesture, push my fist away, but usually with a wry expression on her face.

* * *

I was finally fortunate enough to run into Mrs. Miller—or Diane, as she introduced herself—while I was walking Storm one evening, while my neighbor was retrieving her mail. She was a white woman in her sixties or maybe her early seventies with short, frosted blonde hair. I introduced myself and we talked on her driveway for a while about foxes under the shade of her pretty live oak. Oh, yes, she told me, gripping the stack of mail in her hand, I'd heard correctly from Dale. The foxes nested under her backyard deck pretty much every season, though she hadn't seen them in a few months. "Lots of red on them," she said. "Really skittish," she said. She and her husband offered them a wide berth, hardly ventured into the backyard at all the months they set up housekeeping. They liked to observe them from the kitchen window, but even from inside the house they had to be very careful. The foxes sometimes bolted upon sensing their slightest movement. She marveled over the sharpness of their vision. Our conversation veered toward Storm, whom she'd been petting all the while we talked, a rescue from Hurricane Harvey in the Houston area, I told her. Diane and her husband loved dogs, had always raised basset hounds, but their last one died recently. I said I was sorry. I said that she and her husband might consider adopting a beagle, because beagles were hounds too, and because the news had just broken that some 4,000 beagles rescued from a research laboratory in Virginia needed homes. But I ought not to have mentioned the beagles, or the research laboratory, as it prompted Diane to vent about the horrible experiments they must have been conducting on those poor beagles: "Dr. Fauci stuff," she said, shivering as if from the nonexistent cold, alluding to any number of conspiracy theories about Dr. Fauci and the COVID-19 research conducted by the NIAID (National Institute of Allergy and Infectious Diseases) and the CDC. For a split second, I considered whether I should ask her to clarify her remark, then just as quickly reconsidered. I couldn't imagine any conversation between us on the topic of Dr. Fauci going to any good place and, truthfully, I didn't have the stomach for it. I thanked my neighbor for talking to me about her foxes and for looking out for the foxes and I headed with Storm on our way. Oh, hell! I thought as I continued down the one-way street, sniffing at the ripe odors of the nearby drainage canal. Why couldn't this just have been a nice neighborly moment. Why did things always have to be so complicated?

* * *

She's a complicated creature, Eva. A special snowflake, Wendy and I like to call her. She's in seventh grade, as I write these lines, and seems to be in a pretty good place, moodwise. I don't kid myself into thinking that we're out of the woods with her just yet. Still, it's not so bad to be in the woods with our younger daughter. Why is it, anyway, that we're always trying to get *out* of the woods? The woods are a good place to be, I say. She's developed a fierce passion for anime, or maybe its manga. I'm not sure whether there's a difference. I ask her one morning while I drive her to the bus stop whether it's manga or anime she likes, whether there's a difference. She pulls out her earbuds, vaguely annoyed, asks me to repeat the question, which I do. Then she surprises me by explaining the difference between manga and anime in three or four actual sentences. It may be our finest moment together in weeks, I realize, as we reach her bus stop at the corner. "Fist-bump," I say after I park, raising my fist, which she pushes, playfully, away. I watch as she swings open her door, straps on her ridiculously large backpack.

"Look both ways!" I can't keep myself from shouting out my open window for Eva and all her schoolmates to hear, which prompts both a groan and a glare from her quarter. I've embarrassed her, spoiled our moment, yet she never, *never* looks past her regrown curtain of curly hair to check for cars before she crosses the street. Like our gray fox I've still glimpsed only that once, she just dashes straight ahead and hopes for the best, and hell if I'll hold my tongue. Because that's the whole deal, maybe, raising kids or kits. I've figured this much out anyway. At the end of the day, you just want them to look both ways before they cross the street. You just want them to be okay.

Being with Yourself

15

A Highly Selective Field Guide to Florida's Feral Creatures

Florida boasts myriad native creatures—finned, feathered, and furred. You hold many of these nonhuman animals close to your heart: manatees and mahi mahi and alligators and roseate spoonbills and loggerhead turtles and panthers. Oh my! You and your fellow human residents celebrate these native Floridians on T-shirts, coffee mugs, special-order license plates, and in paintings, photographs, poems, and essays, a few of which you've written. Then there are those other creatures, the feral, non-native creatures that make a go of it here the best they can. Some of these critters were introduced to Florida by your human (non-native) predecessors going as far back as Ponce de Leon and Hernando de Soto. Most of these feral/non-native/exotic/invasive creatures (the terminology one chooses often suggests one's feelings about them) aren't so much celebrated by Floridians as they're tolerated, negotiated, controlled, culled, and/or avoided. While, sure, you favor our native Florida animals too—just as you favor native plants—the ones who are "supposed to be here," as you've uttered on more than one occasion, there's something not-quite-right, you increasingly feel, about your derision for our non-native animals conducting their earth business in our company, something that reveals, you're beginning to suspect, a whole lot more about you than the animals in question. In the spirit of collegiality—if not quite love—you wish to offer this brief field guide to Florida's most prevalent feral creatures.

* * *

European Starling. *Sturnus vulgaris.*
 A medium-sized songbird. Greenish-black overall, the speckled feathers iridescent or oily. The bill: pointy, straight, and yellow, weirdly so given the otherwise dark coloring. A flock of a dozen pairs (or maybe

upward of a hundred) were released, the story goes, into New York's Central Park in the late nineteenth century by an aficionado of Shakespeare, this fellow determined to populate North America with every bird species mentioned in the great bard's plays. Starlings now boast one of the largest populations of any bird species on the continent. Somewhere near 85 million individuals thrive currently in diverse habitats everywhere from Mexico and Alaska out west to Newfoundland and in South Florida on the Atlantic side.

Fricking starlings! That's what you usually think about starlings. Thousands upon thousands of these speckled birds will darken broad patches of sky in downright apocalyptic, shape-shifting murmurations. If you're truly unlucky, masses of individuals from this murmuration will alight in one of your backyard trees, outnumbering the leaves, issuing their cacophony of odd (downright unbirdlike) croaks, bleats, gurgles, and carnivalesque sliding whistles, disrupting the blessed quiet you hoped to enjoy over your morning paper on the backyard patio.

Worse, starlings will invade the nest boxes you painstakingly built with saw, hammer, nail, and hinge, outcompeting the native woodpeckers and owls you had hoped to help conduct their love business. You can try to discourage starlings by climbing a ladder and removing their nesting material of leaves and branches before they start their breeding in earnest. You can climb the ladder again next week to frustrate them further. You can even remove the three, four, or five greenish or bluish starling eggs, if you have the stomach for that sort of thing. In any case, you'll ultimately fail at all such efforts. Because you have other things to do, so so so many other things to do, while the starlings are only busy being starlings.

That's the thing about starlings. They're so darned good at being starlings. Much better at it than you are at being you. You might learn something by watching and listening to starlings. Look again at those liquid murmurations oozing across the sky. Listen again to their unbirdlike croaks, bleats, gurgles, and sliding whistles. It's tough not to see and hear something audacious and joyful in starling-ness.

Oh, and that story of the Shakespeare aficionado releasing that first starling flock? That's bullshit, apparently, or at least mostly bullshit, according to research conducted by an English professor, John MacNeill Miller, and his student, Lauren Fugate, published in 2021. But don't let the inconvenient facts discourage you from passing along this story to others kind enough to listen as you prattle on about these feral Florida creatures. It's still a good story, you think—a story worthy of these avian North American conquerors. These fricking amazing starlings.

* * *

Green Iguana. *Iguana iguana.*

A large green lizard with dark black rings on the tail and rows of spikes down the neck and back. Mature specimens sometimes sport orange and pink colorations. Males develop jowls and a throat fan, called a dewlap. Native to tropical regions of South America, Central America, and some eastern Caribbean islands. First reported in Florida in the 1960s, the exotic pet trade the likely culprit. Many released by private owners, who may not have bargained on caring for a creature reaching upward of fifteen pounds and five feet in length and living for twenty years or longer.

The iguana population has exploded since you arrived here in the mid-1990s, to the point that they've long ago crossed the threshold from "exotic" to "invasive." The most positive spin you might put on this is that they're job-creators, as a plethora of iguana removal businesses continue to crop up. "Like all nonnative reptile species," the FWC (Florida Fish and Wildlife Conservation Commission) states in highlighted prose on its website, "green iguanas are not protected in Florida except by anti-cruelty law and can be humanely killed on private property with landowner permission."

The iguanas you cross paths with aren't quite as frightened by you as you think they ought to be. They tend to hold their ground on the sidewalk or street or backyard patio (onto which they enthusiastically defecate) rather than skitter off. They keep absolutely still upon your approach, as if they might think they're invisible, or maybe they believe that between the two of you, *you* are the creature who ought to flee. They seek refuge from the Florida heat by sliding into the municipal swimming pool smack in the middle of open-swim hours. While you stare lazily down at the lane-line through your goggles, a large specimen might give you a jolt by slithering snakelike across your field of view in the chlorinated blue below. If the lifeguard doesn't clear the pool and you're brave enough to continue your exercise, you keep an eye on it the whole while. It will likely settle at the grotto of the deep end, where it holds its breath for what seems like forever. (Iguanas can do so for up to four hours according to experts.)

Iguanas are herbivores, a nice thing to remember during encounters on land or in water. Still, what this means in practical terms is that they'll invade your garden before your seedlings even have time to flower and fruit, defoliating every last leaf on every last branch of your tomato and pepper plants, turning them into hat-racks for the toads opines your adolescent daughter. Here's where your wife informs you that tomatoes are nightshades and that iguanas really shouldn't eat their leaves because they're poisonous. Here's where you reply, "Great, I'll let them know."

Iguanas can't handle the cold. Freezing or even near-freezing temperatures put them into torpor. They'll fall straight out of the trees, often recovering days later once the temperatures rise, as temperatures always do in South Florida. After one recent cold spell, a stunned iguana (which likely fell out of your tall laurel oak) lay on its stomach on your front yard deck for hours. You warn your daughter to keep clear of the medium-sized specimen, as some iguanas carry salmonella and may transmit this life-threatening bacterial infection upon contact. You leave the scaly green popsicle alone to see if it might recover. You go outside to check on your iguana every hour upon the hour. A full day of warmer weather passes and the iguana still hasn't moved. Then another day passes. There's no reason to mourn a dead iguana, you realize. Yet, looming over it, you exclaim— improbably, illogically, even ludicrously—"live, live, live. . . ."

* * *

Cane toad. *Rhinella marina.*

Native to rural and agrarian outposts in South America's Amazon basin and northward to the Rio Grande Valley in southern Texas. Introduced (myopically) to Florida by sugarcane growers in the 1930s and 1940s as a natural pesticide. A large, dare I say fat, toad reaching up to nine inches in length. In addition to insects, cane toads will also eat, well, anything they can gobble down their throats, including other frogs and toads, small birds, lizards, snakes, insects, and the cat food that humans leave outside to nourish our population of wild bird–killing outdoor cats. (See the Feral Cat entry below.)

Pity the poor cane toad, whom you'll likely first encounter smeared across the asphalt of whatever street you happen to be walking upon. Displaced, to be sure, in our bustling metropolitan region of South Florida. You're predisposed to like frogs and toads, having read Arnold Lobel's classic children's book series, *Frog and Toad*. So you learn to spot those orange eyes bounce-bounce-bouncing in the beam of your headlights as it crosses the street. You try your best to avoid squishing cane toads. Yet

Lobel's books didn't prepare you for the havoc cane toads can wreak all the while they manage to avoid becoming roadkill. You panic one day when you notice from the kitchen window something odd about your dog in the backyard, the way she shakes her head, the cottony saliva she sheds with each strange twist of her maw. You rush to her aid and notice her frothy mouth, her visible distress. You think rabies because you've seen *Old Yeller*. You call the veterinarian's office and the receptionist tells you straight away that your dog likely tried to eat a cane toad, which she calls a marine toad, that these exotic toads sport glands across their skin which secrete bufotoxin poison to keep predators from eating them, and that what you need to do without delay is rinse your dog's mouth thoroughly and vigorously with torrents of fresh water from a garden hose for at least ten minutes. You do this and it seems to work, but you still take your dog to the vet, who checks the poor girl's gums, then tells you that no further intervention is necessary, that your dog will be just fine and likely won't be bothering cane toads anymore.

You'll share the dramatic story with a neighbor the next day, how you rescued your poor dog from certain death, but your neighbor remains unflappable. "Oh yeah," he says, "we had to do that to our dog too," as if this is something that everyone in Florida knows, and experiences, that time to time your dog in Florida will attack an invasive toad armed with poisonous skin, which will require your intervention with a garden hose. You'll contemplate how strange it is that dogs have acquired all sorts of advantageous traits over the ages but not the ability to spit, and that maybe, all things considered, this is a good thing. You'll still try to avoid running over cane toads in the street, but you won't try quite so hard anymore. You'll feel bad about this.

* * *

Lionfish. *Pterois voliltans.*

Lionfish, it must first be said, are gorgeously strange aquatic animals. Zebra-striped in purple and white. Eighteen feathery spines laced with venom protrude quite a distance from the dorsal, pectoral, and anal fins, so that lionfish look as much like decorative balloons or piñatas as they do piscine creatures. Native to the Indo-Pacific and Red Sea. First seen inhabiting the nearshore reefs of South Florida in 1985 (no one knows how they got here), proliferating at a randy rate since the mid-2000s. Lionfish are breeders par excellence. Females release two mossy egg masses into the open current, sending upward of 15,000 eggs in each mass to seek their fortune. The larvae hatch and grow into carnivorous eating machines up to a foot or more in length. On the reef, they outcompete native Florida fish, such as snapper and grouper, partly by eating them, fanning their pectoral fins and even blowing water onto prey (the only marine species known to do this) to herd them into position for the kill. Lionfish will prey upon fish over half their own size. That lionfish can decimate populations of native algae-eating fish crucial to maintaining reef health is of particular concern. Meanwhile, few aquatic predators (including sharks) seem willing to prey upon lionfish, which would mean taking on those toxic spines. And who could blame them?

This leaves only you.

The FWC encourages you to remove lionfish to reduce their negative impacts to native marine life and ecosystems. Hook and line doesn't work. Lionfishing is a spearfisherman's game. Spearfishermen, and women, who impale lionfish by the hundreds from nearshore reefs, are Florida's eco-warriors. They occupy a moral high ground that approximates the high ground held by your neighbors who carry buckets along the tideline, scouring the beach for plastics and other trash they lean down to collect while other beachgoers lounge about or take selfies, or take selfies lounging about. When you glimpse a diver emerge from the reef or bridge-piling from your own small boat, a spiny assortment of lionfish shish-kebabed to her spear, you power down to idle and shout a hearty, "Thank you!"

You're not a diver or a spearfisherman. But you like to eat. Lionfish flesh, you learn, is free of the toxin of lionfish spines, perfectly safe to eat, succulent as snapper. In the spirit of civic duty, you buy lionfish on the relative cheap at your local Whole Foods grocery store. The fillets, as advertised, are delicious. You sauté them with lemon, capers, butter, and parsley. You coat them with Mexican spices and stuff them into tortillas along with guacamole, tomatoes, and cheese to make the fish tacos your younger daughter savors. You dredge them in flour and egg to prepare them Francese, serving the golden-fried fillets atop a bed of linguine.

* * *

Wild hog. *Sus scrofa*.

Also called feral hog, feral swine, wild boar, or, most evocatively, piney woods rooter. Introduced to the Florida peninsula by the first Spanish conquistadors in the 1500s, maybe by Hernando de Soto himself. Wild hogs now live in every Florida county, the statewide population exceeding 500,000 individuals, second in size only to Texas. Adult hogs can weigh over 150 pounds and reach six feet in length. Considered invasive.

"I'll have to get out there and bust a cap in him." This is what the young, male, white, ginger-bearded Everglades National Park ranger says to you at the Shark Valley Visitor's Center, just off the historic Tamiami Trail highway. You've just told him that you were somewhat surprised to see a rusty-haired wild hog rooting around the sawgrass just off the bicycle trail. The scruffy berm of the bicycle trail was lined with behemoth alligators, too, which you expected to see. Their distended stomachs looked like they might contain a wild hog or two. The ranger's words about busting a cap in the wild hog takes you aback as you're relatively new to Florida. You don't know yet that wild hogs are non-native Florida creatures, that they possess ravenous appetites and eat pretty much anything, that they cause terrific damage to native grasses and other groundcover because they don't so much graze upon them as they rip them out by their roots with their broad snouts, leaving swaths of bare muddy earth in their wake the size of football fields, that they consume the eggs and chicks of ground-nesting birds in the wetlands, plus sea turtle eggs and hatchlings along the coast, that their feces—chock-full of harmful bacteria—pollutes waterways and transmits disease to native animal species. The ginger-bearded ranger tells you all this while you nod and make listening noises.

"Thanks for letting us know about it," he says in closing, jotting down the precise location of your sighting in his spiral-bound notebook so he might bust a cap in the feral creature after the park closes for the day.

You don't eat meat for any number of reasons, but when your Trinidadian friend invites you and your family some months later to dinner, which features wild hog, you make an exception. Because you don't want to be rude, and it's not a factory-farmed animal, and, sure, you're curious about the taste. (He tells you, incidentally, that plenty of people, though not him, eat iguana in Trinidad, too, which they call Caribbean chicken.) He tells you that he hunted the wild hog at a private wild hog hunting operation near Lake Okeechobee. A quick internet search reveals scores upon scores of wild hog hunting charters throughout the state on cattle ranches and other private property featuring diverse habitats ranging from palmetto and pine woods to open prairie and swampland. Hunting runs year-round and licenses are not required as wild hog is considered a "nuisance" species. Several of these outfits guarantee a kill and will process and even taxidermy your prize for an extra charge.

Most hunters use rifles or shotguns, but you can also use a bow, crossbow, or even a spear or knife if you're into that sort of thing. You can hunt from a blind, stalk your prey on foot, or ride a swamp buggy or other ATV. Some hunters deploy hunting dogs to sniff out wild hog. The Southwest Florida Water Management District, in fact, sponsors dog-assisted hog hunts on district property to thin the feral hog population. The FWC, too, allows for wild hog hunting in various wildlife management areas across the state. You detect a degree of cognitive dissonance between the claims about wild hog's nuisance status and Florida's wild hog hunting industry, a private and state-sponsored enterprise. The 500,000-plus wild hogs roaming every county of Florida, that is, must constitute a threat to the embattled natural environments of the state; yet monied interests clearly depend upon and maintain this feral population.

At your friend's barbecue, you and your family sit along two conjoined picnic tables in his West Palm Beach backyard beneath towering slash pines and shorter exotic fruit trees he's planted to remind him of Trinidad. Your friend deposits an enormous slab of charred wild hog meat onto an oversized aluminum foil-lined sheet pan in the middle of the conjoined tables. It's not totally clear which part of the beast this slab represents, and you try not to wonder too much about it. Other guests tear into the slab straight away (this is clearly not their first wild hog barbecue), forking great chunks of meat onto their paper plates. The flesh, you notice, looks juicy and oleaginous as it peels so easily by fork from the slab. You serve yourself a healthy portion, eat the entirety of it along with macaroni and cheese. Wild hog, you discover, is delicious. But you probably ate too much, because you barely make it home in time to vomit violently into the toilet. In fairness, your wife and kids ate the wild hog and don't feel sick. Your digestive system isn't used to meat proteins anymore. Your gastrointestinal distress probably says more about your own constitution than it does about wild hog meat or your friend's cooking. Still, you won't be eating wild hog again.

* * *

Burmese python. *Python bivittatus.*

One of the largest snakes in the world. Those caught in Florida average between six and nine feet in length. Tan, with dark blotches along sides and back. Semiaquatic, hence their love of your Everglades. Pythons in the Florida wild started out as pets, enough escapees or releases to establish a robust breeding population. These voracious predators today hunt a wide array of native mammals, birds, and reptiles, including alligators, threatening the balance of this already embattled ecology. Their taste for the endangered Key Largo woodrat and the competition they present to the endangered indigo snake is of particular concern. Pythons have become such a problem that the FWC contracts licensed hunters to help thin the population and have even instituted the Florida Python Challenge, an annual ten-day python "removal" competition boasting a grand prize of ten thousand dollars. Participants, after completing the required online training, use air guns and/or captive bolt weapons to dispatch as many pythons as they can locate.

Here's the tricky part. Locating pythons. All you hear about pythons are two, seemingly contradictory, factoids: (1) they're taking over the Everglades, and (2) they're nearly impossible to find. You can be standing practically right on top of a big one in the brush or muck and never know it's there, you've heard tell on countless newscasts. You think back at those dark blotches along the sides and backs of pythons. Good camouflage in the Everglades apparently. Ten thousand dollars notwithstanding, you have no desire to dispatch pythons with an air gun or captive bolt weapon. You have no desire to *see* a python in the Everglades, or anywhere else. But you do find yourself marveling over the python's skulky ways, so different from the ways of that other non-native animal resident of Miami-Dade County, the peacock—screaming their presence both aurally and visually. You wonder. Are you, by nature, a python or a peacock? A python, most definitely a python. Sealing yourself behind the closed door of your study as you do. You don't care much for attention. Have you been too much of a python? While python-ness works terrifically well for pythons, it's worked less well for you maybe. Trouble is, you don't like (figurative) peacocks. Who does? Even so, there might be something to be said for cultivating, in careful proportion, the life strategies of both pythons and peacocks.

* * *

Florida rat. *Rattus Floridus.*

There's no such thing as a Florida rat per se. You've made this up. Still, "Florida rat" is how you refer to all these chunky rodents you spy outdoors. You do this, it takes some time to realize, to maintain the fiction that the rats you see may be the native and endangered woodrats (which build impressive twig and branch domiciles in the hardwood hammock of Key Largo) or even the arguably native, and far more prevalent, palm rats, rather than the feral Norway rats that have proliferated across Florida's cities and suburbs. It feels better to think of Florida rats as naturally occurring rather than invasive creatures, out there foraging upon the fruits of palm, cocoplum, Geiger tree, and mango (all of which they do eat) instead of whatever's inside your trash bin (which they also eat). Even so, you feel "zero at the bone," to quote Emily Dickinson, every time a Florida rat captures your gaze, skittering across paved road, electric line, or live oak branch, usually at dusk or dead of night when it thinks no one is looking.

They ask so little of us, really, Florida rats. They lay low, daytimes, in the shaggy heads of sabal palm foliage, or in some woodpecker's abandoned slash pine nest cavity, or, sure, in your overgrown vegetable garden, backyard shed, or under your foundation. They start rooting around at night to stake their modest claim. You don't live in Florida long before noticing the rats you learn to call Florida rats; next, you notice the black rectangular rat poison traps perched inconspicuously under shrubs near the corners of homes and buildings. Because no one likes a rat. Still, it isn't such a pretty thing to think about, a poor rat bleeding out internally from the poison we trick them into ingesting. So you try not to think about it. When this proves unsuccessful, you acknowledge the necessity of the eradication efforts, given the amorousness of Florida rats, the pathogens they transmit, the native mammals they outcompete for nuts, grains, and berries, the damage they may do to the wiring on your roof, to the roof itself, and to the insulation beneath, should they manage to breach your defenses. All the same, you wonder whether our enthusiasm for killing Florida rats may be outsized, precipitated by the cultural baggage we carry vis-à-vis rats dating back to the Black Death (bubonic plague), which was honestly more about the fleas than the rats; what's more, recent research attributes the Black Death, quite possibly, to a human parasite having nothing to do with fleas or rats at all, but whatever.

Something there is inside you that can't help rooting for these much-maligned Florida mammals.

Rats, to put it clinically, are cognitively advanced social animals. A group of rats is called a mischief. When they're happy, they relax their ears, which droop and pink up with color. They rate rather high on the scale of personal hygiene for a nonhuman (or even human) animal, licking their fur clean for hours upon hours of the day, even licking clean other rats in their mischief to reinforce social bonds. Rats mourn their significant dead. Rats are fantastic swimmers. Rats vocalize in ultrasonic frequencies to communicate a wide array of emotions, including fear, joy, and pain. The Florida city you've called home for nearly thirty years is the Spanish phrase for "rat mouth," which sounds much better in Spanish.

You sit one evening on a wicker chair beside your wife in your lighted screened-in backyard patio. She's reading while you're only pretending to be reading, because what you're truly doing is admiring the day's last light purpling the cumulous clouds across the horizon. The natural light finally oozes below your sightline, but just as you're about to turn your attention back to your book, you spy that unmistakable silhouette of a Florida rat streaking across the electric wire above your wooden fence (that naked tail dangling below). You shudder, per usual, but then you simply trace the creature's progress with your eyes. You keep still and hold your breath, partly because you've just glimpsed a Florida rat, but mostly because you worry that if you react more demonstrably to the sighting, your wife might glimpse it, then insist upon calling one of the manifold pest control services capitalizing upon our fears of any nonhuman creature we may encounter. Silently, you urge this feral Florida rodent along its peaceful way.

Go, Florida rat, go! . . . go! . . . go!

* * *

Muscovy duck. *Cairina moschata.*

A large, dark-feathered duck reaching nine pounds or more. Sports red, "warty" protuberances about its face called caruncles. Native to Mexico, Central and South America, and parts of Texas. Common across much of North America, and especially prolific in Florida, occupying a niche somewhere between exotic and invasive. Can crowd out and outcompete native species (avian and otherwise), transmit disease, and damage property, yet also beloved (especially the fuzzy ducklings) by several of Florida's human citizens. Mothers and toddlers frequently feed these waterfowl at manufactured ponds, canals, and even parking lots. They enjoy the protection of the federal Migratory Bird Species Act, but the U.S. Fish and Wildlife Service has put out a control order on them, giving private landowners broad authority to "remove or destroy" Muscovy ducks, nesting materials, and/or eggs from their property.

You notice these ducks almost immediately upon moving to South Florida. They're difficult to ignore, given their numbers and the slow, insouciant way they amble across asphalt streets to reach a new section of drainage canal, manufactured pond, or home lawn. Most drivers respect the right-of-way of Muscovy ducks, but not all drivers, the ones who see them as out-and-out nuisances, you suspect. Muscovy roadkill is a common sight, the greenish and purplish-black feathers of the squished creatures riffling in the breeze.

You harbor neither fondness nor animus for these exotic ducks. You do worry a bit about the welfare of the smaller, and fewer, native mottled ducks, whether and to what extent they're being bullied by these non-native bruisers. You certainly wouldn't encourage Muscovy ducks by feeding them in the manner that you feed painted buntings and cardinals. Which may be why you take notice of the elderly, diminutive Black woman walking back and forth through your neighborhood with plastic shopping bags full of whole loaves of bread, then take notice of her at various canal overpasses, the pond in front of the nearby hospital, and even at random roadside puddles. She tears ribbons of the bread she carries and feeds these ribbons to the Muscovy ducks that congregate at her feet, some of them swishing their broad tails, a gesture that indicates excitement you decide. You notice that she shoos away the native white ibises, who also congregate about her feet, her sympathies extending duckwards you glean, more so than native birdwards. One day as she passes your house on the sidewalk, you offer her a ride home, or a ride to wherever it is she's going. It's so hot today and she looks so tired and sweaty under the weight of her shopping bags. Even so, you're surprised when she takes you up on the offer. Her name is Daisy you learn during that first drive, which impels you (moronically) to say, "Hey, I guess I'm driving Miss Daisy." She directs an expression your way that betrays annoyance and amusement in ambiguous proportions.

For the next several years you will ferry Daisy at least once or twice a week to and from her various feeding stations and/or her small, ground-floor apartment, depending upon when you happen to cross her path while driving. In exchange for your efforts, she periodically offers you strange gifts—socks, deodorant, out-of-season holiday knickknacks—which you suspect she picks up at the local nonprofit food and resource center where you've seen her waiting outside in line. You accept these gifts because you'd be a jerk to refuse them. It's the same reason you help Daisy to feed the Muscovy ducks, who truly ought not to be fed by us. Daisy disappears well into her nineties after ten or so years of your routine, her phone disconnected. You know that she must have passed away, or perhaps (you hope), one of her children, two of whom you've met, all of whom live in England, have retrieved her. You're not a sentimentalist, so you don't take over Daisy's Muscovy duck feeding efforts in her absence. Yet it's not so easy to ignore these creatures. In certain local parking lots, they'll recognize your car and waddle over for their shards of stale bread before you can make a clean getaway. They'll make pleading gestures with their necks and warty faces, even swish those broad tails. Your heart will break a little every time you deny them, then will break a little more, mostly for Daisy, once these ducks finally get wise and give up on you.

* * *

Feral cat. *Felis catus.*

An unowned, unhomed domestic cat, which generally avoids human contact. A somewhat nebulous distinction exists between feral cats and those owned, homed domestic cats that nonetheless roam the outdoors unchaperoned; some unwritten proviso in Florida's social contract regards this free-roaming cat ownership practice as vaguely acceptable.

You notice the robust population of outdoor cats (feral and otherwise) shortly after you move to the Sunshine State. Outdoor cats in all shapes, sizes, and colors amble nonchalantly through your neighborhood and yard, and somewhat more sheepishly (probably the feral variety) about your college campus, strip mall, and community parks. You take notice of these outdoor cats mostly because you like wild birds and you don't like outdoor cats, because you can't like both wild birds and outdoor cats. The American Bird Conservancy estimates that cats in the United States kill over 2.4 billion birds (!) every year, making cat predation the largest human-caused threat by far to wild bird populations in the country. Both your daughters like to pet the friendly outdoor cats they meet on your neighborhood walks, which you allow even though it bothers you.

Removing cats from the outdoors seems a no-brainer to you. Yet outdoor cats—by virtue of having insinuated themselves into our social lives thousands of years before the birth of Christ—have their fierce proponents in Florida and elsewhere. This hits home upon spotting so many feral cat feeding stations under shrubs in your neighborhood, beneath picnic tables at local parks, and even under the foundation of a classroom building on your university campus. Trap, Neuter, Release (TNR), you learn, is an actual program endorsed by your Florida county and most other Florida counties to "stabilize" the population of feral cats. Once trapped, neutered, and vaccinated, an ear of these feral cats is notched to indicate that they've been sterilized and vaccinated; then, these wild bird killers are released back to the location where they were trapped. The American Bird Conservancy, The Audubon Society, The Cornell Lab of Ornithology, and pretty much every other wild bird organization, plus other wildlife organizations, plus you, staunchly oppose TNR programs.

You don't personally know anyone who advocates for TNR, until you do. She's your new dental hygienist. Roughly your age. White. Plump. Affable. It doesn't take long during your cleaning for her to work into your conversation her feral cat volunteer efforts. She spends a good bit of money and time tending to various feral cat feeding stations in the area and trapping new cats without the telltale notch on an ear. Clearly, this is her thing. She goes on and on about the poor feral cats while you sit there stewing over the welfare of the poor wild birds. You're about to bring up the birds. How could you not? Yet you hold your tongue, partly because this new dental hygienist is so earnest and, well, nice, and partly because she's plying your mouth with sharp dental instruments. This dental hygienist will take care of your teeth for years, and she'll always bring the conversation around to the poor feral cats and her heartfelt labors to improve their hardscrabble lives. There's not much else going on in her own life you suspect. So you'll make affirmative listening noises, mostly, as the little vacuum doohickey slurps up your saliva. You'll feel shitty that you can't bring yourself to stand up for the wild birds.

* * *

Egyptian goose. *Alopochen aegyptiaca.*

Not a goose, but a cross between a duck and a goose, called a shelduck, because this is a thing. Native to sub-Saharan Africa, the Nile valley, and parts of the Middle East. Introduced to parks, zoos, aviaries, and private properties in the United States as ornamental waterfowl. Now common in California, Texas, and Florida. Designated as an "established species" by the FWC. Larger than Muscovy ducks and smaller than swans, Egyptian geese sport stocky bodies with brown and gray plumage, a rufous patch around each eye, and an iridescent green "speculum" at the rear of their wings, visible at rest. Bills, legs, and feet are pale pink.

You don't notice these linebacker-sized waterfowl until 2018 or so, when their numbers proliferate in your South Florida zip code. Overnight, it seems, they establish permanent residence on your college campus, breeding along the cattail and bulrush edges of the manufactured ponds. Your first thought is that they're prettier than those Muscovy ducks with their warty faces. Your second thought follows close behind: these guys will sure give those Muscovy ducks and iguanas a run for their money. Friends and colleagues ask you about these new "ducks" roaming around your university and town, because they think you know a lot about birds, but you're just as perplexed as they are by the sudden appearance of these exotic creatures. They're pretty intimidating, on account of both their size and their robust vocalizations, which range from trumpeting quacks to honks and hisses. They lumber boldly across campus between the ponds while students offer them a wide berth, as if they were the most popular clique on campus. You learn that Egyptian geese can deteriorate the habitats they've infiltrated, threatening native species through feeding damage and the diseases they may spread through their prodigious feces. You learn that students at a separate local university considered them overly aggressive toward humans and native ducks and petitioned to have them removed, calling them "demon ducks," while residents of a behemoth senior living community in the same county fought to protect the nests of breeding pairs when they were threatened with eviction. You wonder what you might glean from these local stories: the intolerance of the young or their greater eco-awareness? The eco-myopia of the elderly or the affinities all of us develop with individual creatures in our sphere, despite their provenance? You're not quite sure yet how to feel about Egyptian geese, these relative newcomers. You want to agree with those anti-Egyptian geese students. You share their concerns about invasive species, the integrity of local ecosystems, the well-being of native Florida creatures. But then you spy an Egyptian goose pair from your campus office window waddling across the parking lot below, six or seven of their fuzzy young trailing behind, and you find yourself worrying over those poor goslings (or shelducklings). All those feral cats about certainly constitute a threat. And that hot asphalt beneath the blazing subtropical sun. Doesn't it scald their tiny, webbed feet?

* * *

Human being. *Homo sapiens.*

Non-native and invasive, excepting descendants of the Calusa, Timucua, Pensacola, Apalachee, Guale, Potano, Ais, Ocale, Tocobaga, Jeaga, Matecumbe, and Mayaimi. Population sparse through the early part of the twentieth century. Spurred on by Henry Flagler's construction of the Florida East Coast Railroad, stretching all the way from St. Augustine to Key West by 1912. Willis Carrier, improving upon John Gorrie's 1848 invention, patents his electricity-powered compressor for air conditioning in 1906. Additional advancements make portable window units affordable and widespread in Florida by the 1950s. The human population increases precipitously. The statewide human population now exceeds 22 million. Humans in Florida now pose a considerable threat to native species and ecosystems.

You join this year-round population in 1996, migrating from the Northeast to a county near the southeastern toe-tip of the peninsula. You anticipate a slow-paced, southern lifestyle that you've heard so much about but are quickly disabused. The human temperament hews closer to New York City than you anticipated. Humans here, you learn, drive at breakneck speed, rarely yield to pedestrians or cyclists, and are quick to lay on their horns. Humans here, you learn, may carry firearms on their persons and may discharge them upon the slightest provocation. You learn to approach other humans in Florida with caution. Humans here, you learn, can be quite mean and/or stupid, hence the memes, "Florida Man" and "Florida Woman." Humans here, you learn, can be quite kind and/or smart. You seek out the kind and/or smart humans and avoid the other sort best you can. You wonder if non-native creatures like you—animals human and nonhuman—might live in place in such a way, for such a time, as to acquire at least honorary native status. You wonder about the binary, itself, the limitations of any such reductive catalog. In any case, you and your wife raise three kind and smart children here. You hope that they, like you, will stay in Florida.

ACKNOWLEDGMENTS

Heartfelt thanks to,

Laura Strachan, peerless agent and friend

The editorial team at the University Press of Florida, especially Janie Chan for glimpsing what this book could be

The three anonymous readers of the manuscript assigned by the press, for their thoughtful comments and suggestions

Kim Heise, for allowing me to use an image of her beautiful painting, *Slash Pine and Red-Bellied Woodpecker*, for the cover of this book

The literary magazine editors, who published versions of several of these chapters, giving me the crucial confidence to persevere with this longer work and who include: Simmons Buntin and Elizabeth Dodd (*Terrain.org*, "The Problem with Pretty Birds," December 23, 2015; "Slashed," May 11, 2020; and "Fox," August 3, 2023), Tom Jeffreys (*The Learned Pig*, "Macroalgae Matters," January 21, 2021), Brendan Curtin and Debra Marquart (*Flyway*, "Yellow-crowned Night Heron," May 18, 2018), Emily Nemens (*Southern Review*, "Starting from Seed," 51, no. 2, Spring 2015: 224–38), Madison Jones (*Kudzu House Quarterly*, "The Last Patch of Florida Land," 5, no. 2, Summer 2015), Scott Slovic (*ISLE*, "My Garden Tour," 28, no. 4, Winter 2021: 1637–49), Jenna Gersie (*The Hopper*, "Summer Animals," 2, 2017: 30–34), and Sands Hall (*F&M Alumni Arts Review* 4, Spring 2015, 71–77).

The poets whose work I've excerpted: Wallace Stevens, "Of Mere Being," from *The Palm at the End of the Mind: Selected Poems and a Play*; Mary Oliver, "October," from *New and Selected Poems: Volume One*; and Anne Pierson Wiese, "Profile of the Night Heron," from *Floating City*

Fellow writer-friends, for the inspiration of their work and their support of mine and who include Mike Branch, Joni Tevis, C. B. Bernard, David Keplinger, Janisse Ray, Susan Fox Rogers, Susan Cerulean, Erika Dreifus, Pearl Abraham, Margot Singer, Brittany Ackerman, Rachel Kadish,

Adrienne Brodeur, Toni Jensen, Anna Solomon, Jonathan Rosen, Nicole Walker, JoeAnn Hart, Leigh Newman, Yael Goldstein-Love, Tova Mirvis, Emily Nemens, Cathy Salustri, Emily Strelow, Nora Gold, and, of course, my writer-colleagues in the Department of English at Florida Atlantic University (FAU), Stephanie Anderson, Papatya Bucak, Becka McKay, Romeo Oriogun, and Jason Schwartz

Vanessa Bonebrake, John Potts, Kathy Potts, Rachel Sexton, Rachel Bobich, Lisa Childers, Mike Kohner, Ricardo Costabal, Igor Galati, Brian Pawlowski, Rhiannon Wilson, Alexa Gustin, and my entire South Florida swim group at FAU for introducing me to open-water swimming in the Florida ocean

Carl Terwilliger and Donna Leone, of Meadow Beauty Nursery, for continuing to educate and inspire me

My colleagues at FAU in the Department of English and the Dorothy F. Schmidt College of Arts and Letters

Dr. Stephen Kajiura, professor of Biology at FAU, for the generosity of his time in speaking with me about his research on Florida's fascinating sharks and stingrays

My students

My parents, Stephen and Nancy Furman

My siblings, Richard Furman and Dana Friedfeld

And, above all, to my wife, Wendy, to whom this book is dedicated, and to our children, Henry, Sophia, and Eva.

WORKS CITED

Aristotle. *The History of Animals.* 350 BCE. https://www.gutenberg.org/ebooks/59058.
Audubon, John James. *Birds of America.* 1827–1838. New York: Prestel, 2021.
———. "The Florida Keys." *Delineations of American Scenery and Character.* New York: G. A. Baker, 1926.
———. "The Turtlers." *Delineations of American Scenery and Character.* New York: G. A. Baker, 1926.
———. "Yellow-Crowned Heron." *Birds of America.* 1827–1838. New York: Prestel, 2021. https://www.audubon.org/birds-of-america/yellow-crowned-heron.
Bartram, William. *Travels.* 1791. New York: Library of America, 1996.
Berry, Wendell. "Getting Along with Nature." *Home Economics.* Berkeley, CA: Counterpoint, 1987.
Branch, Michael P. *Raising Wild: Dispatches from a Home in the Wilderness.* Boulder, CO: Roost Books, 2016.
Brand, Adele. *The Hidden World of the Fox.* New York: HarperCollins, 2019.
Capon, Brian. *Botany for Gardeners: An Introduction to the Science of Plants.* Portland, OR: Timber Press, 1990.
Carson, Rachel. *The Edge of the Sea.* 1955. New York: Mariner, 1998.
———. *Silent Spring.* 1962. New York: Mariner, 2022.
Cather, Willa. *O Pioneers!* 1913. New York: Vintage, 1992.
Cerulean, Susan. *I Have Been Assigned the Single Bird.* Athens: University of Georgia Press, 2020.
Childs, Craig. *Crossing Paths: Uncommon Encounters with Animals in the Wild.* New York: Sasquatch Books, 1997.
Cooper, James Fenimore. *Last of the Mohicans.* 1826. New York: Midden, 2022.
Cooper, Susan Fenimore. *Rural Hours.* New York: George P. Putnam, 1850.
Corcoran, Mark. "Movement Patterns and Habitat Use of Southern Stingrays (*Dasyatis americana*) at a Tourist Site in the Cayman Islands." https://web.uri.edu/wetherbee/movement-patterns-and-habitat-use-of-southern-stingrays-dasyatis-americana-at-a-tourist-site-in-the-cayman-islands/.
Dillard, Annie. "Living Like Weasels." *Teaching a Stone to Talk.* 1982. New York: Harper Perennial, 2013.
———. *Pilgrim at Tinker Creek.* 1974. New York: Harper Perennial, 2013.
Duarte, Carlos M., et al. "The Soundscape of the Anthropocene Ocean." *Science* 371, no. 6529 (Feb. 5, 2021). https://www.science.org/doi/10.1126/science.aba4658.

Emerson, Ralph Waldo. "Self-Reliance." 1841. *Emerson's Prose and Poetry*, edited by Joel Porte and Saundra Morris. New York: Norton, 2001.

The Encyclopedia of Organic Gardening. Emmaus, Pa.: Rodale Press, 1988.

Faulkner, William. *As I Lay Dying*. New York: Vintage, 1930.

———. *Go Down, Moses*. New York: Random House, 1942.

Ferguson, Patrick. "Stop the Burn: How Sugarcane Field Burning is Devastating Communities in South Florida." Sept. 14, 2022. https://www.sierraclub.org/articles/2022/09/stop-burn-how-sugarcane-field-burning-devastating-communities-south-florida#:~:text=Sugarcane%20field%20burning%20causes%20pollution,wildlife%20caught%20in%20the%20flames.

Frazier, Charles. *Cold Mountain*. New York: Grove, 1997.

Gannon, Michael. *Florida: A Short History*. Gainesville: University Press of Florida, 2003.

Gessner, David. *Quiet Desperation, Savage Delight: Sheltering with Thoreau in the Age of Crisis*. Salt Lake City, UT: Torrey House, 2021.

Haehle, Robert G., and Joan Brookwell. *Native Florida Plants*. New York: Taylor Trade Publishing, 2004.

Harrison, Tony. "Following Pine." *London Review of Books*. Feb. 6, 1986. https://www.lrb.co.uk/the-paper/v08/n02/tony-harrison/following-pine.

Huegel, Craig N. *Native Plant Landscaping for Florida Wildlife*. Gainesville: University Press of Florida, 2010.

Hurston, Zora Neale. *Their Eyes Were Watching God*. New York: J. B. Lippincott, 1937.

Jewett, Sarah Orne. "A White Heron." 1886. *A White Heron and Other Stories*. South Yarra, Victoria, Australia: Leopold Classic Library, 2016.

Keats, John. "Ode to a Nightingale." 1819. *John Keats: The Complete Poems*. New York: Penguin, 1977.

Kimmerer, Robin Wall. *Braiding Sweetgrass: Indigenous Wisdom, Scientific Knowledge and the Teachings of Plants*. Minneapolis, MN: Milkweed, 2015.

Lanham, J. Drew. *The Home Place: Memoirs of a Colored Man's Love Affair with Nature*. Minneapolis, MN: Milkweed, 2016.

LaPointe, Brian. Qtd. in Bethany Augliere, "Too Much of a Good Thing: Poor Water Quality Leads to Toxic Levels of Seaweed." https://www.fau.edu/owl-research-and-innovation/fall-2021/too-much-of-a-good-thing/.

Leopold, Aldo. *A Sand County Almanac*. 1949. New York: Oxford University Press, 2020.

Lobel, Arnold. *Frog and Toad Together*. New York: HarperCollins, 1979.

Lynfield, Geoffrey. "Yamato and Morikami: The Story of the Japanese Colony and Some of Its Settlers." *Spanish River Papers* 13, no. 3 (Spring 1985). https://assets.speakcdn.com/assets/2845/srp_spring_1985.pdf.

Macdonald, Helen. *H is For Hawk*. London: Jonathan Cape, 2014.

Matthiessen, Peter. *The Snow Leopard*. New York: Penguin, 1978.

McIver, Stuart B. *Death in the Everglades: The Murder of Guy Bradley, America's First Martyr to Environmentalism*. Gainesville: University Press of Florida, 2003.

McKibben, Bill. *The End of Nature*. New York: Random House: 1989.

Meloy, Ellen. *The Anthropology of Turquoise: Reflections on Desert, Sea, Stone, and Sky*. New York: Pantheon, 2002.

Melville, Herman. *Moby-Dick*. 1851. New York: Norton, 2017.
Miller, John MacNeill, and Lauren Fugate. "Shakespeare's Starlings: Literary History and the Fictions of Invasiveness." *Environmental Humanities* 13, no. 2 (2021): 301–22.
Oliver, Mary. "October." *New and Selected Poems: Volume One*. New York: Penguin Random House, 1992.
———. *Owls and Other Fantasies: Poems and Essays*. Boston, MA: Beacon Press, 2006.
Osorio, Rufino. *A Gardener's Guide to Florida's Native Plants*. Gainesville: University Press of Florida, 2001.
Pacoureau, Nathan, et al. "Half a Century of Global Decline in Oceanic Sharks and Rays." *Nature* (Jan. 27, 2021). https://pubmed.ncbi.nlm.nih.gov/33505035/.
Peterson, Charles H., and Melanie J. Bishop. "Assessing the Environmental Impacts of Beach Nourishment." *BioScience* 55, no. 10 (Oct. 2005). https://academic.oup.com/bioscience/article/55/10/887/274435.
Peterson, Roger Tory. *Eastern Birds*. New York: Houghton Mifflin, 1934.
Physiologus. 2nd century AD. https://www.gutenberg.org/ebooks/14729.
Pollan, Michael. "Against Nativism." *New York Times Magazine*, May 15, 1994, 52.
———. *Second Nature: A Gardener's Education*. New York: Grove, 1991.
Pranty, Bill. *A Birder's Guide to Florida*. Asheville, NC: American Birding Association, 2005.
Raven, Catherine. *Fox & I: An Uncommon Friendship*. New York: Spiegel & Grau, 2021.
Ray, Janisse. *Ecology of a Cracker Childhood*. Minneapolis, MN: Milkweed, 1999.
———. *The Seed Underground: A Growing Revolution to Save Food*. White River Junction, VT: Chelsea Green, 2012.
———. *Wild Spectacle: Seeking Wonders in a World Beyond Humans*. San Antonio, TX: Trinity University Press, 2021.
Reiley, Laura. "Shell Game." *Tampa Bay Times*. April 11, 2018. https://projects.tampabay.com/projects/2018/special-report/shell-game-panhandle-apalachicola-wild-oysters-aquaculture/.
Renkl, Margaret. *The Comfort of Crows: A Backyard Year*. New York: Spiegel & Grau, 2023.
———. *Late Migrations: A Natural History of Love and Loss*. Minneapolis, MN: Milkweed, 2019.
Rilke, Rainer Maria. *The Duino Elegies & The Sonnets to Orpheus*. 1923. New York: Vintage, 2014.
Saad, John. *Longleaf*. Brattleboro, VT: Green Writers Press, 2017.
Sanders, Scott Russell. *Staying Put: Making a Home in a Restless World*. Boston, MA: Beacon Press, 1993.
Savoy, Lauret. *Trace: Memory, History, Race, and the American Landscape*. Berkeley, CA: Counterpoint, 2015.
Scott, Damon. "Manatees Were Once Important Seminole Food Source." *Seminole Tribune*, April 1, 2019. https://seminoletribune.org/manatees-were-once-important-seminole-food-source/.
Shetterly, Susan Hand. *Seaweed Chronicles: A World at the Water's Edge*. Chapel Hill, NC: Algonquin, 2018.

Sibley, David Allen. *The Sibley Field Guide to Birds of Eastern North America*. New York: Knopf, 2003.
Smith, Miranda. *The Plant Propagator's Bible: A Step-by-Step Guide to Propagating Every Plant in your Garden*. Emmaus, PA: Rodale Press, 2007.
"The Soundscape of the Anthropocene Ocean." *Science* 371, no. 6529 (Feb. 5, 2021). https://www.science.org/doi/10.1126/science.aba4658.
Stevens, Wallace. "Of Mere Being." *The Palm at the End of the Mind: Selected Poems and a Play*. New York: Knopf, 1967.
Thoreau, Henry David. "The Succession of Forest Trees." 1860. *Thoreau: Collected Essays and Poems*. New York: Library of America, 2001.
———. *Walden; or, Life in the Woods*. 1854. Boston, MA: Beacon, 2004.
———. "Walking." 1862. *Thoreau: Collected Essays and Poems*. New York: Library of America, 2001.
Twain, Mark. *Adventures of Huckleberry Finn*. 1884. New York: Norton, 2021.
Valdez, Dolen Perkins. *Balm*. New York: HarperCollins, 2015.
Wallace, David Foster. *The Pale King*. New York: Little, Brown, 2011.
Walton, Dan, and Laurel Schiller. *Natural Florida Landscaping*. Essex, CT: Pineapple Press, 2007.
Wang, Mengqiu, Chuanmin Hu, Brian B. Barnes, et al. "The Great Atlantic Sargassum Belt." Science 365, no. 6448 (July 5, 2019): 83–87. https://www.science.org/doi/10.1126/science.aaw7912.
White, Evelyn C. "Black Women and the Wilderness." *Literature and the Environment: A Reader on Nature and Culture*, edited by Lorraine Anderson et al. New York: Addison Wesley Longman, 1999.
Whitman, Walt. "Song of Myself." *Leaves of Grass*. 1855. New York: Penguin, 1961.
Wiese, Anne Pierson. "Profile of the Night Heron." *Floating City*. Baton Rouge: Louisiana State University Press, 2007.
Wilkerson, Isabel. *The Warmth of Other Suns*. New York: Random House, 2010.
Williams, Joy. *The Florida Keys: A History & Guide*. New York: Random House, 1987.
Williams, Terry Tempest. *Refuge: An Unnatural History of Family and Place*. New York: Pantheon, 1991.

Andrew Furman is professor of English at Florida Atlantic University and teaches in its MFA program in creative writing. His fiction and creative nonfiction frequently engage with the Florida outdoors and have appeared in such publications as *Prairie Schooner, Oxford American, Southern Review, Santa Monica Review, Ecotone, Willow Springs, Poets and Writers, Southern Indiana Review, Potomac Review, Terrain.org, Flyway,* and *Florida Review.* He is the author, most recently, of the novels *Jewfish* and *Goldens Are Here* and the memoir *Bitten: My Unexpected Love Affair with Florida,* which was named a finalist for the ASLE Environmental Book Award. His novel *The World That We Are* will be released by Regal House Publishing in 2025. He lives in South Florida with his family.

www.ingramcontent.com/pod-product-compliance
Lightning Source LLC
Chambersburg PA
CBHW021732220426
43662CB00008B/818